Voices of Innovation—Payers

As the health delivery landscape in the United States evolves in a post-COVID-19 era, both incumbents and new entrants are reimagining models of care. Technology and medical advancements are transforming the way care is delivered and experienced, and changes in regulations and incentives across the industry are redefining how the healthcare system works and interacts. As a result, care delivery is undergoing several transformations: from sick care to preventative whole-person care, from intermittent to continuous care, from facility-based settings to omnichannel offerings through virtual care and video or telephonic technologies, and from standardized to personalized solutions. In addition to healthcare providers, payers are also redefining their role in care delivery through provider ownership, technology, and provider enablement to deliver higher-value care to members. While the payer community has been slow to innovate, they now have an opportunity and an incentive to play an active role in reimagining the future of care delivery. In the past year alone, significant disruptors have entered the provider space threatening the existence of payers, specifically self-funded programs such as Amazon and Walmart. This has served as a giant wake-up call that healthcare has shifted.

Now, more than ever, there is an emphasis on the patient and clinician experience. Perhaps hastened by the pandemic, the race is on for innovations from the payer community to improve patient and provider engagement. Unlike other players, payers have end-to-end visibility into individual care needs and utilization patterns across providers and settings. This perspective can provide informed choices around optimal care models, unlock value through improved health outcomes, and lower the total cost of care for members and customers.

This book is loaded with numerous case studies and interviews with healthcare leaders from the payer community, helping stakeholders understand how to leverage innovation leading them to superior business and clinical outcomes. The book also discusses how and why data is key to innovation activities and how partnerships are key to using data effectively.

Voices of Innovation—Payers

Opportunities for Creating Solutions to Improve Member Experience and Health

Edited by
Edward W. Marx and Sakshika Dhingra

Foreword by Sachin H. Jain, MD, MBA
Introduction by Cliff Deveny, MD

Routledge
Taylor & Francis Group

A PRODUCTIVITY PRESS BOOK

Designed cover image: ©Shutterstock Images

First edition published 2024
by Productivity Press
2385 NW Executive Center Drive, Suite 320, Boca Raton FL 33431

and by Productivity Press
4 Park Square, Milton Park, Abingdon, Oxon, OX14 4RN

Productivity Press is an imprint of the Taylor & Francis Group, an informa business

© 2024 selection and editorial matter, Edward W. Marx and Sakshika Dhingra

ISBN: 978-1-032-46504-3 (hbk)
ISBN: 978-1-032-46502-9 (pbk)
ISBN: 978-1-003-38198-3 (ebk)

DOI: 10.4324/9781003381983

Typeset in Garamond
by Apex CoVantage, LLC

Contents

Foreword

Of all the words we use in healthcare, *innovation* might be my least favorite.

In board rooms, C-suite offices, and hospital corridors, people speak often about innovation. They say we need more of it. They say innovation will make healthcare more efficient, accessible, and affordable. That it will produce better patient outcomes.

But too often, when you ask people who preach the gospel of innovation, what kind of innovation they're specifically talking about, they fall silent. They're sure innovation will save healthcare, but they're murky on the details.

When people say we need innovation, what they often mean is that we need to ensure people do their jobs and perform their roles in the way they were designed. What they're really calling for is the healthcare system to work as it was intended.

This isn't really all that innovative.

I've long argued that innovation in healthcare requires a two-pronged approach. First, there's *Big I Innovation*. This is innovation on a grand scale. Switching to electronic medical records, embracing managed care models, and providing care via telemedicine are all examples of *Big I Innovation* that are making healthcare more accessible, affordable, and efficient.

Small i innovations rarely get the same attention as their *Big I* siblings, but they're just as important. *Small i innovations* are process improvements. Checklists in operating rooms, equipment standardization, and regular auditing of patient charts by payers are all examples of *Small i innovations* that have led to improved outcomes and reduced costs.

Looking at successful innovations and studying unsuccessful ones, it's clear to me that the key ingredient that actually improves healthcare is *radical common sense*. Innovating for its own sake is rarely worth the time or money. Instead, innovations should be pursued and adopted based on their ability to make a meaningful difference in the lives of patients.

This book is designed as a comprehensive guide for healthcare leaders who are looking to steer their organizations into the future. The chapters contained herein explore a wide range of topics, from value-based care models and digital transformation to data analytics, patient-centric approaches, and other trends and strategies that are reshaping the payer landscape. You'll find insights from experts who have successfully navigated the challenges of payer innovation, as well as practical advice on how to implement these innovations within your own organization.

Do these innovations improve patient care? Can they be implemented at scale? Are they truly innovative?

I hope that as you delve into the examples ahead, you'll decide for yourself. And find plenty to take away as you seek to shape the future of healthcare into something truly remarkable.

Sachin H. Jain, MD, MBA
CEO of SCAN Group and SCAN Health Plan, Industry Leader

Introduction

I first met Edward W. Marx in 2022 when we interviewed him for a Summa Health Board of Directors position. As the CEO of Summa Health, I find it critical to recruit and engage board members who believe in innovation and transformation. It has been invigorating to add someone to our board of experts with broad healthcare experience and expertise in digital transformation and innovation. When we met, I knew Ed had the right level of expertise to join our board. Having worked with many boards over the years, I am familiar with the need to be relevant and keep up with the digital transformation that is possible today. I believe that innovation will enhance and transform the patient's experience and elevate healthcare outcomes. We are fortunate to have Ed to propel our organization and industry forward.

Ed has a deep history in healthcare when it comes to innovation. In fact, he has a reputation for collaborating with teams and developing innovative solutions to maximize technical and digital investments. Early in his career, he and his team developed the first two-way NICU video solution so parents could have 24 × 7 interactions with their sick babies. Later, Ed's teams would develop creative solutions that helped save lives and improve the quality of care at multiple organizations, including Texas Health Resources and Cleveland Clinic.

If you have followed Ed, you understand he does not sit on his laurels but continues to be a catalyst pushing the industry forward. As the chief digital officer for Tech Mahindra, his teams developed the world's first complete virtual care platform. In 2023, Ed became the chief executive officer of his own healthcare advisory and solutions firm and has flipped the traditional consulting model, further differentiating their go-tomarket strategy and offerings from traditional competitors.

Ed has also leveraged a variety of media tools to further encourage not just innovation but digital transformation. He is an avid blogger, and his essays have over 100,000 visits. His podcast, DGTL Voices, is ranked in the top 3%. He has written several healthcare best-selling books plus a "coffee table" book on running and a collection of stories from his first 50 years titled *Extraordinary Tales of a Rather Ordinary Guy*. His book on patient experience with Mayo Clinic Press is set to be released in 2024. He and his wife, Dr. Simran Marx, plan to release a book in 2024 on romance in marriage.

After the success of the 2019 healthcare bestseller *Voices of Innovation*, Ed shared he was working on a payer edition and asked that I write this introduction. How could I say no? I understand first-hand the importance of innovation in all aspects of healthcare from payer to biotech to providers to research and clinical trials. As part of Summa Health, we provide SummaCare, a highly rated, complete portfolio of insurance products for members of our community and region.

I met Sakshika through Ed, and what stands out about her is that in this vast and complex landscape of healthcare, she gets the powerful position payers have and the role they're supposed to play, that is orchestrators of the next best action for a patient.

Having grown up around healthcare professionals, Sakshika has dedicated her own career to the dynamic world of payers, and with a background in sociology, management, and digital transformation, she has excelled in every role she has undertaken. The golden thread in Sakshika's illustrious career has been her patient-centricity and her unwavering focus on patient engagement.

Sakshika is known for her commitment to getting work done and creating lasting change, be it through spearheading groundbreaking technology implementations or tirelessly working toward a more accessible healthcare landscape.

With this book, Sakshika and Ed invite you to join them on a journey through the ever-evolving landscape of healthcare with a focus on payer organizations. Together, we will explore the limitless possibilities of innovation, drawing from the wisdom of distinguished and accomplished healthcare professionals who have dedicated their lives to the advancement of the field.

What makes this book even more special is that 100% of all author royalties goes directly to Summa Health so we can continue to invest in cancer care.

Cliff Deveny, MD
President, CEO Summa Health

Acknowledgments

I dedicate this book to two healthcare technology leaders who were as innovative as they come. Paddy Padmanabhan and Timothy Stettheimer. They both left this earth too damn early. But not before leading innovation efforts across the globe.

Paddy co-wrote "Healthcare Digital Transformation" with me. It became the best-selling healthcare book in 2020 and 2021 and remains a well-worn college textbook. When I was diagnosed with cancer, he flew out across the country to visit me. What else can be said?

Timothy and I served as leadership academy faculty for our professional organization. We became fast friends given our profession, fitness pursuits, and spiritual connections. When I confided my life troubles with him, he ran toward me and not away. What else can be said?

I am also thankful for my co-author Sakshika Dhangra. We met a couple of years ago via an introduction from the CEO of Tech Mahindra. While I served as her mentor for one year, I learned as much from her. An innovator herself, she did much of the heavy lifting for the book you are holding.

Edward W. Marx

First and foremost, I want to extend my deepest thanks to my brave and beautiful mother Kamal Dhingra for raising me in the best way possible with limited means, for teaching me that true fulfillment comes from serving others and that anything is possible if we work and pray hard enough. I would like to express my heartfelt gratitude to my husband, Vivesh Sharma, whose patience and understanding sustained me through the long hours that went into this work. He truly is the wind beneath my wings.

A special mention to my five-year-old son Aveer who is a continuous source of love, light, and respite. His unwavering belief in my abilities has been my greatest motivation. I am deeply appreciative of all the healthcare professionals in my family, especially my sister Geetika Dhingra, my colleagues, friends, and mentors that are my sounding boards for contributing to the realization of this book. They have helped build my perspective on innovation in healthcare and continue to influence it.

To all those who have touched my life in various ways, for those who have believed in me when no one else did, I am profoundly grateful.

I owe a tremendous debt of gratitude to my mentor, my friend, and co-author Edward W. Marx for giving me this tremendous opportunity to work together and contribute to a cause that is even closer to my heart now than it was when we started working on this book. He is a constant source of inspiration. Finally, I would like to dedicate this book to my beloved dad, Rakesh Dhingra, who we lost to cancer on April 16, 2023. Papa ji, I miss you every single day.

Sakshika Dhingra

All author proceeds for this book go to Summa Health to help cure cancer in their names.

Rakesh, Paddy, and Timothy

About the Editors and the Contributors

Brandy Bailey (Humana) is the Associate Vice President of Integrated Operations at Humana, focused on the strategy and design for LTSS market operating models and integration points with Medicare. She has nearly 20 years of experience serving vulnerable populations through the lens of both provider and payer, with an emphasis in MLTSS strategy and operations. Prior to Humana, Mrs. Bailey was the Senior Vice President of Home and Community-Based Services for Valir Health, where she started and led as plan CEO a fully integrated program of all-inclusive care for the elderly. Mrs. Bailey is passionate about reducing administrative burden and complexity across the healthcare landscape and empowering vulnerable seniors to age in place with dignity.

Julie Bonello (Integrate Health) is the founder of Integrate Health, an advisory firm helping organizations leverage digital platforms for population health and the transformation to value-based care. She has had a distinguished 30-year chief information officer career most recently with Presbyterian Healthcare Services, New Mexico, and Rush Health, Chicago. She also has held leadership positions in consulting, HIM, revenue cycle, nursing, and research and has been an active member of the CHIME Public Policy Committee for the last five years.

Dawn Carter (Centauri Health Solutions) is a director of product strategy at Centauri Health Solutions. Her career in healthcare spans 28 years, which most recently includes extensive experience in developing revenue integrity software solutions focusing on encounter management, risk adjustment, and social determinants of health for the Medicare Advantage, Medicaid, and commercial health plan markets. She also provides risk adjustment strategic advisory consulting services for these markets. Prior to that, her experience spans all domains of healthcare and revenue cycle, including health plan claims/EDI, enrollment and provider systems administration, finance, compliance, and healthcare applications development. Her experience also includes multiple teaching engagements in medical administration, billing, and coding. She is a passionate and prolific industry speaker, author, blogger, and subject matter expert in claims, EDI management (X12/HL7), risk adjustment, and social determinants of health. She is currently pursuing a master of science in healthcare administration and is a fellow of the American Association of Professional Coders (AAPC).

Nicole Denham has been a nurse for 17 years, and **Bonnie Matthews** a nurse for 25 years. They worked together for over a decade in a cardiac critical care unit at a hospital outside of Atlanta, GA. Both quickly moved through the health system into areas of management, clinical education, and process improvement. In 2014, they took a leap of faith and combined their expertise and their passion for making an impact in healthcare on a broader scale and started a clinical consulting firm called COR consultants. COR has worked with healthcare technology organizations across the United States, focusing on the clinical optimization of products and services. Bonnie earned her master's in nursing education from Duke University and is certified as a Lean Six Sigma Green Belt. Nicole earned her master's in healthcare administration from Penn State and recently became a fellow of the American College of Healthcare Executives.

William Epling President and CEO, (SummaCare) joined SummaCare as president in August 2020, bringing more than 30 years of experience in the healthcare delivery and managed care industry. Prior to joining SummaCare, he most recently served as the president of EnvisionRx Options in Twinsburg. Prior to EnvisionRx Options, Bill held a variety of leadership roles, including president at WellCare of Ohio, Inc. and president and CEO at HomeTown Health Network. At WellCare of Ohio, he is credited with launching and developing government-sponsored programs in Ohio for multiple Medicare and Medicaid product lines. At HomeTown Health Network, a provider-sponsored health plan, he successfully grew the number of covered lives from 5,000 to more than 200,000.

Sakshika Dhingra (Humana) is a strategy director with Humana, currently focused on serving their Medicaid membership. She has spent most of her career serving different population groups while working for multiple leading payer organizations across the country. She is a results-oriented healthcare leader with a passion for implementing innovative solutions that simplify member experience.

Tanvir Khan (NTT DATA) serves as the chief digital officer of NTT DATA. He leads the digital offering portfolio and adoption of technologies across the company, as well as its clients, to deliver better business outcomes. With more than 25 years of experience in the IT industry, he is a thought leader in digital transformation, associated core technologies, and value realization. He is also a hands-on IT practitioner with five patents and four pending patents in AI and automation. As a spokesperson for NTT DATA Services, Tanvir shares his insights with clients, media, and analysts on topics ranging from generative AI to emerging global service delivery locations. Tanvir has been with NTT DATA for over 10 years and has worked closely with most clients in his capacity as the president of Health Plan and Life Sciences, Service Delivery leader over the infrastructure, workplace, and BPO services, as well as the leader of intelligent automation and data services. Prior to joining NTT DATA Services, he held global leadership positions at Dell and Wipro Technologies.

Fred W. Kopplow is an influential executive leader and a driving force in the realm of digital patient engagement, business development, and telehealth strategy. Currently, he occupies a pivotal role, lending his expertise to advise digital start-ups committed to enhancing health outcomes. Fred is a trusted guide in this capacity, steering payers, providers, and digital technology solutions toward creating captivating and streamlined patient journeys that seamlessly integrate into the digital health stack. With a rich background spanning consumer, telecommunications, insurance, and health industries, Fred has garnered extensive experience and insight. His senior leadership roles at Blue Cross Blue Shield Michigan, Better Health, Integrated Health, and State Farm Corporation have shaped his multifaceted expertise.

Fred remains on the cutting edge of healthcare evolution, consistently demonstrating a proven leadership and innovation track record. His contributions include advancing digital patient engagement, pioneering accessible telehealth solutions, and simplifying transformative technologies.

Carrie Kozlowski is the COO and co-founder at Upfront, a mission-driven healthcare technology company focused on guiding every patient to the care they need. In her role, she partners with leading healthcare enterprises to help them drive financial, operational, and clinical outcomes through better patient engagement. Over 25 years, she has combined real-world clinical experience with entrepreneurial drive to lead strategy, operations, and talent development at organizations focused on population health.

Krishna Kurapati is the founder and CEO of QliqSOFT. Kurapati has more than two decades of technology entrepreneurship experience. He started QliqSOFT with a strong desire to solve clinical collaboration and workflow challenges using artificial intelligence-powered digital technologies across the US healthcare system.

John Lee, MD, is an experienced clinical informaticist practicing emergency medicine. He has successfully served as chief medical information officer (CMIO) at several healthcare organizations. Widely respected within the health information technology (IT) and informatics communities, Dr. Lee's accomplishments were recognized with the prestigious 2019 HIMSS/AMDIS Physician Executive of the Year award. He currently provides health IT consulting services through his firm, HIT Peak Advisors.

Tina HsinTing Liu (NTT DATA) serves as the strategic advisor of NTT DATA with focus on healthcare strategies, digital transformation, applied intelligence, innovative solutions, IP development, and practice growth. Tina has more than 20 years of deep healthcare industry domain expertise in providing data-driven insights to support leadership decision-making, enabling rapid activation of optimal solutions. Tina has successfully managed numerous large-scale projects for the C-suite, developing and executing plans for implementation of the nextgeneration business intelligence programs. Prior to joining NTT DATA, Tina served in various leadership positions at New York's health systems, health plan, national actuarial, and global consulting firms. She is listed in Marquis Who's Who in America, holds a CPA and an MBA, and has a design thinking certification from MIT.

Elbridge Locklear is Summa Health information technology executive with more than 25 years of experience delivering innovative solutions to internal and external customers by providing strategic technology vision, development, implementation, and oversight for all information systems. He assimilates and develops high-performing teams by delivering effective strategic planning and setting clear expectations for performance. He leads with a style that produces increased team motivation, improves productivity, and drives accountability. His career spans various industries with progressive moves, providing opportunities to expand technologically, leadership, and strategic expertise across all information systems. He has extensive experience in healthcare, consulting, banking, telecommunications, and manufacturing, driving strategy, leading change, and building world-class technology operations, particularly those that provide quick, agile resolutions for critical customer needs.

Edward W. Marx (Marx Advisory) is a healthcare best-selling author of multiple books around innovation, transformation, and experience. His writings reflect his deep expertise gained while serving as CIO of the global Cleveland Clinic and NYC Health & Hospitals. He is an advisor for startups and multinational companies and sits on the boards of multiple health systems. He advises governments on digital transformation strategies. When not working, Ed competes internationally for TeamUSA Triathlon and is on pace to climb the Seven Summits.

Manish Mehta is the vice president and CTO for Healthcare & Life Sciences North America at Eviden. Entrepreneurial executive, offering years of progressive experience as a strategic thinker and executor. He is also a technology enthusiast and a fullstack leader who excels in building strategic relationships with clients in healthcare, product engineering, technology, and other industries. Manish is focused on evangelizing and strategically advising clients on large-scale modernization, digital strategy, automation, and AI and new technology trends like blockchain, Microservices, distributed computing, cloud, and so on.

Carol Palackdharry Senior Physician Consultant, multiple organizations: Dr. Palackdharry is board-certified in medical oncology and has three decades of experience in all aspects of the healthcare biome. She participated in academic and private practice, bench and clinical research, physician education, and pharma, and was Assistant Dean of the University of Toledo. The past 20 years were spent as an executive in data analytics, medical management, and creating new CMMI innovation models. Known as a consummate leader and patient advocate, she creates environments of trust, transparency, inclusiveness, and opportunities for continuous improvement.

Anna Pannier (Centauri Health Solutions) is vice president of IT and Integration at Centauri Health Solutions. She is an operationally aligned technology and informatics leader with over 20 years of experience, helping organizations innovate, adopt new technologies and processes, integrate technologies and organizations, and develop high-performing teams. She is a fellow in the American College of Healthcare Executives and a certified healthcare CIO.

Vishakha Sant (Global Head Product— Healthcare, Life Sciences, Payer Service Now) is a talented and accomplished leader with experience in strategy, market growth, and optimization of digital technologies for integrated healthcare delivery systems. She is passionate about driving high-quality, affordable healthcare without compromising outcomes.

Taylor Seymore (Doctorite) is the supervising behavioral health navigator at Doctorite inc. She has over a decade of working in healthcare settings with a focus on developing and implementing behavioral health programs. Ms. Seymore has a passion for advocating for clients' medical and behavioral needs. She also currently works providing in-home counseling services to families in partnership with government agencies and is pursuing an MSW.

Arvind Sivaramakrishnan (Karkinos Healthcare) is the CIO of Karkinos Healthcare based in India. He holds the responsibility to drive IT strategy and digital transformation and design the digital roadmap of the company. Karkinos Healthcare is a specialist end-to-end, technology driven, oncology-focused, managed healthcare platform.

"Jay" Jayanthi Subramanian (Doctorite Inc.) is the chief executive officer and cofounder of Doctorite Inc., a behavioral health company delivering behavioral care management services to clinics, by licensed and certified behavioral health navigators, using wholly owned proprietary technology platform and app, across various states in the United States. She has more than three decades of experience working as a clinical, operational, and compliance leader, primarily in the post-acute healthcare industry. She has worked as a health technology leader, enabling clients to comply with new regulatory mandates and developing innovative solutions. Prior to founding Doctorite, she worked as vice president of Healthcare Solutions at Capgemini. In the past, she has served in the American Occupational Therapy Association (AOTA) and is certified by the National Council of Certified Dementia Practitioners (NCCDP).

Mike Treash currently leads the data transformation of a $2.7 billion company. He is a data evangelist for using advanced analytics to drive deep business insights and change the healthcare consumer experience. While not innovating in the data space, he is the executive leader of operations and technology at a provider-based health plan.

Bobbi Weber is the vice president of Portfolio Management and Field Strategy at QliqSOFT. Bobbi is a lifelong learner who is passionate about enabling healthcare transformation. She has 20+ years of healthcare experience in care delivery, consulting, healthcare IT, and market strategy.

Voices of Innovation Series

Voices of Innovation. We published the original *"Voices of Innovation . . . Fulfilling the Promise of Information Technology in Healthcare"* in the Spring of 2019. Little did we know that a few months later, Covid would completely disrupt life as we knew it. Innovation and Digital Transformation became everyday vernacular and *Voices* went on to sell very well. Our publisher returned in late 2022 asking for a 2nd Edition. The publisher made a good point in that there were so many new stories of innovation born from the pandemic, it would help the industry to update the book. We updated almost half of the content with Covid inspired innovations. *Voices, 2nd Edition*, was published in July 2023.

Voices of Innovation, the Series. With the success of the books, we heard requests from many in the Payer community for a *Voices* book of their own. Like their provider counterparts, Payers also long to transform and innovation is a catalyst to spark change of such magnitude. The beauty of *Voices* is that the books remain a set of global best practices where peers openly share their playbooks for transformation around a common structure for innovation that is easily adoptable for any sized organization. A leader can pick up a copy of *Voices* and instantly have access to a tried and tested framework for innovation with multiple "case studies" of how other payer organizations have succeeded, complete with results. This is the reason for the success of all the *Voices* books. The publisher created *Voices* as an ongoing series where further editions can be created and the series expanded into Life Sciences, Med Tech and AI.

Voices of Innovation—
Payers Prologue

Everyone talks about innovation, and we can all point to random examples of innovation inside healthcare information technology, but few repeatable processes exist that make innovation more routine than happenstance. How do you create and sustain a culture of innovation? What are the best practices you can refine and embed as part of your organization's DNA? What are the potential outcomes for robust healthcare transformation when we get this innovation mystery solved? Through timely chapters from leading experts, the first edition showcased the widely adopted healthcare innovation model from HIMSS and how providers could leverage it to increase their velocity of digital transformation. Regardless of its promise, innovation has been slow in healthcare.

The payer edition leverages the same framework and construct but zeroes in on the payer and payvider community. There is more emphasis today than before on the concept of member and clinician experience. Perhaps hastened by the pandemic, the race is on for innovations that will help address clinician burnout while better engaging patients and families. Loaded with numerous case studies and stories of successful innovation projects, this book helps the reader understand how to leverage innovation to help fulfill the promise of healthcare information technology in enabling superior business and clinical outcomes.

Everyone agrees that we need more innovation in healthcare to include within the payer community. Just as the provider side, we are woefully behind other industries when it comes to member and user experience. The long-time battles between payers and providers have not helped change this. I have not met a person who does not have a negative story regarding their insurance company. While not all of the angst is justified, it is fair to say we can do many things to help create a better overall experience.

You will find great ideas in this book and see examples of how some payers are indeed transforming via innovation. Most importantly, you will be delighted to see the innovations that are helping improve the quality of care and overall patient safety. You will discover examples of how member experiences are being improved, fueled by technological innovations. You will find examples of how operations are being streamlined to reduce costs and improve workflows.

Over the last several years, we have seen payers cross into becoming not just the insurance vehicle but the prover of care also. In fact, payers control most provider groups today. Similarly, many providers have begun to add their own payer capabilities toward the same objective—to manage the premium dollar by controlling the payer and provider capabilities. These organizations are known as payviders. You will read several case studies directly from payviders as this newer business model has been forged by innovation.

One last item worth noting as we began to compile this book of payer innovation, highlighting global best practices, was how closely payer organizations kept ideas to themselves. In the provider culture, there is a desire and willingness to share best practices. Ultimately, all provider organizations are trying to do the same things in terms of bringing high-quality healthcare to the communities they serve. You will find executives from even competing providers come together routinely to share ideas and learnings that might improve the quality of care and patient safety. We did not see this on the payer side. While this is likely an intentional move to preserve a perceived competitive advantage, it may inadvertently stifle the speed of innovation and adoption. If true, members and the communities they live in are hurt the most.

As with all *Voices* titles, 100% of author proceeds are donated to charities whose focus is to eliminate cancer. *Voices of Innovation—Payers* will fund cancer care at Summa Health, an integrated delivery system based out of Akron, Ohio, where I serve on the board of directors.

Innovation Framework

There is no perfect framework for innovation. HIMSS developed the framework which serves as the construct of the book. We found that the framework is practical and easy to follow. You can decide on what innovation framework works best for you. A brief description of the innovation framework follows:

Blend Cultures. Include the organization's larger community and ensure that institutional leaders are engaged and supportive of the proposed innovative strategies.

Use People with IT. Do not create an over reliance on people or on technology; use both resources in concert.

Create Roadmaps. Develop a plan for the functions required to innovate and encourage effective communication between functional experts for strategic clarity.

Collaborate and Listen. Listen for ideas that will potentially solve a problem or present an opportunity to collaborate with stakeholders and galvanize your network.

Communicate and Eliminate Barriers. Cross communication is essential to promote innovation. By stripping virtual or physical barriers to communication, ideas have a better chance of being realized.

Stress Simplicity. Do not over complicate a solution to a problem; keep the following principle in mind: "When you have two competing theories that make exactly the same predictions, the simpler one is better to implement."

Recognize and Reward. Recognize or reward the efforts of stakeholders to innovate even at the smallest levels.

Co-create Solutions. Appreciate the complexity of attention that innovation requires and expose the organization to demands from all stakeholders.

Chapter 1

Blend Cultures

Include the organization's larger community and ensure that institutional leaders are engaged and supportive of the proposed innovative strategies.

One of the first things you need to do to improve the odds of innovation success is to ensure support and engagement from key organizational leaders. Innovation is hard to do in a vacuum. Often it takes a team, some of whom are directly involved and others who provide resources and political cover. As you embark on your innovation, take inventory of key decision-makers, influencers, and culture. Identify both the individuals who will help you and those who might hurt you. The more organizational community and leadership engagement you develop, the higher the likelihood of overcoming the obstacles that will be on your path to innovation.

THE NURSING PROCESS STRENGTHENS CLINICAL OPTIMIZATION | BY BONNIE MATTHEWS AND NICOLE DENHAM

Amidst the dynamic landscape of healthcare, the collision of challenges and opportunities has profoundly influenced the state of our industry today. Parallel to workforce shortages, healthcare institutions are navigating elaborate financial issues, as they work to harmonize the increasing costs of delivery within the confines of limited resources.[1] The pursuit of optimized patient outcomes remains an unwavering priority, compelling healthcare leaders to seek technology solutions to achieve this elusive trifecta. Given

DOI: 10.4324/9781003381983-1

the intricacies of the present day, pioneers within the industry must develop products that stress simplicity and seamlessly integrate people, processes, and innovation. Traditional IT models may not be enough to make an impact in the world of clinical technology. By utilizing the framework of the nursing process, vendors and all stakeholders within an organization can effectively collaborate to strengthen clinical optimization.

A Clinician's Perspective

The origin of our individual careers is the same. We had a passion for cardiac nursing, and both worked at a multi-campus healthcare system outside of Atlanta. Even as nurses at the bedside, we continually sought opportunities to be involved in process improvement that would influence both the clinicians and the patients in a positive way. We continued to grow in our roles, and in 2014, we decided to start our own consulting firm to make an impact in healthcare on a much broader scale. Since then, we have worked with both start-up and enterprise organizations to support their valued customers around the country. Our team brings years of experience partnering with healthcare technology companies to offer a unique clinical perspective. Due to our background in patient monitoring, we possess a distinctive expertise in implementing best practices for data movement both within and outside the hospital walls. In a collaborative approach, we optimize the delivery of healthcare solutions from strategic planning through client success evaluation and serve as a liaison between the vendor and their customers.

As an organization that focuses on clinical optimization, we have been successful for nearly a decade by utilizing the framework of two processes. By combining two of the most important elements in the healthcare industry, business, and the delivery of care, we can ensure that the vision of our clients is being implemented.

1. ***The People, Process, and Technology Framework:*** This concept developed in the 1960s as the golden triangle has taken on several iterations to include other elements such as data and platforms.[2] This is a common mantra used by organizations, but in our experience, it has not always been used correctly. While all four elements need to be in congruence with one another, there is a methodology that must be considered early in your endeavor. If you attempt to place *technology*

on top of a broken *process*, it will fail every time. If you focus on the collection of *data*, and not how it is distributed to the *people*, it will fail every time. If the team composition that your *technology* and *data* impact changes, your *process* must change, or it will fail every time. We will highlight these concepts more as we talk about *Product Roadmap Mishaps*.

2. ***The Nursing Process (ADPIE Model):*** Something of critical importance to us as clinical consultants is to continue to utilize the foundations of nursing practice as we guide our clients. The nursing process, or ADPIE model, is a systematic method using a "client-centered approach," "goal-oriented tasks," and "evidence-based practice recommendations".[3] We have altered the elements of the ADPIE model (to assessment, development, planning, implementation, evaluation) while staying true to the framework, to guide our consulting process. Change your perspective from caring for a patient at the bedside to the design and implementation of a healthcare technology product, and the process is still very applicable. This model allows us to blend the development lifecycle of a product with a very clear roadmap for success to ensure clinical optimization and adoption.

Product Roadmap Mishaps

Building a product roadmap is an essential process used to plan and outline the development, evolution, and future course of an innovation. This process has historically been completed in silo from the end user, which can create stakeholder misalignment and lack of adoption. Throughout our years in consulting, we have encountered product roadmaps that lack essential elements and ultimately lead to unnecessary mishaps.

Miscalculated Return on Investment

Understanding ROI is a crucial consideration when planning a roadmap, and we have encountered contrasting scenarios while addressing the concept. At times, health tech companies lack the comprehension of the true diversity within the payer network. The complexity will continue as more healthcare organizations are dipping their toes into value-based care contracts and advanced payment models. We are often brought in downstream when a client is "turning off the subscription" to try to save the account. These are common pitfalls we see:

- **ROI has not been properly discovered**, illustrated, or categorized into clinical, financial, and organizational benefits.[4]
- **Lack of strategy for feature prioritization.** You must consider the voice of each stakeholder as it correlates to the global ROI before you jump into product modification.
- **Measuring success is not formalized** (key performance indicators (KPIs), customer relationship management (CRM) documentation, white paper production, post-implementation evaluation).

Incorporating ROI considerations into your product roadmap ensures that you are making informed decisions that align with your business's financial and strategic objectives. When this is executed properly, business cases can be developed, and preventative measures can be taken with "at-risk" customers. This will also provide you with opportunities to upsell to your existing client base.

Ineffective Client Handoff

The handoff across the sales cycle is not a new concept. Many organizations use a customer relationship management (CRM) tool to simply consolidate client information, rather than utilizing that data to provide continuity through implementation and beyond. Imagine this scenario: the sales team of a health tech company spends months diligently meeting and pitching their product to key members of an organization. They get the inside information on who can champion the purchase of the solution, and the sale finally closes. The sales team jumps right to the next client, and this is often where the proverbial ball is dropped. Your valued client should be handed off effectively and efficiently to different members of your team to ensure that you are able to keep your promise of a seamless integration. All members of your internal team need to collaborate to simplify continuity. Some key reasons that we have seen projects fail with a lack of handoff are the following:

- **The sale is considered the only win.** If your primary focus is not on the implementation and adoption of your product, you will almost guarantee a failed client relationship.

■ **A solidified handoff process is not established** and does not include
the correct subject matter experts throughout the vendor organization,
who can interact with your client's team members in a timely manner.

■ **Clinical products that do not have a clinical team**. This clinical team truly understands how to assess the existing and intended
workflows, training needs, and user-group needs. Without the ability
to communicate and hand your client off to a group of clinicians who
bring expertise and empathy, you are missing a key component to
success.

One-and-Done Training

In the start-up world, creating a robust training program is often an after-
thought. Even some enterprise organizations have heavily depended on the
traditional model of clinical rounding in-services. This model, which we
refer to as the one-and-done approach, is antiquated, unsustainable, and
does not lend itself to clinical adoption.[5] With a new initiative every week,
it is difficult to maintain an enthusiasm for learning, especially when a
generic training is disseminated to all users. A training program should be
an integral part of any healthcare technology roadmap. It should be customized, usergroup specific, and packaged as a simple learner-guided bundle of
education. This will allow for short-term efforts to match long-term business
goals. We have seen repeated product and implementation failures for these
reasons:

■ **Forgetting that healthcare works in shifts**. Your vendor support
should extend beyond bankers hours. Night and weekend shifts require
the same time and attention as day shifts.

■ **Not considering each end user**. A one-size-fits-all approach to education is highly ineffective when multiple disciplines will utilize your
product in different ways. Function overload happens when all features
of your product are thrown out to all disciplines, even when it is not a
part of their workflow.

■ **Not scaffolding education.** The most effective way to simplify training is to create short pockets of training that are learner-guided and
do not interfere with productivity. Your training materials should be
designed to move from learning to understanding to performing in
order to solidify clinical adoption.

Not engaging essential team members at essential times on the roadmap is a huge mishap. There is often a loss of organizational tacit knowledge, customer KPIs, and key stakeholder information. This creates a downstream impact on the vendor organization that has a serious financial impact and frustrates team members.

The Nursing Process

Assessment

In the realm of healthcare, everything hinges on a thorough assessment that includes subjective and objective data. The assessment of the current state requires a holistic approach to properly design a product and roadmap that solves a clinical need. The assessment needs to be completed from the provider and patient perspectives to properly identify any end-user gaps. The review of best practices, policies, and procedures should be understood and incorporated throughout the product lifecycle. This level of evaluation allows for identifying any potential risks that exist for the patient and the organization. The refinement of the vendor KPIs will be built upon the clinical, financial, and organizational benefits, which will provide measurable metrics that can guide future decision-making and create a seamless transition through the phases. When our organization is engaged to help health tech companies, we generally start with performing a basic SWOT Analysis. This analysis aids decision-making, goal-setting, and formulating strategies to protect the vendor and the emerging technology.[6] We build ROI for companies with three concepts in mind:

1. Value-based care (VBC) will impact the future of your business.
2. Demonstrating cause (solution) and effect (benefit) is essential.
3. Storytelling adds to the impact of any ROI calculator.

Development

During the previous phase, we have likely identified dozens of problems and potential solutions. A client handoff tool should be used to document the project from its inception. Here is where it becomes very important to pause this forward momentum and focus on developing a structure for a collaborative implementation. Clinical judgment will be used to analyze the data collected and determine actual and potential problems. What are the KPIs for this implementation, and how do you blend your organization's KPIs with your clients KPIs? You LISTEN. Here is where breaking out of those silos will set your product and your organization up for success. Bring the right stakeholders to the conversation BEFORE the project kicks off to ensure collaboration. If the clinical team weighs in on how to utilize a product without input from the IT department, how efficient is the data-driven piece of technology? If the workflow is designed with only the chief financial officer and biomedical engineering at the table, how likely is clinical adoption to occur? New clinical protocols and guidelines, based on quality metrics and set by the entire healthcare team, will ensure that the common goal of improving patient outcomes is met. Many metrics are directly correlated to financial benefits and the specific ROI calculator. The last fundamental step in this phase is to ensure that after all the work is complete, the end user understands how to utilize your product. During the development phase, customized training materials are created within an education plan that is ready to be delivered inside the organization's ecosystem.

Planning

The planning phase is the time to formulate an individualized plan of care or project charter. This will fit nicely into the templated structure for a collaborative implementation. Vendors often find themselves staying out of discussions about governance and leadership on the project, even though one of their most important KPIs should be to ensure that their product is utilized according to its purpose, while meeting the needs of all members of the healthcare organization. The plan will involve steps and strategies needed to achieve the desired goals and will consider the client's unique preferences. The modification of related policies and procedures is matched to evidenced-based best practices. How do you ensure that your product fits seamlessly into a clinician's workflow, while maximizing efficiency, focusing on cost savings, and improving patient outcomes? The workflow design is engineered to highlight the desired technology utilization and ROI benefits and solidify adoption.

Implementation

This phase is the actionable part of the process. We have carefully and painstakingly designed a roadmap that supports implementation but make no mistake that this was uniquely customized for THIS client. The deployment of training materials will depend on multiple elements that you should have gathered during the previous phases. Considerations of the types of training materials will be based on the specific end users. The methods of training delivery, virtual or in person, will be based on factors such as staff availability and presence of a clinical education team. They are all-inclusive and are built to support initial onboarding, annual competency, and remediation. Keep in mind that even the most detailed and thought-out implementation plan will not consider every hiccup along the way. This is why Go-Live support is essential to a successful implementation. This does not have to mean weeks of boots-on-the-ground presence. A carefully thought-out education plan that includes creative methods for vendor support can counter the need for costly service recovery initiatives and lack of clinical adoption leading to a broken relationship. Project governance is an integral part of a successful implementation, and at times this needs to be driven by the vendor to achieve the overarching goals.

Evaluation

The end of the nursing process is one of the most important phases. The evaluation process should be laid out within the product roadmap with specific milestone triggers and should be both formative and summative. Best practice for evaluation must include end-user adoption statistics, identification of compliance issues, and effectiveness of the overall training program and have a carved-out relaunch phase. Measuring success should be formalized and documented and build the client-vendor relationship.

If these goals are not met, a gap analysis should be performed, and further action is required to enable healthcare professionals to incorporate the product into their workflows. The evaluation phase is a great time to understand the success of the overall program and to seek opportunities for improvement (OFIs) to further refine the product roadmap. When conducted effectively, the evaluation phase closes the loop for all the stakeholders. The transformation at the client site becomes a robust reference point, serving as a foundation for developing impactful marketing collateral.

Blending Cultures. A Call to Action

In the world of healthcare technology, where every single product that is designed will directly impact a patient or a frontline worker, we must emphasize blending cultures. This allows our solutions to deliver maximum value and the best human experience. The nursing process provides a structure that will prevent siloed decisionmaking and promote collaboration among all key stakeholders. Healthcare organizations desire cost-effective solutions that allow them to see a rapid return on their investment. Patients deserve innovations that will consistently improve outcomes. Providers need a simple solution to counter daily challenges and support their work-force shortages as they deliver patient care. Health tech leaders must consider the nursing process a necessary part of the product life cycle, from early stages of design to evaluation of utilization, in order to strengthen clinical optimization.

References

1. *Top Issues Confronting Hospitals in 2022*. American College of Healthcare Executives Learning Center. August 28, 2023. https://www. ache.org/learning-center/research/about-the-field/top-issues-confronting-hospitals/top-issues-confronting-hospitals-in-2022.
2. Olmstead, L. *The People, Process, Technology (PPT) Framework*. Whatfix Blog. Published June 27, 2023. https://whatfix.com/blog/people-process-technology-framework/.
3. Toney-Butler, T. and Thayer, J. *Nursing Process*. National Library of Medicine. April 10, 2023. https://www.ncbi.nlm.nih.gov/books/NBK 499937/.
4. Thusini, S., Milenova, M., Nahabedian, N. et al. The Development of the Concept of Return-on-Investment from Large-Scale Quality Improvement Programmes in Healthcare: An Integrative Systematic Literature Review. *BMC Health Services Research* 22: 1492 (2022). https://doi.org/10.1186/s12913-022-08832-3.
5. Denham, N. and Matthews, B. *No More "One and Done": A New Approach to Training*. Association for the Advancement of Medical Instrumentation Conference. June 2020. Presentation.
6. Siddiqui, A. SWOT Analysis (or SWOT Matrix) Tool as a Strategic Planning and Management Technique in the Health Care Industry and Its Advantages. *Journal of Biomedical Science* 40(2): 1–8 (2021). https://doi.org/10.26717/BJSTR.2021.40.006419.

CLEVELAND CLINIC AND OSCAR HEALTH INNOVATE THE PAYVIDER MODEL | BY EDWARD W. MARX

A Unique Partnership Is Shaped. One of our digital teams' first tasks was to operationalize a truly innovative payer-provider relationship unlike any other. Cleveland Clinic teamed with Oscar Health to develop the nation's first "digital payer plan"—to try and take an outlandishly expensive, outrageously complicated insurance system and restore its focus on the needs of the member. The exclusive provider would be our medical staff, and it would run on Oscar's digital platform. Clearly to make this work, our operational, clinical, and finance teams did the heavy lifting. As the business and clinical process discussions began, we wanted to ensure that all the digital components necessary to enable a great patient and member experience were there from the very start.

The resulting insurance product would engage members in their health and proactively guide them through their experience. Instead of passing higher costs on to individuals and employers, the focus was to empower members to access and choose better, more affordable care. Oscar itself rejected the usual route of broad network contracts of varied quality and chose to partner with a select few of the best hospitals and doctors like Cleveland Clinic to give members a curated experience. We knew we could only enable this kind of deep integration and member experience by leveraging the best of our combined digital capabilities.

The new Cleveland Clinic | Oscar health plan would bring us both closer to our vision of what better healthcare looks like. We believed that strengthening the quality of care and access to it requires a relentless focus on the member/patient. By linking a member engagement platform like Oscar to our first-rate health system, we could deliver a seamless, unified healthcare experience—one that will improve health outcomes and lower costs and make it easier than ever for the member to navigate the system.

A New Payvider Design. We agreed to digitally enable all patient and member experiences with these über-goals:

- Every new Cleveland Clinic | Oscar member will be matched with both a Cleveland Clinic Care Team—a dedicated primary care doctor and care managers—and an Oscar Concierge team, with a nurse and three care guides.
- Every new Cleveland Clinic | Oscar member will have free, 24/7 access to Doctors on Call and Cleveland Clinic's Express Care Online,

optimized care search tools, and a beautifully designed mobile experience that empowers them to be in control of their care.
▪ Every new Cleveland Clinic | Oscar member will have access to our
prestigious Cleveland Clinic network, with over 3,500 full-time physicians and 14,000 nurses across 140 specialties and subspecialties, a 165-
acre main campus and community hospitals, family health centers, and
health and wellness centers in the five counties of service around North
Ohio.

Design Begins. While we had aligned incentives and a clear vision, the
potential for friction remained high. Two bold organizations—one based
on 100 years of tradition and the other a relative newcomer, collaborating
on a first-of-its-kind partnership. Optimism was high. Over the next several
months, our engineers, designers, clinicians, and data scientists worked side
by side to ensure every touchpoint delivers easy, affordable, and guided
care.

Blending and Bending Cultures. With an aggressive timetable laid
out, it was time to get to work. There were no illusions that one culture
would acquiesce to the other. In fact, that was never the direction. Rather,
we would allow both parties to work the way they do best and blend and
bend as needed for collaborative success. In order to preempt any challenges related to culture, we were proactive to help ensure success. These
were the steps we took.

▪ Team Selection. We only selected the best from each of our organizations to work on this endeavor—not just as individual contributors but
more importantly, on how well they would work with one another.
▪ Introductions. We brought the teams together, and everyone had a
chance to share their backgrounds, their experience, and their role on
the team and their professional why.
▪ Inclusivity. Everyone had a voice. No matter how small or big the individual role, every member was expected and encouraged to speak up.
Being quiet on this team was not an option.
▪ Conflict Resolution. We insisted that all inevitable conflicts be worked
out at the earliest time possible and directly with the individuals
responsible. We had no time for backdoor conversations and silent
escalations. We had to avoid the needless chatter and energy
waste from gossipers. We preferred and practiced respectful direct
confrontation.

- Escalations. We set up a process for immediate escalations when conflicts could not be resolved easily. All these were dealt with transparently and swiftly. While it took a couple of turns to perfect, the process was smooth and swift when needed.
- Togetherness. Initial meetings were held at each organization's headquarters for two reasons. One is to get to know the organization more deeply, a better understanding of the people and culture. Second, it naturally caused deeper engagement with one another and developed a shared sense of destiny.
- Team Charter. While there was an early draft to get things going, now that we developed deeper connections, we revisited and updated. The charter was short and simple so as not to create too much bureaucracy or operational burden. For instance, we agreed to adopt agile methodologies but stopped short of mandating that teams outside of our digital structure operate exactly like us. This may have been the ideal state, but it harkens back to the blend and bend, not break a particular division culture. While digital teams were particularly adept with agile, this was something new for our clinical counterparts as an example.
- Routine Updates. We leveraged agile processes here where we had daily stand-ups, so there never was a time, when we were hit with a devastating surprise. We dealt with decisions swiftly and attempted to proactively remove blockers.
- Process Training. As shared, while not mandated across all divisions, we did provide ample training and coaching opportunities related to agile. Whatever design, engineering, and project management process you adopt, it is critical to provide continuous training to the teams.
- Executive Sponsorship. We ensured that executives remained highly visible and engaged throughout the creation of this new organization. It was critical to the culture that teams knew the importance of the work we were doing and were reminded of the why.
- Fellowship. We know the adage "Work hard—play hard." We took ample time to break bread when together and engage on a personal level where we could. Relationships are the key to any kind of success, especially when trying to blend and bend cultures.

Outcomes. The collaborative effort to create a first-of-its-kind, highly engaging, digitally powered payvider model was a great success. There were times when we would get agitated and frustrated, but those times were rare, especially given the complexity of this effort. The NPS scores for both patients and members were high. Quality outcomes were improved. In the first few years, we did not attract as many enrollees as envisioned, but the numbers climbed and still continue to grow. I think with any new insurance product in a crowded field, an uptick will take some time. That said, the product was revolutionary when first delivered, and now we have similar competing products emerging but not as fantastic as the Cleveland Clinic–Oscar model.

We know this success could not be achieved without a joint, relentless focus on blending cultures for shared success. If innovation through blended cultures can be achieved in the healthcare payer space, it can be accomplished anywhere!

ALIGNING YOUR ORGANIZATION'S BELIEF SYSTEM | BY SAKSHIKA DHINGRA

A well-blended culture isn't a pleasant side effect of two or more distinct entities coming together to progress a common goal forward with creative and innovative problem-solving. "Blending cultures" is, in fact, an essential catalyst and a success strategy that must be sought, deliberated, and applied to drive innovation across industries.

This "blending cultures" strategy becomes even more foundational to achieving success in an industry such as healthcare where "human experience" lies at the center of every aspiration. We humans perceive each experience with our own cultural lens, which is unique to every community, every region, and every society. So naturally blending cultures within the healthcare industry holds immense potential for fostering innovation and driving the development of groundbreaking solutions. The fusion of diverse perspectives, expertise, and approaches from different areas within payer organizations or even different payer organizations can lead to the much-needed transformative changes in healthcare delivery, technology utilization, patient care, and cost management. This convergence facilitates the creation of novel strategies, services, and systems that address multifaceted challenges.

Diverse Perspectives and Problem-Solving

Bringing together payer organizations with distinct cultures nurtures a melting pot of ideas. Each entity might have unique methods of addressing challenges, and combining these approaches can spark innovative problem-solving. Diverse perspectives help in reimagining existing processes and finding creative solutions to complex healthcare issues.

Aetna's integration with CVS Health is a perfect example. The merger aimed to combine CVS's retail healthcare services and Aetna's insurance expertise. The goal was to create innovative care delivery models, such as HealthHUBs within CVS stores, offering an array of health services beyond traditional pharmacy services.

Enhanced Collaboration and Knowledge Exchange

When cultures blend, collaboration becomes enriched. Different organizational cultures often bring varied expertise, experiences, and knowledge. This amalgamation can lead to the cross-pollination of ideas, fostering an environment where sharing best practices, technological advancements, and methodologies becomes more prevalent. Cigna's acquisition of Express Scripts exemplifies the successful blending of cultures within payer organizations. By merging their health insurance services with pharmacy benefit management, they aimed to revolutionize healthcare delivery. The fusion allowed them to leverage data analytics, technology, and patient-centric services to enhance outcomes and optimize costs.

Holistic Member/Patient-Centric Solutions

Blending cultures enables payer organizations to develop more comprehensive, patient-centric solutions. For instance, Anthem's creation of IngenioRx, an in-house pharmacy benefit manager, exemplifies blending cultures to drive innovation. This initiative aimed to internalize pharmacy benefit management, allowing Anthem to control costs, improve member experience, and integrate pharmacy and medical benefits more effectively.

Innovation in Technology Adoption

Combining cultures also accelerates the adoption of innovative technologies. For example, integrating data analytics from one organization with another's expertise in telemedicine could lead to advanced predictive analytics for better patient outcomes and more efficient care delivery.

Another great example that drives this point home is Humana and CenterWell. CenterWell Senior Primary Care and Humana Insurance Services collectively drive innovation forward by combining expertise in senior-focused care, insurance services, technology integration, and a commitment to preventive health measures. Their collaboration epitomizes a holistic approach to healthcare, emphasizing patient-centric care, innovative insurance solutions, and the integration of technology to improve health outcomes. Together, they aim to redefine the healthcare experience for seniors, fostering better health, increased accessibility, and improved overall well-being.

Approach

Blending cultures for innovation at an organizational level involves integrating different cultural elements, values, and perspectives to foster creativity, adaptability, and problem-solving. This process can lead to a more innovative and dynamic organization. Here's a step-by-step guide on how to think about and implement this approach:

1. **Understand Your Own Current Culture:** Start by thoroughly understanding your organization's current culture, including its values, norms, and traditions. Once done, identify the cultural elements that support or hinder innovation.
2. **Assess the Need for Cultural Blending:** Consider the reasons for blending cultures. This could be due to mergers and acquisitions, expansion into new markets, or a desire for increased innovation. Clearly define the goals you want to achieve through cultural blending.
3. **Cultural Mapping:** If you are blending cultures from multiple entities, map out the key elements of each culture. This includes values, communication styles, decision-making processes, and leadership approaches.
4. **Identify Common Values and Goals:** Look for shared values and goals among the different cultures. Identify areas of common ground that can serve as a foundation for blending. These shared values can become the basis for a unified culture that encourages innovation.
5. **Define New Cultural Values:** Develop a set of cultural values that reflect the desired innovative culture. These values should encompass the best elements of each culture while aligning with the organization's innovation goals.

6. **Leadership Alignment:** Ensure that leaders and key influencers in the organization are aligned with the vision for a blended culture. Leaders should model the desired cultural values and demonstrate commitment to the cultural blending process.

7. **Communication and Transparency:** Effective communication is crucial. Clearly and transparently communicate the reasons for cultural blending, the new cultural values, and how this change will impact employees and the organization.

8. **Inclusivity and Participation:** Involve employees in the process of cultural blending. Encourage them to provide input and share their perspectives. Inclusivity fosters a sense of ownership and commitment to the new culture.

9. **Training and Development:** Offer training and development programs to help employees understand and adapt to the new culture. This can include cultural sensitivity training, leadership development, and innovation-focused workshops.

10. **Recognition and Rewards:** Align recognition and rewards systems with the desired cultural values. Recognize and celebrate employees who exemplify the innovative culture.

11. **Feedback Loops:** Establish feedback mechanisms to continually assess the effectiveness of cultural blending. Regularly solicit input from employees and be open to making adjustments as needed.

12. **Tolerance for Experimentation:** Foster a culture that tolerates experimentation and accepts that not all innovations will succeed. Encourage employees to take calculated risks and learn from failures.

13. **Cross-cultural Teams:** Form cross-cultural teams to work on innovative projects. Diverse teams can bring different perspectives and approaches to problem-solving, leading to more innovative solutions.

14. **Measure Progress:** Develop KPIs to measure the organization's progress toward its innovation goals. This may include metrics related to product development, employee engagement, and customer satisfaction.

15. **Celebrate Success:** Celebrate successful innovations that result from the blended culture. Highlight and share stories of how the new culture is driving positive change.

16. **Iterate and Evolve:** Recognize that cultural blending is an ongoing process. It requires continuous assessment, refinement, and adaptation to remain aligned with the organization's evolving goals and external changes.

Blending cultures for innovation is a complex and dynamic process that requires time and commitment. When done effectively, it can lead to a more innovative, adaptable, and culturally rich organization that thrives in a rapidly changing world.

Food for Thought

We just learned that the right culture plays a critical role in upping the innovation quotient of an organization. And organizational beliefs serve as the bedrock upon which this culture can be built. The core values and principles set the tone for the culture, influencing the behaviors, attitudes, and decision-making processes of individuals within the organization. Culture, in turn, reinforces and sustains organizational beliefs. When shared values and principles are consistently demonstrated and practiced within the workplace, they solidify as part of the organizational culture. For instance, if a company strongly values innovation, a culture of experimentation and risk-taking might be fostered to support this belief. When organizational beliefs align with the prevalent culture, it creates consistency in actions, fostering a sense of cohesion and unity among employees. Conversely, a misalignment between beliefs and culture can lead to confusion, inconsistency, and a lack of trust within the organization.

Given the importance of consistent demonstration and practice of shared values and organizational beliefs, I strongly believe the concept and role of a "chief beliefs officer" becomes of utmost value within a company. While this specific title might not commonly exist, the role it embodies can be integral in shaping the identity and direction of an organization. A chief beliefs officer would be responsible for safeguarding and promoting the core values and beliefs that define the organization. They would ensure that these values remain integral to decision-making, strategies, and day-to-day operations. They would facilitate an environment where beliefs in continuous improvement, agility, and creativity thrive.

It's important to note that if your organization is not able to carve out a dedicated chief beliefs officer role, the responsibilities as summarized earlier must be distinctly defined and distributed across various roles such as the CEO, HR, or ethics and compliance departments. As it is, the specific responsibilities and scope of a CBO would depend on the organization's size, its unique culture, and beliefs. Whatever leadership structure is deployed, the principles and steps remain universal.

Blending Cultures Outcomes

As the commentary and the industry examples shared earlier demonstrate, transformation and innovation can be achieved when there is organizational focus and determination. So often, it is not technology that slows down our ability to collaborate and innovate. Rather, it is the softer skills, such as the ability to blend organizational cultures that keeps us from achieving the possible and innovating to create better experiences.

BRIDGING HEALTHCARE INNOVATION: BLENDING CULTURES IN PAYER MODELS | ANONYMOUS

Introduction

The landscape of healthcare is undergoing profound transformations, driven by technological advancements, changing patient expectations, and the need for more efficient and effective healthcare systems. Amidst this evolution, innovative payer models are emerging as key players in reshaping the healthcare ecosystem. One intriguing theme that has gained prominence in this context is "blend cultures." This theme emphasizes the convergence of diverse cultural perspectives, practices, and technologies within payer healthcare innovation. In this chapter, we explore how blending cultures in payer models can lead to more inclusive, patient-centered, and adaptable healthcare systems.

We have witnessed the benefits of blending cultures in non-healthcare verticals, and it was only a matter of time before we caught up, especially on the payer side. The methodology we undertook was in three distinct parts, which, in our experience, are laid out in the following. First, make sure to communicate what "blend cultures" really means for our organization, what is the process that worked for us generally, and then some real-world examples. You will want to modify our experience to fit your organization best.

Cultural Influences on Healthcare

Culture shapes our beliefs, values, and behaviors, including how we approach health and wellness. Cultural diversity is a hallmark of societies worldwide, and acknowledging its impact on healthcare is crucial. Cultural factors influence healthseeking behaviors, treatment preferences, and the way individuals interact with healthcare systems. For payer healthcare innovation, recognizing and incorporating cultural nuances are essential for building trust, reducing disparities, and ensuring equitable healthcare access for all.

The Blend Cultures Approach

The blend cultures approach in payer healthcare innovation involves intentionally incorporating diverse cultural perspectives, practices, and technologies to create a more holistic and adaptable healthcare system. This approach transcends geographic and ethnic boundaries, recognizing that every individual's health journey is influenced by a blend of cultural elements.

Culturally Tailored Communication

Effective communication is a cornerstone of successful healthcare interactions. Payers are increasingly recognizing the importance of tailoring communication to diverse cultural backgrounds. This involves using culturally sensitive language, visuals, and channels that resonate with various populations. For instance, a payer might provide educational materials in multiple languages and formats, ensuring that information reaches and empowers diverse communities.

Bridging Traditional and Modern Medicine

The blend cultures approach encourages the integration of traditional and modern medical practices. Traditional medicine often holds deep cultural significance and wisdom, which can complement modern healthcare approaches. Payers are exploring partnerships with traditional healers and practitioners to offer patients a blend of treatments that align with their cultural beliefs. This not only enhances healthcare options but also respects and validates diverse cultural perspectives.

Technology as a Cultural Bridge

Technology plays a pivotal role in blending cultures within payer healthcare innovation. Telemedicine, mobile apps, and online platforms can bridge geographical and cultural gaps, allowing individuals from different backgrounds to access quality care. Payers are developing user-friendly digital tools that accommodate diverse languages, cultural symbols, and preferences, making healthcare resources more inclusive and accessible.

Cultural Competence in Payer Models

Cultural competence, defined as the ability to understand, respect, and respond to the healthcare needs of diverse populations, is a cornerstone of the blend cultures approach. Payers are reimagining their roles as cultural brokers, striving to create an environment where patients from all backgrounds feel understood and valued.

Culturally Diverse Workforce

One way payers are fostering cultural competence is by cultivating a diverse work-force that reflects the communities they serve. Employing individuals from different cultural backgrounds brings a range of perspectives and insights, enabling more effective communication and care coordination. Moreover, a culturally diverse workforce can contribute to innovative solutions that resonate with various patient groups.

Training and Education

Payers are investing in training programs that equip their employees with cultural competence skills. Healthcare professionals are taught to navigate cultural nuances sensitively, ensuring that care is delivered in a manner that respects individual beliefs and preferences. This training extends to administrative staff, ensuring that the entire healthcare experience, from enrollment to billing, is culturally inclusive.

Overcoming Challenges and Realizing Benefits

While the blend cultures approach holds great promise, it also presents challenges that must be addressed to achieve its full potential.

Addressing Bias and Stereotypes

Cultural biases and stereotypes can inadvertently influence healthcare decisions and interactions. Payers must actively work to address these biases within their systems and promote cultural humility among their staff. This involves ongoing self-awareness, education, and fostering open dialogues about cultural sensitivity.

Ethical Considerations

Blending cultures requires a deep understanding of ethical considerations, especially when integrating traditional practices with modern medicine. Payers must navigate questions of safety, efficacy, and patient autonomy, while respecting the cultural significance of certain practices.

Standardization versus Customization

Striking a balance between standardized processes and customized care can be challenging. Payers need to develop frameworks that allow for flexibility while maintaining quality and efficiency. Technology, once again, can play a pivotal role in creating adaptable systems that cater to individual needs.

One excellent real-world example of blending cultures in healthcare leading to disruptive innovation is the collaboration between Western medicine and traditional Chinese medicine (TCM) in the field of cancer treatment. This innovative approach combines the strengths of both medical systems to improve patient outcomes and quality of life.

Integrative Oncology in Cancer Treatment

Cancer treatment traditionally followed Western medical approaches like surgery, chemotherapy, and radiation therapy. These treatments can be aggressive and often result in side effects, affecting patients' overall well-being.

In recent years, some healthcare institutions and researchers have embraced an integrative approach to cancer treatment by blending Western medicine with TCM. This approach is a result of recognizing the benefits of combining the two medical systems.

Innovation and Benefits

Acupuncture for Pain Management: Acupuncture, a key component of TCM, has been integrated into cancer care to manage pain, alleviate chemotherapy-induced nausea, and improve overall comfort for patients.

Herbal Medicine and Supplements: Chinese herbal medicine and dietary supplements have been used to complement cancer treatment. Certain herbs and compounds are believed to enhance the immune system and reduce the side effects of chemotherapy.

Mind-Body Practices: Techniques such as tai chi, qigong, and meditation, which are part of TCM, are incorporated to reduce stress and improve the psychological wellbeing of cancer patients.

Personalized Treatment Plans: Integrative oncology takes a holistic and patient-centered approach. Healthcare providers work closely with patients to develop personalized treatment plans that consider not only the medical aspects of cancer but also the patient's emotional and mental well-being.

Research and Clinical Trials: Collaborative research between Western medical institutions and TCM experts has led to clinical trials evaluating the effectiveness of various integrative treatments. This research has contributed to the evidence base supporting integrative oncology.

The blending of Western medicine and TCM in cancer care has disrupted the traditional approach to cancer treatment in several ways:

Improved Quality of Life: Integrative oncology has helped cancer patients manage side effects, reduce pain, and enhance their overall quality of life during and after treatment.

Reduced Healthcare Costs: By preventing or mitigating some of the side effects of aggressive cancer treatments, integrative oncology can lead to cost savings in the healthcare system.

Patient-Centered Care: This approach prioritizes the patient's well-being, providing a more holistic and personalized approach to treatment.

Wider Acceptance: Integrative oncology has gained acceptance in many healthcare institutions, leading to more comprehensive cancer care options for patients.

Research and Collaboration: The collaboration between Western and TCM practitioners has spurred ongoing research and clinical trials, leading to further innovations in cancer care.

While the integration of Western medicine and TCM in cancer treatment is just one example, it illustrates how blending cultures in healthcare can lead to disruptive innovation, benefiting both patients and the healthcare industry as a whole. It highlights the importance of an openminded approach to medical practices and a willingness to explore new avenues for improved patient care.

Another great example where blending cultures within payer organizations in healthcare led to disruptive innovation is the partnership between Anthem, one of the largest health insurance companies in the United States, and HealthCore, a subsidiary of Anthem, to create the HealthCore Collaborative.

Anthem and Healthcore—Healthcore Collaborative

Anthem recognized the need to harness real-world data and research to drive innovation in healthcare, particularly in the areas of clinical research and evidence based medicine. HealthCore, a subsidiary of Anthem, specialized in healthcare research and had a culture of innovation. Together, they established the HealthCore Collaborative to blend their cultures and expertise.

Blending Cultures

Cultural Integration: Anthem and HealthCore worked to integrate their cultures by fostering a collaborative environment, where health-care experts, data scientists, researchers, and technology professionals could collaborate effectively.

Shared Vision: Both organizations shared a vision of leveraging real-world data and evidence-based insights to improve healthcare decision-making, enhance patient outcomes, and reduce costs. This shared vision served as a foundation for cultural alignment.

Cross-disciplinary Teams: The collaborative initiative brought together multidisciplinary teams comprising healthcare professionals, data scientists, researchers, and IT experts. This blending of diverse skill sets was essential for driving innovation.

Innovation and Impact

Real-World Evidence: The HealthCore Collaborative leveraged real-world evidence from Anthem's vast patient database to conduct research, analyze outcomes, and identify trends. This data-driven approach disrupted traditional clinical research methods that relied heavily on clinical trials.

Evidence-Based Medicine: The collaboration focused on promoting evidence-based medicine by providing physicians with insights derived from real-world data. This led to more informed treatment decisions, improved care quality, and reduced variations in care.

Cost Reduction: By utilizing real-world data to identify cost-effective treatment approaches and interventions, the collaborative initiative contributed to cost reduction in healthcare, benefiting both payers and patients.

Population Health Management: The collaborative approach facilitated population health management strategies by identifying at-risk patient populations and implementing targeted interventions.

Accelerated Research: HealthCore's expertise in healthcare research and Anthem's access to a vast patient population accelerated research timelines and enabled faster innovation in healthcare.

Patient-Centered Outcomes: The focus on blending cultures to enhance research and evidence-based practices ultimately led to more patient-centered outcomes and improved healthcare experiences.

The partnership between Anthem and HealthCore through the HealthCore Collaborative exemplifies how blending cultures within payer organizations in healthcare can drive disruptive innovation. By fostering collaboration, sharing a vision, and leveraging real-world data, the collaboration transformed the way clinical research is conducted, accelerated the adoption of evidence-based medicine, and contributed to cost reduction and improved patient out-comes. This case demonstrates the potential of cultural integration to disrupt traditional healthcare practices and drive innovation.

The Future Landscape of Healthcare

In conclusion, the blend cultures theme in payer healthcare innovation represents a paradigm shift that transcends conventional healthcare models. By embracing diverse cultural perspectives, practices, and technologies, payers are working toward more inclusive and patient-centered systems. This approach has the potential to reduce health-care disparities, improve patient outcomes, and enhance overall healthcare experiences. As payers continue to blend cultures, they lay the foundation for a healthcare landscape that not only embraces diversity but thrives on it, creating a healthier, more connected world.

You can see the approach we undertook is scalable and transferable. We are certain it will require modifications to best fit your organization but recognize the importance of the first two steps we outlined—clearly articulating the definition and opportunity for "blending cultures" and an easy-to-understand process. Your outcomes will follow.

Chapter 2

Use People with IT

Do not create an over-reliance on people or on technology; use both resources in concert.

Often, we rely too heavily on technology as we embark on innovation. Sometimes innovation starts at the other extreme with people but little incorporation of automation or tools. The best innovations tend to be the result of a strong balance at the intersection of people and technology. Always take an inventory of people and technology to ensure balance. It is the ability to take the best of people and technology, and then melding them together, that ignites innovation.

DISRUPTING LEGACY PROCESSES | BY JOHN LEE, MD

Over the past decade, there has been an avalanche of technology infused into healthcare, especially after HITECH effectively mandated electronic medical records in our healthcare systems. The promise of the effort was that doing so would transform our broken healthcare system. The result has been a mixed bag.

On the plus side, we now have access to information that was previously locked in paper charts. I can't count the number of times that being able to get records and see information from a different encounter or facility has dramatically and positively changed my management. However, there are many well-known negative unintended problems such as note-bloat, alert fatigue, and pajama-time documentation, among many others.

 DOI: 10.4324/9781003381983-2

My observation is that there is a common theme when we discuss our lack of progress in changing healthcare: we are trying to hammer square technology into the round hole of 20th-century medicine. Clayton Christensen wrote about two different types of innovation: sustaining and disruptive. Much of the innovation I have seen in healthcare now is sustaining innovation. We are doing the same things we have done in the past, just faster. More documentation. More alerts. Faster insurance processing. More and faster dysfunctional processes aren't a good way to fix our healthcare system.

What we really need is disruptive innovation. We need to get out of our own way and imagine the best ways to use technology. Consider how technology and disruptive innovation have changed our lives. I recall hearing about the novelty of turning off landline telephone service and going only with cell phone service. Moving to cell phone-based communication wasn't only about simply replacing landline phones with cellular devices. It created entirely new technical and media platforms that are embedded into how we live our lives today.

Compare that example with how we have approached innovation in the healthcare space. Almost all the innovations I have experienced are effectively digital analogs of our paper and analog past. What can we do to do better? How can we truly innovate and disrupt a system that is slowly eating away at our collective health and prosperity?

Prior Authorization

Probably the most prominent poster child of dysfunctional sustaining innovation is prior authorization. It is commonly cited as a top pain point for clinicians. More importantly, it is an enormous contributor to poor patient experience. Think about the typical process. A physician recommends a test, procedure, or therapy. The patient trusts the physician and is ready to proceed. But then there is an effective pause button. Hold on. We have to get this approved. Sometimes the approval is quick. Sometimes it can be very prolonged. All the while, the patient has to put life on hold and hope that their lumbar disc pain, multiple sclerosis, or cancer also hits a pause.

The friction point occurs because the ordering physician must dedicate resources to go on a scavenger hunt looking for various pieces of information and data to populate an authorization. While this process occurs, the patient waits. If there is even a small piece missing, the patient waits longer.

If there is a difference of opinion between the ordering physician and the payer, a live conversation is scheduled between the ordering provider and the insurance company. Again, the patient waits.

The "innovations" typically consist of relying on technology to speed up this process. Prior authorization documentation prepopulates for the ordering provider so the staff doesn't have to go on the metaphorical scavenger-hunt. Insurance companies digitally scrape the authorization request so a human doesn't have to touch the process. I have heard humorous but not unrealistic discussions about the process being subsumed by provider bots "talking" to (or arguing with) payer bots.

However, if you think about the history of prior authorization and its origins in paper, telephone, and fax, we are basically digitizing this process. While we certainly need to improve on the process, perhaps we need to think harder about the process itself. As a health executive colleague of mine noted about this specific theme of innovation, "The road of prior authorization is getting smoother but are we paving the right road?" If we think about the collective cord cutting of POTS in the past 20 years, we realized that traditional landline phones were a "road" that didn't suit our long-term needs. Perhaps we should consider the same thing with the prior authorization process. Why stick with a process that, at its foundation, is based on paper, telephone, and fax technology?

Ultimately, we should consider the reason for prior authorization in the first place. Although many of my physician colleagues and patient advocates argue that the process is one that exists purely to deny payment, let's assume that the real reason is to make sure scarce and expensive resources are used appropriately. If you think about this, the paper/phone/fax paradigm makes at least some sense for 1980. However, with our current digital foundation and the technologies that are currently available, we are (borrowing Henry Ford's famous metaphor) trying to create a faster horse.

Instead, we should use technology within another paradigm. Let's think about the ultimate purpose: appropriate use of expensive resources. If we focus on this, we don't need a workflow based on almost 50-year-old technology. The current prior authorization process involves a series of criteria that the ordering provider has to document: Has an X-ray been done within six months? Has the patient had a certain medication failure? Does the patient have a particularly abnormal lab test? Has the patient had symptoms documented over x number of months? Although the default is to check these at each ordering event, with our current technology, we can collect these data en masse and visualize a particular provider's or group of providers' compliance with these criteria. If we then created a reimburse-ment structure that incentivized compliance, we could manage a whole port-folio of "authorizations" by dashboard. The incentive structure would then nudge providers to the "right" ordering behavior. If we did it right, it would result in the right decision by the provider, immediate access for the patient, lower (or more efficient) costs, better outcomes, and far less pain.

Remote Medicine

Medicine is too difficult to navigate. We have to dedicate two hours of driv-ing, parking, and waiting for a 15-minute (if we're lucky) doctor's office visit. The high fixed expenses of offices, hospitals, and other medical facilities add extraordinary costs. Hence, many have been excited about technologies such as telemedicine, asynchronous patient messaging (aka in basket messaging), and remote patient monitoring (RPM). Collectively, they encompass technolo-gies that theoretically will transform medical encounters in the same ways Amazon has transformed retail consumerism.

Unfortunately, their introduction has not revolutionized the way we deliver care. Yes, telemedicine became an indispensable tool during the COVID-19 pandemic, but its use has plummeted. Utilization is still certainly higher than pre-pandemic levels, but the core of most physician practices has reverted back to the 20th century, in person, in office/hospital care. Patient messaging has become the bane of many physicians' existence, con-tributing to hours of "pajama time." In my work with RPM, I have found the effort is focused on generating measurements and the resultant CPT codes, not on changing outcomes.

I think these are really potentially powerful technologies but we need to reimagine their usage and use them in ways that maximize their potential. Let's not try to make these newer versions of the CPT-based encounters that have fed the medical beast for decades. These tools instead can be low-friction ways to interact with patients and generate really useful insights that can truly transform the experience and improve outcomes. For instance, let us consider heart failure patients with multiple comorbidities. She has had a long hospital stay and multiple medication adjustments. Currently, she would get a typical 1–2-week office scheduled, discharge instructions that are dozens of pages thick, and many crossed fingers. We hope she under-stands all she needs to do to prevent herself from bouncing back to the hospital.

These technologies can bridge the gap with connections and feedback until the next in-person interaction. A pharmacist can reach out to the patient via telemedicine the day after discharge and before the patient takes her first flurry of new medications, potentially preventing a medication error. A smart scale can be deployed to detect that she gained 5 pounds of water overnight, triggering a message to the patient to take another dose of her diuretic. When the smart bottle signals her care team that the patient has not taken her additional dose, someone contacts her to have an oldfashioned phone conversation.

To fully exploit this, we need teams of care and an infrastructure that delegates and efficiently distributes these interactions to the various team members. They must all work at the top of their licenses, and the technologies of telemedicine, asynchronous messaging, and remote monitoring are components of a well-oiled holistic approach, not isolated tools generating charges.

Changing the Mindset

These are but a few examples of technologies that are missing the mark because we are not utilizing technologies in ways that maximize their potential. There are many other examples, but they have a similar theme. We are hamstringing our efforts by relying on frameworks and workflows that match 20th-century technologies and workflows instead of modernizing our approach to match what the current technology can do.

I acknowledge that addressing these mismatches will require significant changes in infrastructure and reengineering of workflows. Most prominently, changes in the underlying payment structure will be required to facilitate such disruptive innovation. We need this disruption. Although it has been said many times over the past few decades, our current trajectory is simply unsustainable. Our healthcare system is already objectively failing our population. We can't afford to fail more.

I firmly believe that the full force of technology cannot be realized until we use technology to change the way we deliver care, not match the technology to how we currently deliver care. We need to move away from making the technology fit our legacy workflows and payment mechanisms with sustaining innovation. We need to reimagine and avoid applying technology to "pave the wrong road." We need to disrupt the *way* we use our technology. Otherwise, we will be creating 21st-century versions of an internal combustion buggy whip.

THE CONVERGENCE OF DATA AND RELATIONSHIPS IS WHERE THE MAGIC HAPPENS | BY BRANDY BAILEY

Have you ever seen a plan just come together? Successful business leaders have. They've seen the magic of great business decisions truly happen when they leverage trusted data to identify improvement opportunities and align passionate purpose-driven people with innovation opportunities and resources to drive outcomes. The adage "Let the dataset change your mindset" is foundational, but having a team who looks beyond the obvious insights of a dataset to see what may lie between and beneath is how you move from change to transformation.

As a gerontologist, my passion for care of our elderly community drives my commitment to explore and foster innovation in healthcare to enable adults to happily and confidently age in place with dignity. In practice, this looks like leveraging data to gain valuable insights into my member or patient healthcare utilization patterns and to work to understand the "why?" of their health journey—as in "Why did my member or patient visit the emergency department three days in a row"? As payers, we deploy integrated care management; social, behavioral, and disease programs; and tools to help gain valuable insights to better understand the patterns with a goal of proactively identifying our member's needs, providing avenues to allow members to engage in their own wellness more effectively, preventing avoidable negative outcomes. One of my most interesting discoveries occurred while reviewing data from a RPM program and provided me an opportunity to unite people and technology to engage in a solution.

RPM is a common tool for payers to help members engage in more effective chronic disease management and often results in the issuance of connected devices to measure basic health indicators, such as blood pressure, pulse oximetry, weight, and blood glucose. Proactive and forward-thinking payers track and analyze the information, setting up business rules to determine if a member's readings from the devices are indicative of an exacerbation or worsening of their chronic conditions, resulting in outreach to encourage the member to get appropriate proactive care. That appropriate proactive care usually results in a primary care providers (PCP) or specialty provider visit to assess the trends such as weight gain, which may be indicative of a congestive heart failure exacerbation or a pulse oximetry reading, which may indicate an acute on chronic exacerbation of chronic obstructive pulmonary disease. The proactive engagement of outpatient care is intended to prevent an escalation or deterioration of the member's condition.

One day, I decided it was time to measure the efficacy of this RPM program and began to dive deep into the data. I wanted to understand what trends were in the member data and were we providing the right outreach at the right time to engage members in proactive care. Based on this analysis, I was able to see member values, triggers, and subsequent outreach, but I also noticed something interesting in the data that was totally unexpected; I noticed insights in the administrative data, not just the health data.

For example, one member whose values were reading in the normal range, thus not triggering any of the system rules and logic that would have resulted in a prompt for the care manager to outreach, had very interesting patterns in their readings. There were multiple readings of their pulse oximeter and blood pressure cuff in the middle of the night, in the early hours of the morning. I found this interesting. It intrigued me, why would someone check their pulse oximeter at 2 a.m. and further why would they check their pulse oximetry repeatedly when their first reading was normal? Upon further investigation, I noted this member was diagnosed with bipolar disorder and began to speculate said member was ramping into a manic episode. Caregivers were deployed to the member's home to on them, and as suspected, the member had fully escalated into a manic episode. We were able to engage the members in treatment and care to keep them safe and prevent hospitalization. This is when my team and I began to realize we had access to data, and the data was talking to us. Were we listening? We began to and that allowed us to better support our members' behavioral health needs more effectively, not just through the values in the RPM device readings but in the patterns of RPM utilization.

This RPM data trend discovery was unintended, but when married with the passion and commitment of an innovative interdisciplinary care team driven to provide holistic proactive care, it became a staple in our toolbox for caring for members with both behavioral health and physical health needs. The interdisciplinary care team became aware of members who had both behavioral health conditions and chronic conditions who were issued RPM devices and began to monitor for data trends, which might indicate more than just a chronic exacerbation, allowing them to proactively engage members and provide them physical and behavioral healthcare. The only way this innovative use of data and technology could have occurred is through the successful convergence of technology and people, where opportunity meets an unrelenting passion for changing the course of some-one's healthcare journey.

This innovation in data application was also additionally intriguing because it provided a way to bring value to members without the introduction of additional programs or tools. As a payer and as a provider, sometimes we can fall into the trap of trying to do too much, and when you try to do everything, you struggle to do everything well and need to focus on the things that matter most. Embracing simplicity for care teams and members becomes key to really being able to drive meaningful outcomes. This outcome revealed an opportunity to do more with what we already had available to us by simply looking at the data with a different lens and putting a whole team's focus behind the purpose.

This lesson was easily applied to and proved valuable in many other areas. Looking deeper into admission trends allowed us to multiply value through our health plan. Moreover, this innovation multiplied passion. Our care team associates are here because they want to improve member health outcomes. It is frustrating for care teams when they do not have the information or tools available to effectively identify, outreach, and engage members. Conversely, when care teams feel they are truly making a difference, they want to be on your team, driving innovation and truly changing the course of people's lives.

Simple Steps

As a passionate healthcare team professional, I offer a few words of advice as you seek to unite people and technology in your own teams. You can experience the same results as we did.

First, Establish Solid Foundations

The key to successful technological overlay in health plan operations is to have a solid process foundation to couple with technology. Applying technology to well-defined processes will maximize your value and enhance your success. Applying technology where you have no existing process or a I was operating in, our health plans and our care management teams had been doing outreach to members to provide chronic disease self-management education and tools for years. This was a core competency of our care management teams and something for which we already had a solid process built. Applying technology, which automated the collection and aggregation of this information and alerts for our care teams via business rules, allowed our care teams to effectively provide oversight to more members, that is, maximizing the value.

Before you adopt a technology that provides a solution for something for which you have no existing process, ask yourself, is this a problem I really need to solve? Certainly, there are many solutions, which can be engaged, but that doesn't mean they will all drive the needed value and may distract your health plan operations from the things that matter most. In the HealthPlan operational world, I commonly see us over adopting technology and interventions in a bid to remain competitive, but what matters most is not how much you do but how well you do the things that matter. This brings me to my next point, understanding what matters most.

Second, Measure What Matters Most

We have an understandable love affair with technology and data. But we can easily overwhelm ourselves and our teams with this and lose focus on what matters most. All too often, I've seen where we can become dazzled with technology and data, and we try to bring on more and more, without consistently evaluating our portfolio to understand what we can consume and manage. This becomes an overload for our teams to administer and our leaders to manage. Understand the key drivers of your member's outcomes and your health plan's success and the key interventions, which are meant to support successful outcomes and measure the ones that matter most. Having a clearly identified strategy for success, measurable key performance indicators, and reports that provide those key insights will empower health plan leaders to drive the people to the data that will allow them to make the most impact.

Third, Connect with Purpose

The final tip I offer is to help your care teams connect the technology and data outputs to their purpose. We live in a world filled with data, but not everyone can see the story behind the data. In health plan operations, many of our associates are caregivers, nurses, social workers, and community health workers, and they all do what they do to make a difference. It is our job to ensure we tell the story behind the data and connect the data to our team's purpose. A practical example for consideration: reducing preventable hospitalizations through a successful RPM program is an expected outcome. But why do we care about preventable hospitalizations? We care, because for frail, older adults, hospital stays can lead to nosocomial infection, reduced functional abilities, and psychosocial setbacks. We care because a day in the hospital is a day not with family and loved ones, and for members who may be in the final years of their life, a single day away is a day too much. But our teams may not be able to draw the parallel that a 2% reduction in preventable hospitalizations could have directly changed the trajectory of a member's life and avoided an institutional placement or that the day or days in the hospital prevented could have allowed them to be home with family for the holidays. As leaders, we have to humanize the data and connect it to our team and their purpose, so they see and, most importantly, feel the value of their hard work.

Use People with Technology Outcomes

The outcomes for our teams and members are immeasurable. As shown, the solution didn't cost more money or have any unintended consequences. Simple to adopt, the speed to execution was near real time. We now look to utilize these same three steps to other challenges we experience, given the lessons we learned and the immediate and positive impact to every stakeholder.

LEVERAGING IT SOLUTIONS AND HUMAN RESOURCES FOR IMPROVED PROVIDER DATA MANAGEMENT | ANONYMOUS

In today's dynamic healthcare industry, provider data accuracy is critical to achieving operational success and customer satisfaction for healthcare providers.[1] Maintaining inaccurate or out-of-date provider information, which can negatively affect plan members and result in subpar service or care, carries harsh penalties for health payers today. Improved provider directory accuracy, accurate claim adjudication, and higher member and provider satisfaction can all be obtained by proactive management of provider data quality. To achieve data accuracy and contextual knowledge, end-user self-service capabilities, data integration, reconciliation, and reconciliation with providers are all crucial. These factors eventually improve decision-making and enable collaborative engagement with providers for better healthcare outcomes.

"Use People with IT" Innovation Pathway in Conduent's PDM

The innovation process that best captures the inspiration behind Conduent Incorporated's new provider data management (PDM) product is "Use People with IT." This route makes use of advanced analytics and cutting-edge artificial intelligence (AI) to gather, verify, and share data regarding doctors' network involvement, demographic changes, and other important details.[7] Conduent's system also includes devoted call-center personnel (people) who contact service providers to confirm any missing or incorrect information, resulting in accurate and current directories. Conduent aims to provide health insurance companies with a single, real-time data source so they can maintain accurate doctor directories, adhere to laws like the No Surprises Act (NSA) and improve overall operational efficiency.

The Integrated IT Solutions—People Skills Basis of PDM

A PDM solution is a healthcare organization's enterprise-wide system for linking and managing provider data.[3] A PDM system combines both IT tools and human expertise. It gathers, verifies, and disseminates provider information using advanced analytics and artificial intelligence (AI). The system serves as the one source of truth for provider data by enabling users to produce, edit, consolidate, analyze, and view provider data in one location. The significance of human abilities in PDM and upkeep cannot be overemphasized.

To guarantee quality and accessibility, data must be regularly reviewed, updated, and corrected in the PDM system.[3] The data stewardship teams are essential to efficiently managing and sustaining provider data. Also, the necessity of the PDM system's seamless integration with existing data sources and its capacity to enhance provider data with data enrichment highlights the requirement for human involvement and experience to guarantee the system operates to its full potential. Hence, a PDM solution combines human skills (such as data governance and data stewardship) with IT technologies (such as AI and advanced analytics) to efficiently manage and maintain provider data.

Conduent's PDM and Aided Compliance with the No Surprises Act

Specifically, when insured individuals unintentionally obtain care from out-of-network hospitals, physicians, or other providers they did not choose, the NSA, a federal statute, creates new safeguards against surprise medical expenses.[4] The law mandates that for certain types of treatments delivered in particular locations, private health plans must apply in-network cost-sharing and pay out-of-network claims. This covers all services offered at in-network facilities, including emergency, post-emergency stabilization, and non-emergency treatments. The NSA also forbids healthcare facilities, including hospitals, from charging patients unexpected medical costs that are greater than the in-network cost-sharing threshold.

The NSA's requirements are in line with Conduent's goal of giving health insurance firms a single, real-time data source. Health insurance firms can more effectively adhere to the NSA's requirements and safeguard consumers from unexpected medical expenses by having accurate and current data on providers' network status and costsharing information. Also, Conduent's services can help health insurance providers operate more effectively as they deal with the intricate legal requirements and claim and billing procedures for out-of-network services.

Emphasis on Using Both IT Solutions and People Skills

Conduent's PDM solution employs advanced analytics (IT) and AI to gather, validate, and disseminate information about doctors' network participation as well as other data points.[2] It also emphasizes that if there is any missing or incorrect information, call-center employees (people) are active in contacting the suppliers for confirmation. Conduent's PDM solution seeks to minimize complexity, reduce inaccurate claims payments, increase member happiness, and improve overall operational performance for health insurance companies by integrating AI and advanced analytics with the involvement of call-center employees. This shows how technology and human knowledge can be combined to increase the accuracy of medical directories and guarantee adherence to laws.

The "Use People with IT" innovation pathway is best illustrated by the emphasis on using both IT solutions and people skills. Johnson et al.[5] emphasize the potential of AI to offer information, aid in decision-making, and improve medical procedures. A strategy to harness the power of AI while preserving a cooperative and supportive relationship between AI systems and human healthcare practitioners is by integrating people skills and AI. When discussing the adoption of AI in healthcare, Johnson et al.[5] bring up the combination of AI and people capabilities and place a strong emphasis on the following three fundamental ideas: data and security, analytics and insights, and shared expertise with several elements of the PDM solution being consistent with the preceding principles.

1. **Data and Security**

   The discussion emphasizes the value of complete transparency and trust in both the training of AI systems and the data and knowledge that go into that process. It is crucial to have faith in the results of AI systems as humans, and these systems collaborate more and more. To gather, verify, and convey a doctor's participation within a network as well as other crucial data points, the PDM solution makes use of cutting-edge AI and advanced analytics.[2] This suggests that the solution places a high priority on maintaining data security and accuracy.

2. **Analytics and Insights**

   The idea of "augmented intelligence" is presented in Johnson et al.'s[5] overview, in which AI technologies complement human activity rather than replace it. AI can aggregate data from various sources, reason semantically, and offer insights to aid healthcare workers in making better decisions, such as doctors making diagnoses or nurses planning patient care. To drive essential daily information updates and minimize frequent data errors, the PDM solution makes use of AI and automation.[2] To improve doctor and member satisfaction and prevent unexpected costs, it offers accurate, current information. These characteristics show how AI can be used to support decision-making and offer useful insights.

3. **Shared Expertise**

   Johnson et al.[5] emphasize how AI systems and human experts complement one another. Human professionals teach and support AI, which causes changes in the workforce and calls for new skills. To develop cutting-edge AI models and develop top-notch business applications, skilled specialists with access to the most recent hardware are needed. The PDM solution is said to reduce inaccurate claims payments, bad member ratings, and dissatisfied doctors by minimizing complexity with a single source of truth.[2] This implies that the solution's main goal is to assist healthcare practitioners by supplying precise and trustworthy data using AI-driven data management.

Singhal et al.[6] discuss the outcomes of using large language models (LLMs) to tackle medical questions and reveal that the accuracy of answering medical questions significantly increases as models are scaled up from 8B to 540B. This suggests that technology, in the form of broader language models, can enhance the capacity to provide appropriate responses to medical queries. More importantly, Singhal et al.[6] emphasize the need for teaching prompt adjustment, which includes combining human knowledge and skill, since scale alone is insufficient. The results of Singhal et al.'s[6] analysis demonstrate that on multiple-choice medical question-answering datasets, the Flan-PaLM models, which featured instruction fine-tuning, outperformed the PaLM models across all model size variants. This shows that integrating technology with efficient instruction tailoring, which includes human expertise, might enhance the precision and efficacy of medical questionanswering models. Conduent's AI-driven PDM solution offers advantages that are consistent with the notion that technology and human knowledge can be combined to improve operational effectiveness for health insurance providers and decrease common data errors, increase doctor and member satisfaction, and increase claims auto-adjudication rates.

Emphasis on Personalized Experiences with IT Solutions

A Conduent Incorporated publication emphasizes how crucial it is for HR to combine digital and interpersonal contacts to improve employee engagement and happiness with digital experiences, including self-service alternatives, better human capital management systems, and feedback tools.[7] Outstanding employee experiences boost engagement and loyalty. Conduent's Life@ Work Connect combines employee health, financial, and wellness data with HR data to provide highly tailored experiences that increase engagement and productivity. This is an emphasis that can significantly help to consistently improve the organization's current PDM solution in the ways highlighted in the following.

1. **Integrate Digital and Human Interactions**
   While utilizing cutting-edge AI and automation to speed up data management procedures, the solution could still offer choices for human validation and verification of crucial data points. With this strategy, health insurance providers can be confident that the information is accurate and reliable.
2. **Focus on Digital Employee Experiences**
   By implementing digital tools for gathering customer feedback, improving the user interface of human capital management systems, and increasing self-service options for health insurance providers, Conduent can improve the user experience of its PDM solution.

3. Strengthen the Life@Work Connect Platform

Conduent can keep developing the Life@Work Connect platform to fur
ther strengthen its PDM solution. Delivering hyper-personalized experiences entails merging more HR data with employee health, wealth, and
well-being data. For health insurance firms using the PDM solution, the
platform can increase engagement and productivity by enabling employees to make knowledgeable decisions based on their preferences.

Conclusion

Conduent Incorporated's PDM system is a prime example of how human
expertise and IT solutions may be successfully combined to improve healthcare operations. Conduent assures accurate and real-time provider data
by integrating advanced analytics and AI with the assistance of call-center
specialists, assisting health insurance companies in adhering to laws like the
NSA. Through Life@Work Connect, the focus on tailored experiences further
boosts engagement and productivity. The effectiveness and precision of the
PDM solution for healthcare providers will be further increased by fusing
digital and human interactions, emphasizing digital employee experiences,
and fortifying the Life@Work Connect platform.

References

1. Eichler, R., & Cartaino, C. (2023). *A Modern Approach to Healthcare Provider Data Management—Wipro*. Wipro—Transform Digitally with Our Technology and IT Consulting Services. https://www.wipro.com/healthcare/a-modern-approach-to-provider-data-management/
2. Conduent. (2023). *Conduent Broadens Healthcare Payer Portfolio with New Innovative AI-Driven Provider Data Management Solution for Health Plans*. https://www.news.conduent. com/news/conduent-broadens-healthcare-payer-portfolio-with-new-innovative-aidriven-provider-data-management-solution-for-health-plans
3. Verato. (2023). *What Is Provider Data Management?* Verato. https://verato.com/blog/what-is-provider-data-management/
4. Pollitz, K. (2021, December 10). *No Surprises Act Implementation: What to Expect in 2022*. KFF. https://www.kff.org/health-reform/issue-brief/no-surprises-act-implementation-what-to-expect-in-2022/
5. Johnson, K. B., Wei, W. Q., Weeraratne, D., Frisse, M. E., Misulis, K., Rhee, K., Zhao, J., & Snowdon, J. L. (2021). Precision Medicine, AI, and the Future

of Personalized Health Care. *Clinical and Translational Science, 14*(1), 86–93. https://doi.org/10.1111/cts.12884

6. Singhal, K., Azizi, S., Tu, T., Mahdavi, S. S., Wei, J., Chung, H. W., Scales, N., Tanwani, A., Cole-Lewis, H., Pfohl, S., Payne, P., Seneviratne, M., Gamble, P., Kelly, C., Babiker, A., Schärli, N., Chowdhery, A., Mansfield, P., Demner-Fushman, D., . . . Natarajan, V. (2023). Large Language Models Encode Clinical Knowledge. *Nature.* https://doi.org/10.1038/ s41586-023-06291-2

7. Maksimovic, A. (2023). *Conduent's Report Highlights the Need of HR Technology Solutions for Personalized Experiences—CX Scoop.* cxscoop.com.https://cxscoop.com/latest-news/ conduents-report-highlights-the-need-of-hr-technology-solutions-for-personalized-experiences/

PAYER ENABLEMENT IN ACCESSIBILITY AND DELIVERY OF PSYCHOSOCIAL CARE TO ENABLE WHOLE PERSON CARE AND OUTCOMES IN PRIMARY CARE PROVIDER CLINICS | BY JAY SUBRAMANIAN

Context for Enabling Accessibility to Psychosocial Care at Primary Care Providers

The purpose of Whole Person-Centered Care Delivery is to minimize disease progression and disease prevention. Today, the many models of care delivery are focused on increased efficiency and efficacy of care at reduced costs and improved outcomes particularly for chronic disease progression. The care delivery at primary point of care is commonly centered around addressing physical aspects of care (medication, procedures, laboratory and radiology parameters, diet, nutrition, and exercise). However, studies show that physical health outcomes are significantly improved when psychosocial services are integrated into the patient care, resulting in decreased re-hospitalization and visits to ER, thereby reducing cost of care. Psychosocial care commonly refers to include both behavioral (includes mental health) and social determinants of health (SDOH) and will be referred throughout the chapter as psychosocial or separately as behavioral, mental, or SDOH services. One such study shows the benefits of integrating psychosocial care for better health outcomes:

> *"The Additive Impact of Multiple Psychosocial Protective Factors on Selected Health Outcomes Among Older Adults"* in Geriatric Nursing, Volume 42, Issue 2, March–April 2021, in which the study

sample included adults age ≥65 who completed a health survey during May–June 2019 (N – 3,577) and the conclusion of the study demonstrates that the additive properties of psychosocial factors significantly improved psychological and physical health outcomes, maximizing their health potential and enhancing quality of life as they age. The unadjusted annual expenditure reduced up to 40% when psychosocial care is provided with physical care.[1]

Another important reason why psychosocial care needs to be addressed at PCPs point of care is because patients with mental health problems end up visiting their primary provider or the ER before they even think of reaching out to specialized mental health provider. In the past three years, starting from the onset of pandemic in early 2020 till today, there has been a significant increase in mental health and substance and alcohol abuse problems. According to Centers for Disease Control (CDC) data in 2021, more than a third (37%) of high school students reported poor mental health during the COVID-19 pandemic, and 44% reported persistent feelings of sadness or hopelessness.[2] According to 2019 National Ambulatory Medical Care Survey, number of visits to physician offices with mental disorders as the primary diagnosis was at 57.2 million[3] and that number is possibly significantly higher post pandemic. The pandemic has affected the public's mental health and well-being in a variety of ways, through isolation and loneliness, job loss and financial instability, and illness and grief.[4] Anxiety, depression, and stress have risen immensely among the various demographics, and alcohol-induced and drug overdose deaths have substantially increased post pandemic. The rising mental and behavioral health problems are further compounded by the severe shortage of mental health professionals that can meet the demands of mental health crisis across the demographics. Access to mental health services has been a serious point of contention even pre-pandemic and has seriously worsened post pandemic. Although there are emerging initiatives by governmental agencies to address mental and behavioral health issues, health equity, and SDOH to drive a comprehensive care delivery model, it is still only at a nascent stage of conversation or early exploration at best, for the PCPs.

Addressing behavioral health enables increased adherence to care, reduced dependency on opioids, and improved mental health status as some of the factors that influence better whole health outcomes. Screening and addressing SDOH helps understand social factors such as housing, transportation, access to food, and social connections that influence physical health outcomes such as diabetes. Influencing whole-person outcomes requires that

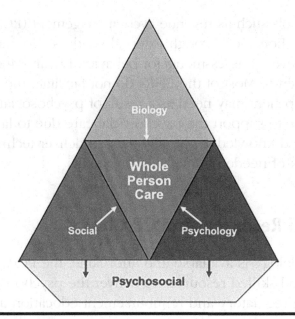

Figure 2.1   Whole Person Care.

the PCPs are equipped with the needed skilled resources, awareness, and training, facilitated by simple-to-use cost-effective technologies for efficiency, insights, and standardization of care. Accessibility to psychosocial care at PCP clinic means that the PCPs have to be adequately supported by cost-effective technologies that drive psychosocial pathways paired with trained resources, provide a framework to build a referral network for follow-up services that are outside the scope of PCPs, and help create an ecosystem that makes the delivery of psychosocial care and whole personcentered outcomes feasible to implement and easy to sustain over time benefiting patients and providers. Before enabling PCPs to implement psychosocial services as part of their routine care, it is important to understand the current processes and challenges experienced by the PCP clinics, and it is split into two main areas:

■ Use of technology
■ Skilled resources.

Commonly Used Technology Software in PCP Clinics

The most used technology by PCPs is the electronic health record (EHR) to document, bill, and report for regulatory and compliance needs. They may use third-party tools such as revenue cycle management (RCM) and billing software either in house or through external vendors. More and more EHRs enable minimal level of assessments for behavioral health and fewer enable the SDOH screenings. Most of the EHRs do not facilitate the access to identified services the patient may need as a result of psychosocial findings. PCP groups are unable to support the psychosocial care due to lack of appropriate technology and knowledge, the high cost to deliver technology-enabled services, and lack of needed human resource skills.

Use of Skilled Resources in PCP Clinics

Even if the technology is available and affordable, the PCPs require dedicated, trained, and skilled resources to deliver the psychosocial care. This requires ongoing regulatory and reimbursement education and consistent use of technology to deliver efficient care, document and ensure accurate reporting for incentives, and train back-up resources to mention a few of the activities needed to successfully execute the program. When starting any new program, the patients must be educated, and outreach must be made over a sustained period to ensure the program is adopted effectively to justify the investment in resources and technology. When there are staffing challenges, the dedicated resources to deliver psychosocial care are most often the first ones to be pulled out from the psychosocial program execution to support other clinic functions. Over time, the program focus diminishes, and the well-intended whole person-centered care is reduced to managing patient physical conditions.

Challenges with Adoption to New Technologies in Clinics

To initiate and successfully execute a new program, over time, in PCP or specialty clinics is challenging, given the over dependency on already short-handed and overworked resources. Implementing and adapting to new technologies is a challenge for most clinics and clinicians. With the emerging popularity of AI in clinical decision-making and health prognosis, clinicians are motivated to use AI; however, the need to learn the associated technology becomes a barrier. There is also the challenge of using many disparate technologies that do not talk to each other forcing the clinic to duplicate some of the processes and data entry multiple times to use each technology. The lack of integrated seamless technology causes additional resistance for clinics to adapt to new technologies, and the clinic becomes over reliant on the overburdened staff to deliver care regardless of inefficiencies. Providing tools such as Patient App for patients to complete assessments ahead of time and engage in care plan activities using technology can also improve both patient compliance and provider efficiency in delivering psychosocial care, especially since the assessments such as SDOH for psychosocial services can appear to be invasive and inhibit patients from truthfully answering in a clinic setting.

To ensure that patient adoption to App is consistent and sustained requires additional time and resource investment from the clinic. Enabling the integration of the care delivery platform and the Patient App provides an easy method to assess, deliver, and measure progress of care delivered. Pricing complexity and add-on costs to implement new technologies deter PCP clinics from adopting new programs that are supported by technologies. The combined effect of inefficiencies, costs, and lack of integrated simple to use technology leads to the failure of new program continuity.

Balancing the Use of People with Sustained Adoption of Technology to Roll Out New Programs

When rolling out a new program, it is imperative to first study the daily processes, challenges, resource availability, and how often and how much of the technology is being used by various resources such as licensed providers, medical assistants, and others. It is equally important to observe how many different times is a process repeated or data entered in multiple software to complete a task such as patient visit, billing, and reporting. If a program such as the psychosocial care is being implemented with the buy--in of the clinic leadership, there still must be sustained efforts to get the buy-in from the field staff. The way to get the field staff's buy-in is to understand their challenges, time constraints, and their comfort with using various technologies. It is equally important to train them in the advantages of a new program and not only how it benefits the patients but how it can be implemented with minimal interruption to their existing workday. It is imperative to understand the technologies used, the functionality it serves, and how the staff perceives the ease of use of the technology to perform their daily functions, to get insights to what is missing and what is needed. Investing in such study will help in increased success of the program implementation and technology adoption.

Our Organizational Objective to Leverage Skilled Resources Paired with Simple and Seamless Technology to Deliver Psychosocial Care

With our pilot clinics, we had an opportunity to study a few different cultures, workflows, and technologies used. We had the privilege of deeply interacting with various staff members to understand their challenges and the mixed use of technologies and numerous spreadsheets to do their tasks. These insights provided us with adequate information to create our care delivery technology platform with simple functionalities that comply with regulations and enable users to use with ease. To make the adoption even better, we spent sufficient time to train the staff in the use of the technology even though they were not the primary users to deliver the psychosocial care. Within the first three months of rollout of the program, we were able to refine our technology platform to leverage additional functionalities that would provide improved trackability and insights for the clinic and care and outcome metrics of the patients. Although we had a robust care delivery platform and integrated Patient App software, we hired and trained resources that were experienced in delivering psychosocial care leveraging technology. We created a psychosocial care pathway to standardize the care and outcomes and enabled the clinic team to review the metrics on an ongoing basis. The adoption of the Patient App by patients has been challenging given the demographic population we are currently serving which is the elderly. However, we are working toward increasing adoption of the bilingual Patient App for better tracking, insights, and improved resource efficiency. We built technology efficiencies over time to support the care delivery and established weekly call cadence to keep the clinic staff in the loop and actively engaged in the program's success.

In healthcare delivery, it is imperative to engage the staff regularly about the new program to build success, even with the use of the most advanced technologies, to ensure patients receive consistent messages from all members of the team and the human connection especially important for psychosocial care. Most importantly, we quickly initiated the integration of our platform to the EHRs to minimize process duplication and data entries. We automated billing and invoicing to reduce the need for manual spreadsheets. Within our platform, we have built efficiencies for the care team to document using Voice to Text feature, robust Telehealth capability, and enabled voice calls and SMS functionality without ever having to leave the platform or use other software to complete the care.

In our recent enhancement, we have integrated generative AI models based on care team inputs to provide clinicians with personalized recommendations that speed clinical assessments and minimize gaps in care. Over the course of the first few months of the pilot rollout, with consistent delivery of care and connected team collaboration, we were able to minimize duplications of processes and data entries to make the services seamlessly available to the clinic. We built standardized processes that embed within the clinic workflow. We built training modules and methods to ensure our skilled resources are consistent in their care approach. We also trained the designated clinic staff as back-up resources in case of challenges or demand from patients. As an organization, we remain committed to ensuring the clinic team is aware and actively engaged in the delivery of the program without feeling overburdened to be the PCPs of the psychosocial program.

To elaborate further about our training program, we recognize that there is a serious shortage of mental health professionals and hence sourcing well-trained and limited availability of resources from the industry may not be the only way to meet the needs of the ever-growing demands of the patients to help them with their psychosocial needs. Hence, in our organization, we have built a training module that helps scale and skill individuals with prior patient care experience and life skill to undergo our training program with hands-on mentoring to ensure the care delivered is within the bounds of their training.

Need for Improved Regulations and Reimbursements

As we invest in the end-to-end delivery of psychosocial care for PCP clinics, we will also need to explore with payers and governmental agencies about the various reimbursement and regulatory mandates that incentivize appropriately the delivery of such psychosocial programs to attract more PCPs to adopt the program. It would be important for various value-based models to rigorously measure integrated psychosocial services with the physical care to determine future reimbursement models. It would be beneficial for the payers to refine the processes, the components of psychosocial care, and the reimbursement codes, build a framework for SDOH community provider network, and minimize the fear of denials and appeals among the providers if the services are delivered in compliance. Most often, the PCP providers are fearful of denials and the need to spend additional time of their resources to get reimbursed the few dollars that the payers provide for the extensive services delivered. This deters the providers from considering the psychosocial intervention as part of their patient care, which in turn prevents patients from receiving whole person-centered care. The outcomes continue to be measured for the physical care, and we continue to incur high healthcare utilization and costs with no real solution.

Call to Actions

Incorporating psychosocial care as part of holistic healthcare delivery and outcomes require the following broader vision and action from the healthcare industry:

1. Payers to relook at the existing reimbursement models and develop a rigorous incentive program for providers to include psychosocial care delivery on a scalable basis, influencing a higher volume of patients than what is needed for HEDIS (The Healthcare Effectiveness Data and Information Set) measures today to drive integral adoption.
2. Payer to build awareness and support frameworks that enable providers to adapt to the inclusion of psychosocial care in a structured way defining requirements that ensure there is standard care delivery and metrics across providers.
3. The incentive program to adopt psychosocial care delivery needs to be standardized across various payer systems rather than differing degrees of payment, causing confusion and deterring providers from implementing the program.
4. Engaging a group of providers based on a few select regions or states to participate in pilot programs may provide the payers with substantive amounts of data that drive future policy design.
5. Facilitate technology-enabled service provider organizations to participate in incentivized pilots to expand and make outreach in areas of lesser accessibility to psychosocial services.
6. Build a collaborative training curriculum and qualifiers for community organizations can engage to build a robust pool of resources to serve the various populations.

Conclusion

In summary, we in our organization believe that there needs to be many more organizations that come together in their concerted efforts to influence whole-person care and outcomes. We need to be committed in our awareness building both among payers and providers to generate the momentum needed to make psychosocial care as seamless part of our healthcare delivery and not as a special program. Psychosocial health that includes behavioral and social health is not a want but a need of our times today, and separating them from the physical healthcare will not serve well in long term, especially after the end of pandemic as sharp increase in behavioral health problems, rising homelessness, and food insecurities continue to plague the communities across the country.

References

1. Musich, S., Wang, S. S., Schaeffer, J. A., Kraemer, S., Wicker, E., & Yeh, C. S. (2021). The additive impact of multiple psychosocial protective factors on selected health outcomes among older adults. *Geriatric Nursing, 42*(2), 502–508.
2. https://www.cdc.gov/media/releases/2022/ p0331-youth-mental-health-covid-19.html
3. https://www.cdc.gov/nchs/fastats/mental-health.htm
4. https://www.kff.org/coronavirus-covid-19/ issue-brief/the-implications-of-covid-19-for-mental-health-and-substance-use/

CLOSING GAPS IN HEALTHCARE IS A HIGH-TECH, HIGH-TOUCH ENDEAVOR | BY ANNA PANNIER AND DAWN CARTER

In the realm of healthcare, the concept of "closing gaps in care" lies at the core of providing comprehensive and effective treatment to patients. However, despite the best intentions, the system is not infallible, and sometimes individuals slip through the cracks.

Machines beeped and whirred softly in the background as Mrs. Anderson lay in her bed, anxiously awaiting her discharge papers. At 76 years old, she had experienced a life-altering fall at her

*humble home just a week before. Fractured ribs and a sprained
ankle were painful reminders of her vulnerability, but they paled in
comparison to the uncertainties that lay ahead.*

*The discharge nurse handed her a stack of paperwork filled with
detailed instructions and a list of follow-up appointments, including a visit to her primary care physician (PCP) and a referral for
rehabilitation services. As Mrs. Anderson carefully studied the documents, confusion began to cloud her weary eyes. It surprised her
that she found this so disorientating having taught middle school-
ers for 25 years. The medical jargon seemed like an indecipherable
language, leaving her feeling lost and overwhelmed.*

*Days turned into weeks, and the chaotic rhythm of life carried
Mrs. Anderson along. The appointment with her PCP came and
went, as she had unwittingly let it slip through the cracks of her busy
schedule. The rehabilitation referral also fell victim to her ever-
growing to-do list. Meanwhile, the simple act of walking up the stairs
or completing basic household tasks became increasingly challenging for her aging body.*

*As the days passed, the support Mrs. Anderson needed at home
diminished. Her children, burdened with their own responsibilities,
found it difficult to spare the time and energy to tend to her needs.
Then, on an unassuming afternoon, fate dealt her a devastating
blow. Mrs. Anderson lost her balance once again, but this time,
the consequences were far graver. The impact of the fall resulted
in a broken hip, a shattered pelvis, and a severe head injury. As
the ambulance rushed her back to the hospital, her face reflected a
mosaic of pain, regret, and the heart-wrenching knowledge that this
outcome could have been prevented.*

This unfortunate tale of Mrs. Anderson's experience serves as a stark
reminder of the urgent need to close the gaps in care within our healthcare
system. It highlights the vital role of comprehensive support, clear communication, and meticulous follow-up care in ensuring the well-being of patients,
especially those in vulnerable circumstances.

Partnerships between health plans, hospitals, people, and technology can
combine to make a difference in closing these gaps. While both hospitals
and health plans share the goal of providing quality care after discharge,
their specific responsibilities and approaches may differ due to their distinct
roles in the healthcare system. Now, however, more than ever, there is an
opportunity to establish partnerships that can solve these complex needs.

Gaps in care refer to deficiencies or inadequacies in delivering comprehensive and timely healthcare services to patients. These gaps can occur at various points along the care continuum and encompass several areas, including provider networks, care coordination, preventive services, chronic disease management, medication management, health literacy, and patient engagement.

Technology has long been a focus of our efforts in closing gaps in care at discharge. Early in a hospital stay, health plans are alerted to a member's admission and status. Hospitals and health plans have algorithms alerting staff to higher-risk patients that may need additional support. Upon discharge, hospitals leverage their electronic medical record (EMR) and health information exchange (HIE) to facilitate the secure exchange of patient health information, including follow-up needs, and provide health education. Health plans and hospitals provide portal and mobile applications for patients to review and share information. Patients have access to home monitoring provided by hospitals and home-care providers. Technology is abundant; however, technology alone is insufficient for closing the gap.

In conjunction with technology, members with post-discharge needs can benefit from having an assigned care coordinator working on behalf of the health plan and discharging health system. So what can this look like?

Let me introduce you to Shelly, our techenabled care coordinator. Shelly's responsibilities include conducting comprehensive assessments of activities of daily living, developing personalized care plans, coordinating appointments, and serving as a point of contact for patients and their families. She acts as an advocate for patients, addressing their needs, concerns, and questions.

At discharge, Shelly receives an electronic version of the discharge materials and follow-up care needs in her purpose-built workflow system. She is well versed in behavioral interviewing, patient education, health literacy, the local market, and virtual provider resources. Shelly reaches out to Mrs. Anderson and her approved children by phone and text, placing emphasis on building trust and gaining a deep understanding of the patient's needs, available supportive resources, risks, questions, and aspirations. Shelly takes as much time as is needed. She may have multiple contact calls and interactions. This personalized approach ensures that Shelly can tailor her assistance to address the specific challenges faced by the patient.

Shelly takes on the responsibility of creating and managing the required follow-up appointments, with a strong emphasis on closing the loop on all open items. Behind Shelly is a combination of people, technologies, and processes that support her work. Leveraging technology, Shelly coordinates follow-up appointments on behalf of the patient, securely transferring documentation to healthcare providers, obtaining required signatures and approvals, and ensuring that any friction in the process is reduced or eliminated.

This high-tech, high-touch model of care coordination seems almost magical, but it is already happening in among a limited number of innovative markets where health plans and hospitals are partnering with technology-enabled service organizations that can manage closed-loop referral needs. Although technology still plays a critical role, it cannot close the gaps in care without the human touch of care coordinators. The synergy between the two creates a powerful combination that enhances the patient's experience, improves health outcomes, and reduces avoidable healthcare utilization.

Some Results

- Reduced readmissions
- Improved patient and family survey feedback
- Increased in-network referral volumes
- Meaningful collaboration among payer and providers
- Expansion of virtual care options to address provider network gaps

From an experience map perspective, many technology aspects are working behind the scenes to enable a successful on-stage performance for our care coordinator.

Collaboration and information sharing are keys to ensuring that all parties involved are working toward the common goal of delivering comprehensive and coordinated care. Secure information exchange is at the center of this, serving as a hub to EMRs, referral management, and payer systems. Through collaboration between the health plan and health system, member admissions and discharges are flagged for appropriate intervention. By analyzing vast amounts of patient data, AI algorithms identify patterns, predict risk factors, and provide insights that inform care coordinators' decision-making processes. EHR connections move the needed information into clinical workflows. Data subscriptions provide seamless handoffs in transitions of care and referrals. This data-driven approach enables care coordinators to proactively identify patients who may be at higher risk of adverse health events, allowing for early interventions and targeted support.

Closed-loop referral management requires a purpose-built workflow tool. This tool can parse data from direct secure messages or take data from HL7, efax, and portals. It includes a comprehensive database of providers and access to direct scheduling where possible. It tracks the lifecycle of every referral. It includes omnichannel engagement capabilities and customer relationship management best practices. Data analytics and AI further enhance the effectiveness of care coordination, seeking hot spots, bright spots, and performance metrics.

Care coordination requires a strong local market presence that connects the hospital to the provider for the regular blocking, tackling, and support needed in providing good care handoffs. Hospitals and health plans are so busy with their core capabilities, partners that are white labeled to represent the hospital and/or health plan can focus these efforts and establish relationships and engagement in the local community.

Closing the gaps in care requires a multifaceted approach that combines technological advancements, dedicated care coordinators, and collaborative partnerships. By leveraging technological advancements, such as EHRs, secure data exchange, telehealth, referral management systems, and data analytics, healthcare providers can enhance communication, improve access to information, and facilitate care coordination. Care coordinators play a crucial role in bridging the gaps, serving as advocates for patients and guiding them through the complex healthcare landscape. By embracing these strategies, healthcare systems can make significant strides in providing patient-centered care, reducing adverse events, and improving health outcomes.

In the Alternative Model for Mrs. Anderson's Discharge Using Technology and People

The discharge nurse handed Mrs. Anderson a stack of paperwork mirroring what was viewable from her mobile phone or patient portal. It included instructions and a list of follow-up appointments, including a visit to her primary care physician (PCP) and a referral for rehabilitation services. Mrs. Anderson's confusion was alleviated by her ability to replay the recording of her nurse's directions, and through her ability to share this with her children. The nurse's instructions included the name and contact information of her care coordinator, Shelly, who she should expect to hear from shortly.

Upon returning home, Mrs. Anderson already had a message on her answering machine and a text from Shelly, her care coordinator. Her children were also included in the text message. Shelly and Mrs. Anderson had a call shortly after she returned home. Shelly was able to pull Mrs. Anderson's daughter into the call as well.

Speaking with Shelly was the first time in a long time Mrs. Anderson hadn't felt rushed, confused, or worried. They even had an opportunity to talk about her granddaughter's upcoming wedding and how important it was for her to attend that and to remain as independent as possible in her own home. Together, they identified extra support she needed to be safer at home, and identified organizations in the community that Shelly would coordinate with to help replace a stair handrail and add bathroom safety bars.

Mrs. Anderson's daughter was able to take her to her PCP appointment, and it was arranged that the rehab would come to her home twice a week for 6 weeks. In between, Mrs. Anderson continued to have weekly contact with Shelly, sharing how she was doing with her exercises and activities around the house. At the end of 6 weeks, Mrs. Anderson was feeling stronger and safer in her home. She was so thankful for the great care she had received from her local hospital, providers, and health plan. Now she looked back at her fall as an opportunity to get her life back in order.

Mrs. Anderson's story serves as a powerful reminder that no patient should fall through the cracks of the healthcare system. It is our collective responsibility to implement these innovative solutions and ensure that every patient receives the comprehensive care they deserve. This holistic approach not only improves patient outcomes but also enhances patient satisfaction and reduces healthcare costs. It is through these collaborative efforts and the relentless pursuit of closing gaps in care that we can create a healthcare system that is truly patient-centered, efficient, and effective. Together, let us strive to build a future where no patient falls through the cracks and where comprehensive and compassionate care is accessible to all.

Chapter 3

Create Roadmaps

Develop a plan for the functions required to innovate and encourage effective communication between functional experts for strategic clarity.

There is an unsubstantiated fear that plans and order run counter to the innovation spirit. Effective roadmaps actually serve as beacons or markers that help innovators navigate their way without being distracted and thrown off course. Plans do not stifle innovation but rather provide necessary guardrails to ensure focus and completion. Too many great ideas were never realized as resources and passion dwindled from an unnecessarily long journey.

CREATING ROADMAPS | EMPATHY AS A FOUNDATION FOR CHANGE | BY TAYLOR SEYMORE

How do we help the people we serve thrive? The world of healthcare is changing quickly, not only in technological advancements but also in the challenges patients are facing. As progress in healthcare has greatly improved outcomes for patients, it has also resulted in new demographics with unique and often difficult-to-address needs. Working, for example, with individuals managing complex behavioral challenges such as severe and persistent mental health, substance use, and cognitive impairments compounded with significant physical care needs has pushed the boundaries of the available healthcare systems. The populations I have been privileged to serve represent some of the most vulnerable among us. My experience has convinced me there is a healthcare crisis in lack of access to resources

DOI: 10.4324/9781003381983-3

and in understanding of the needs of the people being served. To address this crisis, behavioral healthcare practices are being more commonly implemented into all healthcare settings. The practice of behavioral health is meant to help bridge the gaps in accessing and engaging with care. Through the implementation of behavioral healthcare practices, I have witnessed patients change their lives and work toward goals they may have given up on. One resident was able to, at the end of his life, publish a poetry book he had been working on since the age of 16. Another contacted his brother who he hadn't spoken to in nearly a decade after a falling out. When behavioral health is implemented, healthcare moves toward holistic and person-centered care practices. Patients engaged in behavioral healthcare are enabled to treat each other and their environment with love and respect. Innovation in healthcare technology is not exempt from the benefits the practice of behavioral healthcare can bring to patients and practitioners alike.

Providing care for others is often an impossible job, as anyone who has spent time working as a healthcare provider knows. The resources, funds, education, and support needed for care settings to work efficiently for residents and those who care for them just are not there. The added challenge of finding resources for those who often can't engage in the care they need is a recipe for poor health outcomes and an even worse quality of life. I have spent a decade advocating for patients, and while I have at times been successful, the single most impactful factor to a person's ability to engage in care is the empathy they receive from those providing care. Empathy is, on its surface, a basic concept, but implementing care with empathy requires the constant practice of self-reflection and accountability. It is the duty of providers to model and practice empathy in all interactions and to practice self-reflection and accountability. Through the consistent practice of empathy, an exponential growth can be made in understanding the needs of patients, and with that understanding comes an ability to build roadmaps in healthcare technology that will address larger societal concerns and allow for the impact of innovation to be much greater.

Empathy has become a popular buzzword over the last few years as mental health has become less stigmatized and more accessible to the average person. Of course, its definition and implementation have been widely obscured as is common when a term hits mainstream use. In my experience, empathy is as much a feeling as an action. Utilizing empathy requires taking a step back and allowing others to be as they are without judgment. Practicing empathy has been a lesson in letting go of control and ideas of

how life should be lived. Healthcare innovators are bound by duty to provide opportunity, resources, and support regardless of an individual's ability to engage in what is believed to be healthiest for them. Empathy is the
foundation of change but for that change to address the needs of patients,
innovation must also address the behavioral factors preventing those most in
need of care from getting it. The principles of behavior are as follows:

1. Behavior is action, everything we do both consciously and unconsciously.
2. Behavior is a form of communication and is reflective of both past and
   present experiences.

These two principles, when examined, allow us to make some assumptions
about the people in care. I have found that these assumptions can drive systems that improve quality of life.

1. **People are all doing the best they can with the tools they have.**
   When the two principles of behavior are applied to this assumption,
   the historical, environmental, physical health, and mental health experiences of the patient are considered. Person-centered care can then
   begin to be taken into account in the development and implementation
   of innovation in healthcare. This first assumption is the most important as it helps to define empathy. When it is assumed, each person is
   doing their best to survive and thrive, each interaction can be started
   with a focus on positive problem-solving. This assumption can be difficult to remember in times of stress and conflict, but it must go beyond
   first interactions and times of positive growth and be applied each
   time there is an interaction with or about a patient. In my personal
   experience, this assumption is the initial step to building rapport and
   implementing changes in the care patients receive. Assuming everyone
   is doing their best with the tools they have is a potent reminder that
   patients are, first and foremost, human.
2. **Humans have the same basic needs to feel accepted, supported,
   safe, and that they have purpose.** While assumption one lays the
   framework for applying empathy to care, assumption two is the first
   stepping stone in building roadmaps that invite person-centered innovation. As defined in premise two, behavior is a form of communication
   and is reflective of both past and present experiences. Behavioral patterns develop around the patients' attempts to feel their basic needs are
   met. Maladaptive behaviors often occur when patients have experienced

that their needs will not be met without the use of unsafe communi-cation tools such as aggression or refusing care. When I applied this assumption to my own interactions with patients, I saw an immedi-ate change in the way care was perceived. I was driven to think more deeply about the things that help people feel cared for. I began using phrases like "I'm proud of you," "I think you're really amazing," and "I love being able to have you in my life." Not just as a response to posi-tive communication but also during times of calm. It became effort-less to integrate supportive phrases in communication, and the results rippled far beyond the walls of the care home.

3. **Maladaptive behaviors are a result of not feeling our core needs are met.** As noted earlier, maladaptive behaviors are behaviors that are unwanted and a result of patients feeling unsafe, unsupported, that they are not accepted, and/or that they have no purpose. Maladaptive behav-iors lead to impairments in patients being able to engage with the care and support they need to improve or maintain their physical and mental health. Understanding the function of maladaptive behaviors or which core need is not being met is imperative to ensuring innovation in healthcare stays focused on the patients' needs. When these core needs are considered in problem-solving, innovation becomes exponentially more applicable and accessible to everyone.

4. **Humans are both immensely complex and incredibly simple.** It can be overwhelming to consider how to construct a roadmap when taking only core needs into account, but when considered in conjunc-tion with the first three assumptions, it can help to define the problem to be addressed. If only the core needs of the patient are considered, a clear pathway cannot be built; innovators must also consider the factors, which are impacting a patient feeling their core needs are being met. These factors include but are not limited to a person's environment, social life, or internal experiences. How each person will react to the challenges placed before them will be unique to that individual, but the factors that prompted maladaptive and protective behaviors are often the same. When empathy is applied to this assumption, those looking to affect change in the healthcare universe can look beyond the behav-ioral responses of patients and address the barriers to healthcare in a person-centered manner.

Creating Roadmaps and Empathy. When empathy acts as the foundation of innovation, solutions become person centered. I have witnessed that when these principles and assumptions are applied, the lives of people most in need of the support of the healthcare system can change drastically.

Most of the patients I have supported have had little trust in the healthcare system. Driven by both fear and experiences of maltreatment and discrimination, their reluctance to engage with healthcare is understandable. It is not, however, safe or healthy or promotes a high quality of life. With empathy as a building block, social factors that contribute to an individual's ability to engage in care can be addressed. Factors such as environment, finances, and social connections highly inform a person's ability to engage in care and should be addressed when constructing roadmaps for innovation in healthcare technologies. Social factors can act as a lens to clarify goals and recenter focus back to the most important factor in healthcare, the people. Innovation drives the world forward, but innovation without empathy is more likely to drag patients back. To truly move forward, technology in healthcare needs to revolve around the holistic needs of the patients and that can start with creating roadmaps that prioritize empathy and behavioral health as informing factors.

DESIGNING AN INTEGRATED OPERATING MODEL FOR VBC SUCCESS | BY JULIE BONELLO

Value-based care (VBC) transforms the healthcare business model to a new way of delivering and financing quality care. It requires a new way of working, redesigning existing structures, people, and processes, similar to start-ups in that new organizational structures, governance, staffing, and processes are needed for transformation. While the Population Health strategy defines the "what" of value base care, it is the operating model that defines "how and by whom" to achieve success. Both are needed for transformation.

Steven Jobs commented that

> it is a disease thinking that a really great idea is 90% of the work and that if you just tell all the other people, here is the great idea, they can go off and make it happen. The problem with that is there is a ton of craftsmanship in between a great idea and a great product. It is the process that is the magic.

The VBC craftsmanship is in developing an operating model framework that translates the strategy into an implementation and service roadmap enabled through a team of people passionate about the strategy. Importantly, it is achieved through payer-provider partnerships designing and delivering on contracts that deliver high quality, cost-efficient, and seamless healthcare delivery for different patient populations.

This chapter describes the work of Rush Health and Access Community Health Network, two passionate organizations, who each worked on the "how" they developed sustainable operating models with a focus on technology to successfully implement their different Population Health strategies in close partnership with the payers.

- Rush Health is a clinically integrated network of physicians and hospitals working together to improve health through high-quality, efficient health services. Rush Health contracts with payers to cover the spectrum of patient care from wellness and prevention to disease management and care management. In 2015, Rush Health developed an operating model framework with a focus on technology to successfully begin VBC with pay for performance (P4P), shared savings, and bundled payment contracts.
- Access Community Health Network (ACCESS), founded in 1991 to provide primary and preventive care services in targeted areas on Chicago's South and West sides with high levels of poverty and poor health outcomes, has grown into a diverse network of 35 health centers that serves more than 170,000 patients each year across Chicago and suburban Cook and DuPage counties. As the nation's sixth largest network of federally qualified health centers, ACCESS continues to innovate and evolve its care delivery model to address the total health needs of our patients. In 2014, ACCESS developed a Medicaid managed care operating model transitioning 150,000 patients successfully to VBC.

The first step in beginning the operating model is assembling the great team with a cross section of talent across all stakeholder areas and letting them operate within a trusted environment of challenging each other to make something great. Steven Jobs comments on the value of a great team through a metaphor of a tumbler polishing rough rocks into beautiful stones,

> that through the team, through that group of incredibly talented people bumping up against each other, having arguments, having fights sometimes, making some noise, and working together they polish each other, and they polish the ideas, and what comes out are these really beautiful stones.

Great teams at Rush Health and Access Community Health Network bumped up against each other to design VBC products that improved care, and their leaders, Brent Estes, CEO, Rush Health, and Donna Thompson, CEO, Access Community Health Network courageously provided a safe environment for the team to design "polished" VBC products. Each leader elevated technology as a strategic advantage and ensured that technology best practices were built into the "what" and "how" of the operating model. Importantly, the IT teams were passionate, valued participants adding to the polished product where technology could be efficiently leveraged for new VBC delivery models. This chapter identifies how IT best practices were built into the Rush Health's operating model.

Operating Model Components

1. Strategy
   The transition from fee for service (FFS) to VBC is a journey to accept more financial risk across an organization's commercial and government payer contract portfolio. An organization will only move to VBC when clinical and financial processes are in place to manage risk and ensure the quality of care delivered. The operating model is the vehicle for designing and implementing these new processes to accept more risk.
   VBC programs hold providers accountable for improving patient outcomes while managing costs. VBC reimburses providers based on the quality of their care while FFS reimburses providers on the quantity of their care. With FFS, providers are paid for each service regardless of the outcome and effectiveness of the treatment. They are incentivized to provide more services. With VBC, providers are reimbursed based on quality but have financial risk if the quality and cost do not meet VBC program requirements. There are four major contract payment steps along the continuum in transitioning to more risk. Nationally, most VBC contracts are still with P4P and Shared Savings programs:

   ■ P4P—Providers are still paid under FFS, but they are provided an additional payment or bonus based on meeting specific quality targets of the VBC program.
   ■ Shared Savings—Providers are still paid under FFS but can gain a percentage of the financial savings if quality and cost saving targets are met (upside risk) and/or share in the losses of financial overrun if targets are not met (downside risk).

- Bundled Payments—Providers are held accountable and reimbursed for a predetermined single payment of services during an episode of care. Providers are accountable for the quality and cost of the episode, and all programs require care coordination to manage services within the episode.
- Partial or Full Capitation—Providers receive a fixed "per patient, per month" payment to cover all healthcare services (full capitation) required for an individual. Providers are at financial risk of managing the health outcomes of their patients. Often, under partial capitation, contracts exclude services that continue to be paid under FFS. Partial capitation generally includes primary care services, preventative services, basic diagnostic services, some specialty services, and care management.

Strategy: Integrating IT into the Operating Model

a. Ongoing Contract Strategy—The contracting team at Rush Health regularly included the clinical, financial, administrative, and technology stakeholders to "polish" the VBC product design in partnership with each payer product. The information technology team regularly met with their payer counterparts and with the separate health system IT teams to agree on technology requirements and resources required across different IT platforms. The integrated design plans were developed together with the respective areas throughout the course of the year. At Rush Health, it became common to discuss technology initiatives at payer contract design meetings.

b. Ongoing Population Health Technology Platform and Plans—The Population Health Technology platform included the separate IT platforms of all network members and payers. A key component was building interoperability and sharing data across the platforms, so care could be managed across the continuum of care regardless of technology or EHR.

   The technology plans were aligned and updated based on the contract strategy and associated new care delivery models, the redesigned clinical, financial, and administrative workflows, and the performance measurement requirements. Another key component was detailing all new end-to-end workflows in leveraging technology for each contract program. The technology plans were updated to include new EHR workflow requirements; new software capabilities to manage the care of patient populations; new capabilities to manage the patients and providers enrolled in the network;

interoperability enabling data to be shared in real time with providers and payers; and an analytics platform with robust data collection, analytic, and reporting capabilities measuring and managing the performance of each value-based program. Technology enhancements were standardized across VBC products, and new digital innovation products were considered within the context of the current population health technology platform capabilities and need. The updated technology plans were signed off by all member IT departments and by payer partners.

2. Structure and Governance

   Accountable care organizations (ACOs) and/or clinically integrated networks (CIN) are legal structures for managing the care coordination, quality, and cost of VBC contracts. ACOs are legal entities comprising a network of providers and hospitals that share responsibility for the care coordination, quality, and cost of a one VBC program or population. A CIN is a legal organization that is a collaboration between hospitals, their employed physicians, independent physicians, specialty providers, and other care providers who collectively contract with payers to coordinate care, ensure quality, and manage cost based on clinical protocols and guidelines. CINs are subject to anti-trust laws meant to promote market competition.

   ACO/CIN organizations create separate structures to support the legal clinical integration requirements: clinical protocols, care coordination, population health management, performance management, and financial alignment. Departments often include clinical, quality, care management, legal and compliance, contracting, finance, provider services, information technology and analytic services. As the CIN is formed, the integrated responsibilities between the CIN and the member organization responsibilities are determined in order to minimize duplication. ACO/CIN employees work collaboratively with all payers and network provider organizations to support cross-network services. ACOs and CINs are not mutually exclusive and can be used together for different VBC programs.

   The ACO and CIN governance structures are similar, although the CIN has broader responsibility governing contracts. Governance involves all participating partners including hospitals, physicians, and other care providers; promotes physician engagement and participation; and includes consensus-driven partnership across all parties. Often the board governance aligns with the organization structure and includes a finance/contracting committee, quality committee, technology committee, and provider services committee reporting to the board of directors.

Structure and Governance—Integrating IT into the Operating Model

a. Building the IT Structures—A priority at Rush Health was building the IT and analytic departments with the responsibility to design the Population Health Technology strategy with collaborative relationships with member IT departments, payers, and third-party partners. Under the CIN IT and analytics leadership, all worked collaboratively to develop and implement an integrated technology and analytics strategy that integrated all IT platforms. The success relied on executive leader support from of all participating CIN partners who participated on a board technology committee. Shared responsibilities were identified across all the IT teams to ensure collaboration.

b. Clear Roles and Responsibilities—Rush Health worked to define clear population health roles and responsibilities between the CIN and member organizations where separate population health departments and IT resources existed in health systems for FFS business. Without clarity, it was hard for the IT teams to implement both a FFS and a VBC population health technology strategy. It was hard to collectively engage all to implement one polished product regardless of payment structure. While collaborative IT working relationships existed with shared responsibility, blurred lines of responsibility led to confusion and delays.

c. Governance—Rush Health elevated technology into their board structure by forming a dedicated committee and including information technology leadership in all other board committees: population health, finance, quality, and provider services. The dedicated Health Information Technology Adoption and Optimization Committee was charged with "maximizing technology value, establishing common goals and platforms, promoting collaboration and knowledge sharing, and developing an interoperable health system platform that empowers individuals to use their electronic health information to the fullest extent; enables providers and communities to deliver smarter, safer, and more efficient care; and promotes innovation at all levels." The committee provided a foundation for successfully leveraging technology although confusion remained on overlapping technologies and responsibilities between the CIN and the provider organizations. As a result, the CIO worked to define a shared responsibility structure with the health system CIOs, but it is important to determine with all overlapping CIN and health system departments straddling duplicate FFS and VBC staffing models.

d. Digital and Innovation—Over the past decade, separate innovation and digital departments have been formed to transform care delivery by leveraging new or existing digital tools. Without an effort to clearly define the "what" of digital and innovation within the context of population health and VBC organizations, there is increased risk to further fragment care without performance aligned with VBC contract requirements.

3. Network Development and Integration VBC programs require an engaged provider network to drive quality, patient engagement, and care management across the continuum of care. The provider network needs to include primary and specialty providers (employed and independent), and inpatient, post-acute, rehabilitation, long-term, and home-care provider organizations. The provider network must align with the services of program and must have adequate providers to support the size and location of patients served and the breadth of services rendered. ACO/CINs develop and accredit their provider network to accept all contracts including VBC.

Network Development—Integrating IT into the Operating Model

a. Joint Operating Committees—Payers regularly scheduled Joint Operating Committee meetings with the Rush Health team to review the performance of each contract program. Yearly, Rush Health shared the VBC operating plans with each CIN member and Joint Operating Committee meetings regularly scheduled to review performance. Concurrently, IT Joint Operating Committee meetings were scheduled to review the performance of the VBC IT operating plan. The Rush Health IT and analytic departments regularly worked with each organization to ensure technology, and analytics were successfully leveraged for contract performance: care management, patient engagement, quality, attribution, interoperability, and data-sharing requirements. All adhered to strict data submission requirements for timely program monitoring. Yearly Security Risk and Interoperability Capability Assessments were reviewed, and plans approved with each provider network partner.

b. New Care Continuum Partners, Capabilities, and Services—As new VBC products were designed with new partners and services across the continuum, the same operating model methodology and IT platform requirements of implementing interoperable, end-to-end workflows with new IT platforms were extended to all new service partners. Interoperability and security across disparate IT platforms became a critical issue to monitor.

4. Clinical Integration Components

Clinical integration is organizing healthcare delivery among an integrated care team across the care continuum, who work together optimizing patient care, while enhancing efficiency through cost-effective practices. The legal clinical integration requirements include clinical protocols, care coordination, population health management, performance management, and financial alignment, which are built into all VBC contracts.

Clinical Integration Components—Integrating IT into the Operating Model

The Rush Health operating model included IT specifications and work plans for each VBC program clinical integration component. The work plans included goals, metrics, time frames, and resources. The CIN multidisciplinary team, provider organizations, payers, and third-party vendors adhered to the integrated work plans. Everyone knew their value and contribution to improving performance on quality, efficiency, and cost.

a. Clinical Protocols and Guidelines—Clinical protocols and guidelines are developed by clinicians to standardize care and improve efficiency leading to improved patient outcomes. Clinical protocols and guidelines standardize care for specific conditions and for different healthcare settings: disease management, preventative care, palliative care, critical care, clinical pathways, and care coordination. For all Rush Health VBC contracts, the clinical protocols and guidelines were built into the EHRs with interoperability capabilities across all IT platforms and disparate EHRs.

b. Care Coordination—Care coordination is the organized effort across the care team to deliver seamless care to patients. Care coordination services include developing a care plans, facilitating care transitions between health settings, identifying and following up on gaps in care, and ensuring consistent patient communication and follow-up for care guidelines. The care coordinators support effective collaboration and communication across the multidisciplinary care team.

Rush Health built care coordination protocols and guidelines into the EHRs with interoperability across network member EHRs. Rush Health built care coordination dashboards to manage and monitor care across the VBC contracts. Bidirectional data exchange with the payers is implemented for real-time follow-up, increasing care gap closure, improving authorization timeliness, reducing denials, and improving care coordination.

c. Population Health Management—Population health management is the coordinated effort across the care team to improve the health outcomes of a population, considering the influence of social determinants on health outcomes to individualize care.

Rush Health selected one EHR to build registries and dashboards to centrally manage care and measure the health outcomes across the patient populations for all VBC programs. Registries and dashboard were also built into the analytics data warehouse platform with all payer claims and clinical performance data. EHRs were optimized for population health management with the integration of social determinants into a patient's care plan.

d. Performance Management and Reporting—The CIN/ACOs track and report on VBC program performance metrics, including clinical quality, patient satisfaction, service productivity, and cost-efficiency metrics.

Rush Health collected and aggregated the data from payers, the EHRs, and other source systems to calculate metrics benchmarked against required performance standards. The online performance data was made available to all network providers and integrated into the EHR reporting when possible.

e. Financial Alignment—The CIN tracks the differing financial performance across the various VBC reimbursement models to identify specific incentive payments for participating providers and requires a close working rapport with the payers.

Rush Health built a performance monitoring platform with analytic capabilities, reporting, and dashboards available to members to proactively monitor financial alignment of VBC contracts across the network. The design of the data warehouse, analytics, and reporting was critical to ensuring financial alignment and trust for the provider members.

Summary—Getting Started

The great idea of VBC transformation is only 10% of the work while 90% is in the craftmanship of developing a VBC operating model. The operating model is complex because it requires a shared vision and commitment for population health where disparate organizations may be required to adjust their own organization's vision, strategies, structures, and processes to participate. It changes in the payment structures and reimbursement and requires that FFS and VBC services and responsibilities are differentiated. Getting started requires executive leadership from all participating organizations to endorse the great idea. Equally important is to charge and empower a separate, multidisciplinary great team to develop the operating model. A VBC operating model is the vehicle to remediate historical VBC implementation challenges of "how the work gets done and by whom" through designing an operating methodology for implementing the strategy, structure, governance, and network development for clinical integration components. Integrated throughout the model are the technology structures, resources, and tools needed for new workflows, data, interoperability, and analytic capabilities.

Create roadmaps; it worked! The integrated operating model successfully deployed by Rush Health took several years to refine the craftmanship by a passionate great team, committed partners, and strong partnerships with the payers to improve care. It was through the collaboration and a willingness to bump up against each other and continue to polish the model that sustained VBC program success was achieved.

INSIGHTS IN NANOSECONDS | BY MIKE TREASH

Three years ago, the healthcare leader of a major retailer talked to a group of us about strategic initiatives. At the end of the presentation, he was asked about the retailer's data capabilities. He was a healthcare guy new to retail. A smile on his face prefaced his response, which was, "the retailer can generate consumer insights in nanoseconds."

Not sure if he could've lobbed a bigger competitive threat than "insights in nano-seconds." Any company producing insights in nanoseconds is a disruptive force in health insurance. They just have to overcome a few barriers: excessive data and security regulations, nonstandard datasets, underperforming governance practices, immature (but maturing) interoperability mechanisms, highly decentralized and variable data eco-systems, and immense complexity.

"Data rich and insights poor" had been our moniker for years. We had data warehouses but no datamarts. Visual analytics no one looked at. Few people knew the difference between data governance and data mastering. Neither our architecture nor our applications were orchestrated to produce data in real time. As a small organization, we did not invest much capital in data capabilities. Critically, our leaders did not have data-related degrees or data strategy on their resumes. Fortunately, no one in this industry was clearly outperforming the competition solely on the basis of their data strategy.

Fast forward to the present, AI is the rage, and ChatGPT is a potential game-changing disrupter. Data scientist PhDs make more money than many of the consulting partners who hire them. Prompt engineer is an actual job title. Our physicians can explain when to use a data lake versus a data warehouse. Our data hub can pull and push data events in real time (our core applications still struggle with real time). Our analysts are building Power BI visualizations sitting on top of data marts. We just don't govern data; we master data. And generative AI is already disrupting our operating model.

Predictive Analytics

Before we could generate insights in nano-seconds, we needed to generate insights. One of the core elements was a low-tech architecture solution we call our Consumer 360. The Consumer 360 is a data architecture we use to profile a consumer utilizing many data sources. It unifies demographic, medical, pharmacy, marketing, service, and other data sources at the consumer level. Fundamentally, it provides better reporting and a more informed view of the consumer. More importantly and more powerfully, it feeds emerging advanced predictive models with variables. While advanced analytical models require lots of data to train on, the output is the minimum set of variables that best predicts consumer behavior.

With a comprehensive view of the consumer, we are better able to create A-B models. In layman's terms, what is an A-B model? A is the dependent variable or what you are trying to explain, forecast, predict, influence, or create. B represents the independent variables, meaning the things you believe will influence, are associated with, or cause the A variable. The table given here illustrates use cases in a health plan and potential A-B models:

Use Case	Analytical Model
Increase campaign and outreach ROI • Material improvement in campaign activation rates (marketing, HEDIS/STARS, gap closures, pop health, medication adherence)	• A variable: Campaign response rates • B variables: Age/gender, channel preferences, zip codes, HCCs, diagnosis, revenue, medical expense, interaction histories
Decrease consumer inquiries • Reduce the volume of service related inquiries and complaints	• A variable: Consumer interactions • B variables: Age/gender, benefit plans, diagnosis, provider, interaction history, HCCs, zip codes
Decrease benefit inquiry costs • Reduce call handle time using generative AI to retrieve benefit documents and create a response	• A variable: Benefit inquiry response • B variables: Benefit documents, clinical policies, desk-level procedures, other source documentation

In our "model to predict," which healthcare consumers will call us, we have identified body mass index (BMI), age, and zip codes as strong predictive variables when combined. (We are digging deeper into BMI.) Even after normalizing for disease states, those variables remain strong predictors. We have learned that certain age groups, in specific zip codes, who are diabetic, are more likely to complain about their claims and at a higher rate in February through April. We can identify which variables increase the likelihood of a Medicare member staying with us and which variables are strongly associated with those who leave us within the first two years of enrollment. We know which consumers are our most profitable and have deep insights into their behavior and characteristics. And we know which consumers are not profitable and why.

What do we do with these insights? We are reaching out to a priority list of consumers who are at risk of disenrolling because they have not had a wellness visit. We have another list of consumers who are likely to file a complaint about coverage and who we are educating on their benefits. We have lists of consumers who prefer emails over text messages and vice versa. We now better understand which of our consumers are more likely to respond to our medication outreach and which of those campaigns are more effective. We are studying why consumers in Detroit are more likely than non-Detroit consumers to file a grievance and less likely to file an appeal. Interestingly, the results are the same for high-income and low-income Detroit residents.

Why is this information more valuable than generalizable data we can purchase? Simply put, when you use publicly available demographic and market data, you are gravitating to the mean. You are using the same information as your competitors. By building models using data only available to us and sourced via the Consumer 360, we derive insights unique to each consumer and not achievable from public data. Oddly, HIPAA, which restricts the use of health consumer data, is indirectly making the insights only we can derive from that data very valuable.

Insights Not Just Data Monetization

The value of data ranges in a continuum from raw data to structured data to governed and mastered data to visual analytical models to simple A-B models to highly predictive and trained models. That continuum is not necessarily linear. Some raw data is more valuable than structured data. A single lab result in an EMR sourced timely that increases the predictability of a stroke is extremely valuable. When you head down the continuum, visual analytics allows the user to see patterns, and advanced analytics validates those patterns and correlations. The holy grail of insights monetization is the deep insights derived from large datasets where advanced analytics trains a model to identify the most predictive combination of variables.

Let's be clear: monetization doesn't mean selling insights and data on the open market (which, if done wrong, is illegal). Monetization means driving results using insights and data. Automating data extracts into reusable data marts, which reduces redundant data wrangling costs, is an example of monetization. Cutting population health campaign costs by outreaching to priority consumers with higher activation propensity scores is another example. Pacing the investment in channel expansion based on predictive data of who will engage in self-service tools is an illustration of using data to leverage capital wisely. Trading access to a data model for data science expertise is a method of monetization. Selling access to your AI-enabled marketing campaign model to smaller non-competitors is a way to leverage and scale your AI investments.

What About Generative AI?

Generative AI is a perfect example of generating insights in nanoseconds. A consumer asks a Chatbot about vision benefits. Here is the response a simple generative AI model provides:

> HAP Senior Plus Option 4 offers vision benefits that include one routine eye exam per year, coverage for outpatient physician services for the diagnosis and treatment of diseases and injuries of the eye, including treatment for age-related macular degeneration, and coverage for one glaucoma screening each year for people at high risk of glaucoma.[1] The plan also covers one pair of eyeglasses or contact lenses after each cataract surgery that includes insertion of an intraocular lens, and routine corrective eyeglasses or contact lenses once every year.[1] The plan partners with EyeMed to provide routine vision care services, and in-network retailers include Henry Ford OptimEyes, LensCrafters, Target Optical, Pearle Vision, and America's Best. The cost for Medicare-covered eye exams by a primary care physician is a $0 copay, and the cost for Medicare-covered eye exams by a specialty care physician is a $25 copay. For Medicare-covered standard eye wear after cataract surgery, the cost is a 20% coinsurance, whether in-network or out-of-network.[11]
>
> **Citations: 1. Y0076_2023_EOC_
> PPO_Opt_4_004–93.pdf**

That response took generative AI four seconds; it takes one of our call-center reps roughly two minutes to search 400 or more documents of 80 plus pages each. The AI challenge for smaller companies, as usual, is scale. We are training our models on outliers we see every three months while larger companies see the same outliers every three days. Smaller organizations are on the wrong side of the AI monetization game; scale, in terms of dataset size and the fixed cost of data scientists, is working against us. The smallest of the smallest payers are often provider based, which means they potentially have access to the broader dataset of the parent. A broad dataset means more variables, and more variables can translate into better predictive models. In the data strategy game, it's important to understand the value drivers behind monetization.

Insights in Days

"Insights in days" lacks the rally cry and pizzaz of insights in nanoseconds. "Insights in days" means that the discharged Medicare patient with COPD is already readmitted. The diabetic failed the test another week. Prospective Medicare member enrolled in another plan before your campaign launched. The consumer already called to ask why they got charged a cost share for a preventive visit before your email explaining why. On a micro level, "insights in nanoseconds" is about the basics: establishing valid correlations with the variables that drive results, automating the extraction of that data, democratizing the real-time availability of data, and developing visually logical reports.

"Insights in nanoseconds" at scale gets complicated and more capital intensive. Core transaction systems are not real-time data ready; data interoperability is costly, data sharing is more pervasive, but insight sharing is not, and the customer relationship management (CRM) tools that enable real-time messaging are hugely expensive. What is clear is that companies our size are not going to outdo the infrastructure, data science, or CRM of the larger national payers and external threats.

The Need for a Roadmap

How do smaller healthcare organizations with less capital and scale compete in the data economy? The answer is by creating effective and strategic roadmaps. What we have is lots of variables, especially provider-based health plans who can better source variables across the delivery spectrum. For predictive modeling, the more variables you source, the more innovative and unique the insights your data model can derive. In the generative AI game, we have the inside track on use cases and the thing about generative AI; it's not capital intensive to get started. In the short term, generative AI has tremendous promise from automating routine daily tasks to enabling material shifts in self-service. However, advanced generative AI models need large volumes of training data and expensive in-demand prompt engineers to train the models. Smaller health plans will be purchasers of generative AI models, but right now we have to be in the game, so we are informed consumers when it comes time to buy.

Innovation is often dependent on investing in the right things. In the data economy, smaller companies are wise to make the minimum viable investments in the sunk costs of data infrastructure and digital front doors. The better play is investing in what we can innovate and monetize, which are basic A-B models utilizing the array of variables we can source and our subject matter experts who can contextualize data and insights. These investments are less on the tech side and more on the people side, mainly upskilling the data strategy and analytical capabilities of our leaders and our analysts. Roadmaps harmonize and catalyze the organization to accomplish innovation. They serve as dynamic tools that guide progress, facilitate decision-making, and keep everyone focused on the end goal.

NAVIGATING HEALTHCARE INNOVATION FOR PAYER TRANSFORMATION | ANONYMOUS

Introduction

In today's dynamic healthcare landscape, innovation is essential to enhance the efficiency, accessibility, and quality of healthcare services. Payers, including insurance companies and government programs, are instrumental in driving innovation within the healthcare system. The theme of "Create Roadmaps" emphasizes the importance of strategic planning and vision in payer healthcare innovation. This chapter explores the concept of creating roadmaps within payer models, focusing on how this approach can lead to more effective, patient-centered, and adaptable healthcare systems.

Payers as Catalysts for Healthcare Innovation

Before delving into the "create roadmaps" theme, it is crucial to understand the pivotal role of payer models in healthcare innovation.

The Evolving Role of Payers

Traditionally, payers have been primarily responsible for risk assessment, claims processing, and financial management in healthcare. However, the evolving healthcare landscape demands a broader and more strategic approach. Payers have transitioned into key drivers of innovation by shifting toward patient-centered, VBC models and embracing technology as an enabler.

The Impact of Payer Innovation

Innovative payer models have the potential to transform healthcare by improving patient experiences, reducing costs, and enhancing healthcare outcomes. To harness this potential fully, payers must strategically plan and create roadmaps that guide their innovation efforts.

The "Create Roadmaps" Theme: Paving the Path to Innovation

The "create roadmaps" theme signifies the importance of having a clear and well-defined strategy in payer healthcare innovation. By creating roadmaps, payers establish a structured approach that ensures their innovation efforts are purposeful, coordinated, and aligned with the evolving needs of patients and providers.

Strategic Planning

Effective innovation requires a strategic vision. Payers must identify long-term goals and objectives that align with their mission and the broader healthcare landscape. Creating a strategic roadmap involves setting priorities, allocating resources, and establishing key performance indicators (KPIs) to measure progress.

Alignment with Stakeholder Needs

Payer models should prioritize the needs of both members and healthcare providers. Understanding these stakeholders' pain points and expectations is crucial when creating roadmaps for innovation. Payers should seek input from these groups to ensure that their strategies address real-world challenges effectively.

Adaptability and Flexibility

Innovation roadmaps should not be static documents but rather flexible frameworks that can adapt to changing circumstances and emerging opportunities. Payers must be prepared to adjust their strategies as new technologies, regulations, and healthcare trends emerge.

Roadmap Components in Payer Healthcare Innovation

Creating a roadmap for payer healthcare innovation involves several key components.

Technology Integration

Technology is a driving force in healthcare innovation. Payers must outline how they intend to integrate cutting-edge technologies, such as artificial intelligence (AI), telehealth, and blockchain, into their models. This may involve partnerships with tech companies, the development of in-house IT solutions, or the adoption of emerging healthcare technologies.

Data Management and Analytics

The effective use of healthcare data is critical in payer innovation. Roadmaps should detail how payers plan to harness data to improve care coordination, reduce costs, and enhance patient experiences. This may include investments in data analytics tools, data-sharing initiatives, and strategies to ensure data privacy and security.

Member Engagement and Experience

A patient-centric approach is essential for payer models. Roadmaps should outline strategies for improving patient engagement and experiences. This might involve the development of patient portals, mobile apps, and telemedicine platforms that facilitate communication, appointment scheduling, and access to health information.

Value-Based Care Models

Many payers are shifting toward VBC models, which prioritize outcomes and quality over the quantity of services provided. Roadmaps should define how payers plan to transition to these models, including how they will measure and incentivize VBC initiatives.

Challenges and Considerations in Roadmap Implementation

While creating roadmaps for payer healthcare innovation offers significant benefits, there are challenges and considerations that payers must address.

Resource Allocation

Innovative initiatives often require substantial investments in terms of finances, time, and expertise. Payers must allocate resources strategically to ensure that their innovation efforts remain sustainable and effective.

Regulatory Compliance

The healthcare industry is heavily regulated, and innovation initiatives must comply with numerous federal and state regulations. Payers must navigate complex legal frameworks to avoid compliance issues that could hinder their progress.

Interoperability

The seamless exchange of health information between different healthcare systems remains a challenge. Payers must work toward interoperability to ensure that their innovation efforts align with broader healthcare initiatives.

Equity and Access

Innovations in healthcare must be accessible to all, regardless of socioeconomic factors. Payers must consider how their roadmap implementation plans address issues of equity and access to healthcare services.

The Future of Payer Healthcare Innovation

The "create roadmaps" theme holds great promise for the future of payer healthcare innovation.

Improved Member Outcomes

Payer models with well-defined roadmaps can prioritize initiatives that directly impact patient outcomes. By focusing on member/ patient-centric innovations, payers have the potential to improve the health and well-being of the communities they serve.

Cost Reduction

Strategic innovation roadmaps can identify opportunities for cost reduction and resource optimization. By streamlining processes and investing in VBC models, payers can work to reduce the overall cost of healthcare.

Enhanced Collaboration

Innovation roadmaps encourage collaboration among payers, healthcare providers, tech companies, and other stakeholders. These collaborations can lead to the development of innovative solutions that benefit the entire healthcare ecosystem.

Adapting to Change

As the healthcare landscape continues to evolve, payer models with flexible roadmaps are better equipped to adapt to new challenges and seize emerging opportunities. This adaptability ensures that payers remain relevant and effective in an ever-changing industry.

One real-world business case where payer organizations achieved transformation in healthcare by creating roadmaps and leading to disruptive innovation is the collaboration between Blue Cross Blue Shield of North Carolina (BCBSNC) and Aledade, a healthcare technology company focused on accountable care organizations (ACOs).

Case Example: BCBSNC and Aledade—Accountable Care Organizations

Background: BCBSNC recognized the need to transition from traditional fee-for-service reimbursement models to VBC models to improve healthcare quality, control costs, and enhance patient outcomes. Aledade had expertise in helping healthcare organizations establish ACOs and navigate the transition to VBC.

Creation of Roadmap and Collaboration

Shared Vision: BCBSNC and Aledade shared a vision of creating ACOs that would enable primary care physicians to take on more significant roles in coordinating patient care, focusing on preventive care, and reducing healthcare costs.

Strategic Roadmap: The collaboration involved the creation of a strategic roadmap outlining the steps required to establish and support ACOs effectively. This roadmap included defining ACO goals, selecting participating practices, implementing technology solutions, and creating care management processes.

Provider Engagement: BCBSNC and Aledade actively engaged with primary care physicians and healthcare providers to ensure their involvement and commitment to the ACO model. Effective communication and collaboration were key elements of the transformation.

Data and Analytics: The partnership leveraged data and analytics capabilities to identify high-risk patients, track outcomes, and measure the success of VBC initiatives. This data-driven approach informed decision-making and performance monitoring.

Innovation and Impact

VBC Model: The creation of ACOs shifted the payment model from fee-for-service to VBC. Physicians were incentivized based on patient outcomes, preventive care, and cost savings, disrupting the traditional fee-for-service reimbursement system.

Improved Patient Outcomes: By focusing on preventive care, care coordination, and population health management, ACOs aimed to improve patient health outcomes, particularly for individuals with chronic conditions.

Cost Containment: The VBC model sought to reduce overall healthcare costs by avoiding unnecessary tests and procedures, preventing hospital readmissions, and focusing on cost-effective care.

Enhanced Patient Experience: ACOs emphasized patient-centered care, offering patients more personalized care plans, care coordination, and better access to healthcare providers.

Provider Collaboration: The transformation encouraged collaboration among healthcare providers within the ACO network, leading to more coordinated and patient-centric care.

Scalability: The success of the ACO model led to its expansion to serve a broader population, demonstrating scalability and the potential for disruptive innovation in healthcare delivery.

Alignment of Incentives: The creation of ACOs successfully aligned the incentives of payers, providers, and patients, encouraging them to work together to achieve better healthcare outcomes.

The collaboration between BCBSNC and Aledade to establish ACOs represents a real-world example of payer organizations creating roadmaps and achieving transformation in healthcare. By shifting to a VBC model, focusing on patient outcomes, and actively engaging with providers, they disrupted traditional fee-for-service models and improved healthcare quality while containing costs. This innovative approach has the potential to reshape the future of healthcare delivery and reimbursement.

Another great example is the partnership between the Centers for Medicare & Medicaid Services (CMS) and private payers, including UnitedHealthcare, to develop and implement the Comprehensive Primary Care Plus (CPC+) program.

Case Example: Comprehensive Primary Care Plus Program

Background: CMS, the federal agency responsible for administering Medicare and Medicaid, aimed to improve primary care delivery in the United States by shifting from fee-for-service reimbursement to VBC models. Recognizing the potential for transformation, private payers like UnitedHealthcare collaborated with CMS to develop a roadmap for comprehensive primary care.

Creation of Roadmap and Collaboration

Shared Vision: CMS and private payers shared a vision of enhancing primary care by fostering care coordination, patient engagement, and improved health outcomes. They recognized the need to shift from volume-based to VBC.

Strategic Roadmap: The collaboration resulted in the creation of the CPC+ program, which outlined a roadmap for transforming primary care. The roadmap included criteria for participating practices, payment models, performance metrics, and care delivery requirements.

Provider Engagement: To ensure the success of CPC+, CMS and private payers actively engaged with primary care practices, clinicians, and healthcare providers. Effective communication and collaboration were essential for securing participation.

Data and Analytics: The program leveraged data and analytics capabilities to monitor and assess the performance of participating practices, identify at-risk patients, and measure the success of VBC initiatives.

Innovation and Impact

VBC Model: CPC+ shifted the primary care payment model from fee-for-service to VBC. Primary care practices received comprehensive care management fees, performance-based incentives, and shared savings payments, disrupting traditional fee-for-service reimbursement.

Improved Patient Outcomes: By emphasizing care coordination, preventive care, and population health management, CPC+ aimed to improve patient health outcomes, particularly for those with chronic conditions.

Cost Containment: The program sought to reduce overall healthcare costs by focusing on preventive care, reducing hospital admissions, and avoiding unnecessary tests and procedures.

Member-Centered Care: CPC+ encouraged patient-centered care, offering patients more personalized care plans, care coordination, and better access to primary care providers.

Provider Collaboration: The transformation fostered collaboration among primary care practices, specialists, and community resources, leading to more coordinated and patient-centric care.

Scalability: The success of CPC+ led to its expansion to more regions, demonstrating scalability and the potential for disruptive innovation in primary care.

Alignment of Incentives: CPC+ aligned the incentives of payers, providers, and patients, encouraging them to work together to achieve better healthcare outcomes.

The CPC+ program represents a real-world example of payer organizations and government agencies creating roadmaps that led to transformative changes in primary care. By shifting to a VBC model, focusing on preventive care, and actively engaging with providers, they disrupted traditional fee-for-service models and improved healthcare quality while containing costs. This innovative approach has the potential to reshape the future of primary care delivery and reimbursement.

Conclusion

The "create roadmaps" theme in payer healthcare innovation represents a strategic approach to driving positive change within the healthcare industry. By setting clear goals, aligning with stakeholder needs, and remaining adaptable, payers can navigate the complex healthcare landscape with purpose and vision. Through well-defined roadmaps, payers have the potential to drive innovation that improves patient outcomes, reduces costs, and enhances the overall healthcare experience for patients and providers alike.

Chapter 4

Collaborate and Listen

Listen for ideas that will potentially solve a problem or present an opportunity to collaborate with stakeholders and galvanize your network.

Many innovations started by listening, observing, and then communicating ideas and solutions to problems. When you listen, people are more likely to share ideas and provide encouragement. The more you engage others, the more ideas you are likely to catch. Great innovations are typically a result of multiple iterations by numerous individuals invited to participate in ideation and execution. Inviting others to share in your innovation will galvanize support and engagement necessary for success.

One is too small a number for innovation. Innovation is largely a result of a team-of-teams approach to solving a problem or exploiting an opportunity. It can be an ego challenge to have a great innovation and allow others to modify and edit your dream. We can take innovation too personally and become captive to the potential and miss out on something greater. Leveraging others actually frees the innovation to grow and expand beyond what you initially envisioned. There is strength in seeking the wisdom of others.

ANTHEM'S APPROACH IN BIRTHING OF AVANEER | ANONYMOUS

The healthcare sector is usually cautious when implementing new technologies, and blockchain technology has not yet been widely used despite its potential advantages.[1] AI is getting all of the attention recently but

DOI: 10.4324/9781003381983-4

blockchain remains a good foundation for innovation. Aetna, Anthem (now Elevance), UnitedIIcalthcare, and Humana are just a few of the key participants in the health insurance market who have participated in early industry experiments and pilot programs. These pilot projects show how healthcare organizations might work together to investigate the potential of blockchain technology. In the blockchain era, patients will stand to gain greatly. Patients may have greater data ownership and control over who has access to their medical records as a result of the adoption of blockchain-based solutions in the healthcare industry. This strategy promotes a culture of shared responsibility and empowerment by requiring cooperation and consent from patients and healthcare providers to utilize their private keys for accessing medical information on the blockchain.

The network, which focuses on payer-to-payer data sharing, eligibility, and prior authorization, is constructed using block-chain technology and HL7's FHIR specification to improve data access among healthcare institutions.[2] The demand for safe and efficient transactions between healthcare companies is what spurred the use of blockchain in this situation. The network intends to overcome data exchange inefficiencies and interoperability barriers in the healthcare sector. In order to encourage the implementation of cutting-edge technologies like blockchain, the group attempts to involve and align numerous stakeholders, decision-makers, and leaders within the healthcare sector.

When considering how to convince Anthem or American healthcare providers to adopt blockchain technology, the relevance of merging cultures becomes clearer. Blockchain technology will need the active involvement and support of many stakeholders, including institutional leaders, healthcare professionals, IT specialists, patients, and other pertinent parties, for it to be successfully adopted in the healthcare industry. This is the hallmark of "Collaborate and Listen."

Collaborate and Listen

In the context of the HIMSS Innovation model, Aetna, PNC Bank, IBM, Anthem, and Health Care Service Corporation (HCSC) collaborated to create the health utility network that birthed Avaneer Health in June 2021.[3] "Innovation through Collaboration," a joint value, best represents the motivation that led to the formation of Avaneer Health and to incorporate blockchain in its operations.[2] Avaneer Health was created by a consortium of leading industry leaders, including Aetna, Anthem, Cleveland Clinic, HCSC, the PNC Financial Services Group, Inc., and Sentara Healthcare. Avaneer Health's vision is to build a healthcare ecosystem in which payers, providers, patients, and partners can effortlessly connect and securely share information directly with one another, breaking down healthcare boundaries. They intend to accomplish this through collaboration and innovation, working together to increase transparency and interoperability in the healthcare business.

The health utility network sought to use blockchain to address issues with provider directories, healthcare information interchange, and claims processing in the sector. The original members' cooperative efforts and knowledge sharing led to this expansion into a stand-alone company. Co-chair of the Avaneer Health Board of Directors Marvin Richardson underlined that the company was carrying out the idea of a utility network for the healthcare sector.[3] This emphasizes the strategy of bringing together many stakeholders and encouraging an inclusive and collaborative culture. The JPMorgan Chase executive in charge of Avaneer Health, Stuart Hanson, was ecstatic about the chance to contribute to resolving the most difficult problems in healthcare.[3] To advance the plan and create favorable momentum for the business, the executive was eager to collaborate with the Avaneer Health team and industry partners. This shows a focus on developing solutions together and a collaborative approach.

According to Forbes,[4] the Innovation Pathway element that can be credited with encouraging or aiding Anthem, the second-largest health insurance provider in the United States, to use blockchain technology is "Collaborate and Listen." Forbes reported that Anthem, Aetna, HCSC, IBM, and PNC Bank formed a new blockchain-focused cooperation. Their objective was to improve interoperability and partner confidence while assisting in maintaining patient data privacy. These partnerships and collaborations with other businesses in the healthcare sector demonstrate Anthem's willingness to cooperate with others, take into account their knowledge, and collectively explore the potential advantages of implementing blockchain technology. Anthem may benefit from the expertise and perspectives of these partners in blockchain technology by working together and paying attention to other businesses. This knowledge and insight probably influenced Anthem's choice to use blockchain solutions for protecting patient data and enhancing the exchange of medical information. Different businesses could have different work cultures, approaches to problem-solving, and viewpoints on how to use technology. When people come together to work on a shared objective, there is a chance for the interchange of concepts, methods, and practices, which leads to some degree of blending or integrating of cultures.

Allison[5] mentions how leading healthcare providers, including IBM, Aetna, Anthem, HCSC, and PNC Bank, are working together to enhance data exchange and boost the effectiveness of health claims and transactions using a "blockchain-based ecosystem." The partnership intends to improve customer experience and reduce inefficiencies in the healthcare system by utilizing data insights and cutting-edge forecasts made possible by blockchain technology. It's important to note that Anthem, one of the Health Utility Network's founding members, has joined rivals in this initiative to reduce waste in the healthcare sector. Although Allison[5] does not specifically address mixing cultures, the article does emphasize the significance of competitor cooperation and collaboration to overcome shared difficulties in the healthcare sector. In this type of collaborative effort, several groups with their backgrounds and working methods come together to work toward a common objective, promoting a culture of open collaboration and knowledge sharing. This type of collaborative effort can be considered a form of blending cultures. Allison[5] also states that other well-known names in the blockchain healthcare field are vying for the same projects, and Anthem is contributing diverse technologies to the platform together with other members. This shows a readiness to combine different strategies and technological advancements, possibly encouraging an innovative and receptive culture.

Blockchain technology will be used by Anthem to develop a permission-based system that will let patients own their medical records and share them with doctors as needed.[6] To build confidence and facilitate secure data sharing, this strategy demands cooperation and coordination among several stakeholders. Blockchain technology is being tested by a group of healthcare behemoths, including Anthem and Aetna, as a potential remedy for the inefficiencies and data silos in the healthcare sector. This consortium strategy entails getting many organizations together to jointly research and apply blockchain technology. The consortium's members, including Anthem, will collaborate to produce applications. This cooperative strategy promotes information exchange and joint development of solutions to problems facing the industry.

In a British context, the lack of interoperability in the healthcare system, which limits clinicians' ability to deliver quality care, was projected to inspire the adoption of blockchain.[7] With its capacity to handle access control and develop smart contracts, blockchain technology can facilitate easy interchange and quick access to health data across many platforms. Building standardized techniques for data interchange calls for collaboration and cooperation among many healthcare stakeholders. Vazirani et al.[7] address the Office of the National Coordinator for Health Information Technology's (ONC) initiatives to establish a "Use of Blockchain in Health IT and Health-Related Research" competition. Innovative approaches to health record management and patient empowerment through interoperability were sought out in the challenge. MedRec, one of the winning proposals, suggested leveraging blockchain to safely record patient-provider interactions and give patients authority over their data. These joint activities reveal a cooperative and knowledge-sharing attitude as they look into blockchain options for bettering health record administration.

Avaneer Health continues to collaborate with the original organizations to co-develop shared procedures and solutions. This cooperation opens up previously unimagined business possibilities to help solve age-old difficulties and unleash significant cost, procedural, and technological inefficiencies in healthcare.

"Collaborate and Listen" Resulting Interoperability

ONC defines interoperability as the ability of diverse systems in healthcare to exchange health information and efficiently use shared data. This notion emphasizes the significance of smooth data interchange between payers, providers, and other healthcare innovators. Interoperability is a critical prerequisite for Avaneer Health's aim of creating a healthcare ecosystem in which all stakeholders may connect and safely share information. The four levels of healthcare interoperability provide a complete framework for ensuring effective data exchange.

Foundational Interoperability

This level sets the fundamental technological requirements for secure communication between systems or applications. It ensures that one system may communicate and receive data from another. Foundational interoperability is critical for Avaneer Health's mission of tearing down healthcare barriers and enabling seamless interactions between payers, providers, patients, and partners.

Structural Interoperability

This level determines the data exchange format, grammar, and organization. It ensures that data can be correctly and accurately understood by various systems. A common understanding of data structure and organization is critical for effective data sharing and exploitation in the context of block-chain implementation.

Semantic Interoperability

Semantic interoperability is concerned with the development of common underlying models and the codification of data. This entails adopting standardized definitions from publicly available value sets and coding vocabularies to ensure that the data is understood and understood by everyone. Semantic interoperability is critical for ensuring that data is correctly processed and used by all stakeholders in Avaneer Health's mission of enhancing openness and interoperability.

Organizational Interoperability

Factors for secure and seamless data communication and use at this level include governance, policy, social, legal, and organizational factors. Consent, trust, and connected workflows are examples of issues addressed at the organizational interoperability level. Organizational interoperability becomes critical in the combined efforts of Avaneer Health and other industry leaders to ensure a smooth interchange of information between different companies and entities.

In the Absence of a "Collaborate and Listen" Approach

Avaneer[8] acknowledges that when health-care systems and stakeholders are unable to exchange data and collaborate efficiently, providers and patients alike will face serious ramifications as highlighted in the following.

1. **Providers**
   a. Delayed Reimbursement
      The reimbursement procedure for healthcare services might be delayed if data sharing is inefficient. This can put financial hardship on healthcare providers, who rely on prompt payments to stay in business.
   b. Refused Claims
      Inadequate data exchange may result in claims-processing errors or missing information, increasing the chance of claims being refused.

This may result in increased administrative difficulties and revenue loss for providers.

c. Unnecessary Write-Offs

When critical data is not available or provided promptly, providers may be obliged to write off specific services or treatments, resulting in financial losses.

d. Poor Cash Flow

Delays in reimbursement and denied claims can impair a provider's capacity to manage spending and invest in resources.

e. Additional Work

Providers may be required to invest more time and effort in manual processes such as faxing or sending prior authorization requests, resulting in inefficiencies and lower productivity.

2. Members

a. Delays in Care

Inadequate interoperability can cause delays in acquiring previous authorizations or accessing important health information, thereby delaying necessary medical treatments and interventions.

b. Surprise invoices

Inadequate data interchange and communication might result in billing mistakes, allowing patients to receive unexpected or ambiguous invoices.

c. Poor Patient Experience

Difficulties accessing health data or experiencing delays in care can result in a negative patient experience, lowering overall satisfaction with healthcare services.

d. Reduced Outcomes

Providing effective and coordinated care requires timely access to complete and accurate patient information. A lack of interoperability may impede care coordination, potentially resulting in inferior patient outcomes.

Conclusion

Blockchain is viewed as a potentially game-changing technology for safe data transmission, and Avaneer Health's architecture is meant to do this through collaboration and listening to the requirements and concerns of many healthcare stakeholders. By giving insurers quick access to vital data without compromising data security, blockchain can minimize costs and the potential for errors. This feature encourages insurers to collaborate with blockchain technology to enhance cost-effectiveness and data management. It draws attention to some difficulties and opposition to the adoption of blockchain technology, particularly from businesses that profit from collecting and storing data. This opposition stems from apprehension about upending established paradigms. Collaboration and open communication among healthcare industry players, including insurers like Anthem, would be necessary to meet these issues. The adoption of block-chain technology in the healthcare industry requires cooperation across healthcare entities, an emphasis on patient empowerment, advantages for payers, and a coordinated approach to overcoming hurdles.

References

1. Kaltwasser, J. (2022, February 8). *Is Healthcare Ready for Blockchain?* Managed Healthcare Executive. https://www.managedhealthcare-executive.com/view/is-healthcare-ready-for-blockchain-
2. Avaneer. (2022, August 16). *Unlocking the Full Potential of Healthcare—Avaneer.* https:// avaneerhealth.com/ blog/unlocking-the-full-potential-of-healthcare/
3. Landi, H. (2021, June 14). *Aetna, Anthem and Cleveland Clinic Back Blockchain Venture to Improve Healthcare Efficiency.* Fierce Healthcare. https://www.fiercehealthcare.com/tech/aetna-anthem-and-cleveland-clinic-back-block-chain-startup-to-improve-healthcare-efficiency
4. Rosenbaum, L. (2019, December 12). *Anthem Will Use Blockchain to Secure Medical Data for Its 40 Million Members in Three Years.* Forbes. https://www.forbes.com/sites/leahrosen-baum/2019/12/12/anthem-says-its-40-million-members-will-be-using-blockchain-to-secure-patient-data-in-three-years/?sh=32aaf86a6837
5. Allison, I. (2019, January 24). *IBM, Aetna, PNC Explore Medical Data Blockchain for 100 Million Health Plans.* CoinDesk: Bitcoin, Ethereum, Crypto News and Price Data. https://www.coindesk.com/tech/2019/01/24/ibm-aet-na-pnc-exploremedical-data-blockchain-for-100-million-health-plans/
6. Roberts, J. J. (2019, January 24). *Can Blockchain Solvethe Messof Medical Records? IBM Announces Tie-Up with Healthcare Providers.* Fortune Crypto. https://fortune.com/crypto/2019/01/24/ ibm-blockchain-healthcare/
7. Vazirani, A. A., O'Donoghue, O., Brindley, D., & Meinert, E. (2019). Implementing Blockchains for Efficient Health Care: Systematic Review. *Journal of Medical Internet Research,* 21(2), e12439. https://doi.org/10.2196/12439
8. Avaneer. (2023). *Healthcare Interoperability—Avaneer.* https://avaneerhealth.com/healthcare-interoperability/

DON'T LOSE THE "PERSON" IN THE "PROCESS" | BY CAROL PALACKDHARRY

Processes are not enough
For impactful innovation
One must always hold close
A goal to touch the spirit of a patient
A need to reinvigorate the spirit of a clinician
As both feel cast aside
By technology's Game of Thrones
Their patience stretched to
The thinnest of strands
Of wanting to revolt and abandon

Processes are not enough
To demonstrate goodwill and unity
To break real or imagined barriers and discrimination
Seen even by eyes that are blind
Find those that can contribute
Give them a seat at the table
Listen, learn, practice, teach, reach
Because processes are not enough
To reach those in need of healing

My journey of creating innovation and practice change in medicine has spanned three decades. Learning how to be successful was a steep learning curve full of failures. I am an immigrant born in what was British Guiana [now Guyana], raised with different cultural values. I am a brown-skinned woman who went to medical school and into oncology at a time when white males dominated those areas. Sexual and racial harassment in medicine abounded in those years. During the past two decades, I was not only a senior medical executive developing new programs but also an unexpected patient, surviving three life-threatening iatrogenic adverse events. As a 15-year breast cancer and 7-year spinal cord injury survivor, I can't phantom how anyone without medical training could have navigated the system and survived what I experienced. No wonder so many patients die in hospital of iatrogenic causes. We must not lose sight of patient safety.

In 2022, I watched my shy 84 y/o, old-school, never-question-a-doctor, mother die a heartbreakingly painful death with [not from] widely metastatic breast cancer because a thoughtless medical resident made her feel too ashamed to ask for opioid refills for pain relief. She died of hepatocellular necrosis from acetaminophen toxicity, her only form of pain control. We can do better. We must do better. Data can help but only if we also know the actual *patient experience*. To know the patient experience, we must put programs in place to capture it accurately.

After completing a clinical research hematology and oncology fellowship at Fox Chase Cancer Center, I set out to change the treatment of cancers with what was then known as "biologic response modifiers." As a principal investigator for two pharmaceutical companies, the tenacity of oncology clinical researchers of that time to continue through failure and serious toxicities eventually led to the current immune-oncology and molecularly targeted therapies that have revolutionized cancer therapy and patient outcomes. Cancer research taught me innovation MUST include an understanding of the driving forces of ALL parties involved in healthcare. Every subset of the healthcare industry has goals for their companies that matter and therefore deserve a seat at the table of change. The way oncology had to change to advance holds several lessons for innovation of the rest of the healthcare system.

Looking back, *reimagining what data to obtain and how to use it to demonstrate changes in outcomes that were hidden in "total data" analysis,* was how progress in targeted oncology therapy was made. Eventually patient-level individual tumor factors had to be obtained and presented in new types of graphics called "waterfall" and "swimmers" plots. These new data techniques prove remarkable progress, and cures have been made in previously rapidly fatal cancers because of targeted therapy advances in specific patient subpopulations. Witnessing the rapid change, this produced has been bittersweet. Today's oncologists give therapies costing >$10,000 per month without knowing the work by those of us toiling decades ago to help patients survive early immunotherapies that most thought would go nowhere because the toxicities and the way we looked at outcome data masked benefit. Their success is built on our failures. That is how innovation happens. You don't quit if you fail; you dig deep for the reasons, try a different approach, and look at data in new ways to show outcome differences in specific populations.

Upon making the transition into the data analytics and payer policy world, I was forced to grow in a way I never realized I was deficient. In academic practice, I did what I thought was best-given patient circumstances and my own "subspecialist opinion." I never saw bills or knew what financial sacrifices patients were making to get treatment. When utilization review medical directors from the HMOs of the early 1990s called me to question something, I angrily informed them they did not have the credentials to question my decision-making. I had no idea, nor did I question who was footing the bill for my "right" to create "therapeutic concoctions" when faced with failed or contraindications to first-line therapy. I was in the wrong because I did not have the education necessary to have financial and policy discussions. I use my own experience to bring other physicians to the table because *this* is our common bond.

It took working with/for many different stakeholders for me to understand the interplay of the moving parts of medicine, with most stakeholders taking a myopic view of their rights and responsibilities. I think of three primary driving forces. First up is the myopic view of patients. I was a young attending in the pre-2000 era of "supporting patient choice, no matter what." I was never educated about the concept of different premiums for different deductibles, copays, pharmacy benefits, and places of care. This often created a me + patient against the insurance company scenario. I can't count the number of times I told patients [and have had my own doctors tell me] that "we'll figure out a way to get around insurance barriers to our treatment plan." The naked truth is that patients want to pay the minimal premium possible but, if there is a need for medical care, want the best and shiniest new thing for themselves at the places closest and most convenient for them. We need to be taught about health economics, payment policies, financial toxicity, and ethics in medical school, so we, as physicians, stop contributing to payer policy deception. Mic drop.

Second up is a look at those providing healthcare or drugs and devices. Therapy sophistication, job satisfaction, and decreased applicant pools are changing the face of medicine. Those involved in patient care, from hospital janitorial staff to drug company CEOs, are increasingly seeking compensation based on the risk they undertake [not to be confused with risk-based patient outcome models]. Those who provide patient care deserve the same rights as all humans—safe environments, reasonable work hours, protected family time, feeling purpose and meaning in their jobs, and the ability to maintain physical and mental wellness. The long-projected physician shortage has begun. Average wait times for all new patient appointments are more than four weeks across the United States in 2022, with some areas reporting new primary care appointment wait times of more than four months. Both COVID-19-related shutdowns and physician stress from all the deaths have led to physicians leaving practice. Those remaining are revolting against increased administrative demands related to payer coverage policies and varying quality measures. Any innovation that further increases administrative activities will fail. Only innovations openly acknowledging and addressing pain points have a chance of success. In terms of addressing supply shortage, companies that can operate as *medical service extenders* are needed. Terminology is critical. *"Supporting the treating physician"* as the one in control of the patient care plan is critical.

Third is *acknowledging and owning results of HEOR and OECD data.* For me, this was the hardest and most humbling lesson of the transition into executive medicine. This US "crisis in healthcare" has been going on for decades. Prior to the COVID-19 pandemic, the cost of healthcare in the United States was unsustainable with outcomes poorer than most economically advantaged countries that spend far less per capita on healthcare. In the United States, in 2022, the average length of life decreased for the second year in a row. The COVID-19 pandemic accounts for just over 50% of the increase, with mortality measures in lives lost per capita among the highest of OECD countries We should be ashamed of this waste of both money and lives.

When I introduce or bring together a team to create new programs, I start with teaching sessions on OECD data. The feedback from others has been just as profound as it was for me when I learned about healthcare economics: "we wish we would have known this before." People cannot know until they have been taught. It is not a problem just for health plan CEOs, CMS, and self-funded groups. This is a problem for everyone, including physicians and patients. Everyone who is employed and pays taxes has a vested stake in HEOR.

Collaborate and Listen. To reiterate, from my vantage point of having experience as a patient who nearly died from iatrogenic harm, a caregiver who watched my mom die in agony, a senior medical director who designs new programs, and a leader in multiple stakeholder groups, building successful innovation programs [defined as a positive ROI, better outcomes, and increased patient and provider satisfaction] should incorporate the following into whatever process model is followed:

1. *Measure and improve patient safety events and the morbidity and mortality from iatrogenic harm—including iatrogenic harm from what is said to a patient.* What happened to my mom should never have happened. If just one other person never has to suffer like that, at least her suffering was not in vain.

2. *Build programs that are extensions of the treating physician care,* taking the time to build patient trust, address language and cultural barriers, and gather information that there is no time for in-office visits.

3. *Provide needed culturally sensitive services* such as home-care visits, infusions, blood draws, and so on. Compliance and follow-up are improved, and this opens physician time to decrease wait time for new patients to get in.

4. *Teach care managers how to ask difficult questions about barriers and SDOH and then how to listen* before finding solutions. This is not taught in nursing school but requires specific education on cultural and religious beliefs in addition to family circumstances.

5. *Have patient advocates on corporate program development teams.* When I was recovering from surgery, I stopped answering the phone because nurses from four different programs were calling daily to ask the same questions. Simplify patient's lives.

6. *Use physician experts who can reinvigorate client physician and clinician purpose and meaning,* which is why most choose healthcare to begin with.

7. Never increase, but *drastically decrease physician administrative responsibilities.*

8. *Evaluate and find new ways to reevaluate advanced data* to match the real-world patient state as closely as possible and *determine what populations benefit from interventions.*

9. Measure more than the standard decreased cost of care, IP stays, ER visits. *Use new data visualization techniques to demonstrate the impact of personalized interventions.*

This is dedicated to all the patients we failed in our promise to "first, do no harm."

THE SUMMACARE INNOVATION JOURNEY | BY WILLIAM EPLING

Formed in Akron, Ohio, in 1993, SummaCare is one of the region's only provider-owned health insurance companies. While the company began as a product offering for large, self-funded employers in Akron, its integration with Summa Health (hospitals, clinics, and payer) allows the company to continually develop and evolve its care-inspired coverage and introduce clinical programs that facilitate improving health outcomes while improving quality and controlling costs. Today, SummaCare serves a variety of markets across northern Ohio through its 5 STAR Medicare Advantage plans, employer commercial group insured and self-funded plans, as well as individual and family plans on and off the marketplace.

SummaCare operates its Medicare Advantage business in a highly competitive environment, presenting a portfolio of products to a market that changes tactically not only as competitors seek advantage from year to year but over time as the health insurance market is shaped by both regulatory changes and the innovation in health insurance design.

The market for Medicare Advantage plans is a dynamic environment experiencing a significant amount of change. Price pressure is driving an increasingly strong trend toward zero premium and commodity-priced plans (defined as those plans with a premium under $30), while the dramatic expansion of supplemental benefits since 2019 has added a new dimension for competition around non-medical benefits that support improved quality and health outcomes rather than specific medical procedures or clinical treatments.

SummaCare did an analysis of the market for both commodity-priced plans and menu-driven supplemental benefits and identified an opportunity for SummaCare to successfully position itself in the new, emerging market as an industry innovator and leader. To take advantage of that opportunity, and support the continuous innovation to improve health outcomes and provide seniors with flexibility and choice, two new products were developed:

- A commodity-priced plan with a $19 premium named "Jade"
- A menu-driven benefits control pack-age named "Bene-Flex™." The concept is to allow seniors to construct their own supplemental benefits based on their individual health status and needs.

This increased level of competition—price and outcome-supporting benefits—is driving changes in the market for plans, creating opportunities for lower-priced premium plans and placing financial pressure on carriers to provide outcome-driven supplemental benefits in a cost-effective way. Numerous focus groups and introduction of limited offerings in the market indicated broad consumer acceptance of the concept. Additionally, research by Medicare market research firm Deft as well as SummaCare supports that approach with recent studies showing a significant majority of Medicare Advantage prescription drug (MAPD) (plans which are a type of Medicare

Advantage plan that includes prescription drug coverage. You'll have more coverage than with original Medicare, and you don't need to worry about a separate Part D plan) members expressing interest in a menu approach to choosing supplemental benefits.

SummaCare chose to introduce a new MAPD plan, Jade, in 2023, developed to target those individuals who seek to be in control of their healthcare. It was positioned to be attractive among age-ins and those inclined to self-manage their health and healthcare support.

The plan utilizes the Bene-Flex™ supplemental benefits package, allowing members to pick up to five (5) supplemental benefits based on their health conditions and the benefits they believe would be put to the best use given their healthcare conditions and lifestyle needs.

Bene-Flex™ is a flexible delivery approach to maximizing the available supplemental benefits to members while reducing the overall cost of deployment by having members choose a selection of benefits from a menu of choices.

Market research found that Medicare Advantage plan members not only understand the concept but find it more desirable than the traditional delivery of a full slate of benefits.

Research has shown members are not aware of and do not utilize many of the supplemental benefits offered by their plans, driving up general plan costs on a per member per month (PMPM) basis to make the benefits available to all members— regardless of interest in the benefit.

Having members choose their supplemental benefits may reduce PMPM costs while at the same time driving up utilization, thus improving member health out-comes at reasonable costs as those benefits specifically selected will better fit that member's needs and lifestyle.

Enabling members to change their benefits while staying in the same plan may also positively impact member satisfaction and retention.

Medicare expanded the supplemental benefits that Medicare Advantage plans could offer to members beginning in 2019. These benefits are designed to enhance a member's quality of life and improve health outcomes by impacting chronic conditions or supporting wellness. Since their appearance in the market, competition between plans over supplemental benefits has intensified, and two categories of supplemental benefits have emerged:

- **Core or Table Stakes**—these benefits have proven to be exceptionally popular among beneficiaries and are an area of intense competition between plans.

- **Discretionary or "Extra" Benefits**—these benefits are not always well known among plan members and tend to be utilized only when they become aware of them or have an event that causes them to seek the benefit.

Bene-Flex™ is a concept for allowing members to pick the supplemental benefits they believe will give them the most value and best fit their needs for the coming enrollment year—a controlled benefit access feature. The idea is based on a finding of research with Medicare members in another market in 2020. That research found that Medicare-eligible seniors were very aware their healthcare needs changed as they aged, and their Medicare coverage needed to change to meet their needs. Research with members was conducted in the summer of 2021 to understand the acceptance and level of interest in the concept.

The member research found the following facts:

- Members are fully aware and knowledgeable about their Part A and Part B benefits. They tend to focus on discretionary supplemental benefits (as opposed to core supplemental benefits) only when in need of the services covered.
- The concept of being able to choose from different bundles of benefits to better match their plan to their personal health situation was both quickly understood and considered very desirable.
- The ability to pick the benefits in their own bundle was seen to offer significant value. Providing benefits from which to choose in tiers similar to the way drugs are covered was suggested by the participants as a means of controlling the cost between different levels of benefits.

In a study published in January 2022, Deft Research found in a survey of 1,018 Medicare Advantage plan members (the study also surveyed 747 Medicare supplement members, 173 original Medicare members, and 132 age-ins) that more than six in 10 (61%) of the respondents preferred nontraditional supplemental benefit delivery options, with 31% preferring to choose benefits from a menu of options (see Figure 4.1).

The key feature of Bene-Flex™ is that it is designed to allow members to better manage their benefits through a full selection of supplemental benefits rather than just one.

Bene-Flex™ supports the management of benefit-cost through the use of cost tiers, with Tier 1 benefits being the lowest cost to provide, Tier 2

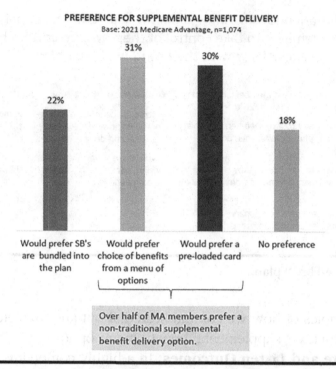

Figure 4.1 Deft findings on Medicare Advantage plan member supplemental benefits delivery.

Source: Deft Research 2022 National Medicare Advantage Supplemental Benefits Conjoint Study

benefits being those that cost more, and Tier 3 benefits being those benefits that are the most expensive.

Bene-Flex™ can thus potentially offer a significantly broader array of supplemental benefits allowing members to build their own supplemental benefit design that best fits their current needs and then be able to modify or change those selections in subsequent years as their needs change.

Three tiers of benefits were structured for Jade members to choose from.

Core benefits such as dental, vision, hearing, over-the-counter (OTC) allowance, Assist America, and visitor travel are included in all plans.

Tier One Benefits. These benefits are less costly to provide. Jade members enrolling in the plan can pick three of them.

Tier Two Benefits. These benefits are somewhat more expensive than the Tier One benefits, and Jade members may pick one of them.

Tier Three Benefits are the most expensive to provide, and Jade members may select just one.

Bene-Flex™ is an innovative way to deliver supplemental benefits.
It empowers members to take control of their own healthcare benefits
and is available **exclusively with the brand new Jade plan.**

- Consumers, including our own members, have told us they want "control" of their healthcare.
- We have designed a way to give members the ability to personalize their plan to meet their unique healthcare needs.
- Members create their own package by choosing discretionary supplemental benefits from a menu of options.
- Members can change their discretionary supplemental benefits annually to meet their changing healthcare needs.

Key features of the new Jade plan:
- Attractive benefits including a low monthly premium, low MOOP & competitive copays for medical and drug
- Table stake supplemental benefits including dental, vision, hearing, OTC, Visitor/Travel & Assist America are embedded

Figure 4.2   Bene-Flex™ plan.

Here are examples of how we communicated about and marketed the Jade plan and Bene-Flex™ supplemental benefit menu options.

Collaborate and Listen Outcomes. In a highly competitive environment, SummaCare analyzed the market; listened to existing members, prospects, and distribution channels; and identified an opportunity to innovate through the development of a low commodity-priced Medicare Advantage Prescription Drug plan, Jade, and a unique, menu-driven supplemental benefit delivery option, Bene-Flex™, designed to allow seniors to build and customize their own supplemental plan design to best fit their needs and lifestyle. By pairing them together, we successfully positioned SummaCare in the new, emerging market as an industry innovator and leader.

REVOLUTIONIZING CANCER CARE | BY ARVIND SIVARAMAKRISHNAN

Introduction

The cancer care burden significantly impacts all stakeholders across the world. The impact is due to key barriers to cancer, which are lack of awareness, lack of time, high associated costs, and lack of accessibility, which cause emotional, physical, and financial stress and strain to the population at large. This impact is growing as the incidence rises.

Healthcare as an industry has been a laggard in adoption of technology adoption and digital innovation. According to the McKinsey Digitization

Index, healthcare ranks among the least advanced in terms of digitization. However, because of COVID-19, there has been an impetus across all segments of healthcare to adopt and embrace digital technologies driving accessibility and affordability.

In the following sections, Karkinos, a "digital first"-driven oncology care provider company based out of India, presents the case study of how the "collaborate and listen" theme has been leveraged to transform oncology care.

Karkinos: About the Company

Karkinos is a healthcare technology company, founded in 2020 in India, specializing in oncology healthcare with the following objectives:

■ Karkinos Healthcare is a health technology platform that supports integration of distributed cancer care.
■ Karkinos is on a mission to provide an end-to-end care solution where no person is deprived of care, for lack of access or affordability.

The company is focused and determined in its mission in providing an end-to-end care from detection to treatment to meet the following objectives.

Karkinos: Innovative Approach—"Collaborate and Listen"

The key challenges in oncology care delivery can be stated in terms of lack of facilities, capacities, expertise, and detection at late stage compounded by lack of accessibility and affordability is a major issue, especially in a country like India.

Karkinos recognized that a holistic and comprehensive transformation is needed to address the challenges faced. But since the problems are widespread and varied, Karkinos adopted a "collaborate and listen" approach to develop a viable and practical solution to cancer care.

Toward This Following Tactical Steps Have Been Leveraged

■ One of the significant advantages that was leveraged was that Karkinos founders have been at the forefront of fight against cancer with stakeholders from Tata Institutions, which include stalwart hospitals such as

Tata Memorial Hospital, an 82-year-old institution dedicated to providing free or affordable cancer care in India; Roswell Park New York; Adyar Cancer Institute; AIIMS Delhi; Tata Memorial Hospital Kolkata and Government Institutions; and so on.

■ The discussion earlier provided a "captive storehouse of experiences," which provided a great opportunity to delve into the problem in terms of identifying the potential areas of transformation by interacting with treating doctors, patients, and other stakeholders of the system.

■ In addition, Karkinos invested significant effort and time by listening intently to the voices of patients, caregivers, healthcare providers, and community leaders, gaining valuable insights into the challenges they faced.

Through the "collaborate and listen" approach, Karkinos was able to build a comprehensive understanding of the landscape, which enabled it to arrive at an innovative solution to transform Cancer Heath, which is a 4D model of care, powered by robust digital platform, which is described in the next sections.

Karkinos: "Collaborate and Listen"—Delivery Model

Figure 4.3 depicts the innovative model, which has evolved with the innovative approach of "collaborate and listen" as explained earlier:

The model given earlier is powered by a robust technology-driven platform as given in Figure 4.4.

The multidimensional approach to cancer care is enabled through a future-ready intelligent platform. The Karkinos platform is a Cloud-native, open-systems-based, and event-driven architecture for healthcare ecosystem with API-driven separation of data, apps, and user experience, ensuring semantic and structural interoperability for needs of the healthcare ecosystem.

Karkinos is among the top 2A0 digital healthcare tech companies implementing India's national health mission—Ayushman Bharat Digital Mission (ABDM), which is fully certified (M1, M2, M3) and has built ABDM compatibility into the platform, ensuring quick readiness and compatibility for partners. Additionally, the platform features an AI/ML-driven insights platform that uses OncoKEEN, proprietary NLP models, and data visualization to discover insights within the data present in the data lake.

Karkinos 4D model

✓ Oncology focused platform

Detect Early

✓ Integrates clinical & research workflows using technology with an academic rigor

Diagnosis:
Democratizing
Precision Oncology

✓ Enables end to end care solutions across the cancer care continuum

Delivery: Integration of
primary health and cancer
care- care closer to home

✓ Strives for affordable excellence in cancer care

Discover new insights

Figure 4.3   Innovative care model: 4D.

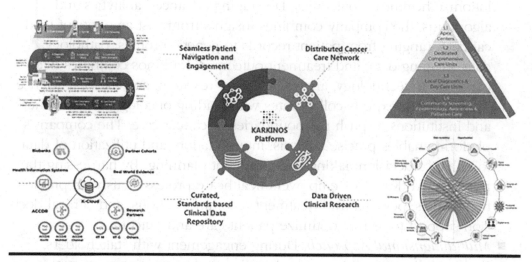

Seamless Patient
Navigation and
Engagement

Distributed Cancer
Care Network

KARKINOS
Platform

Curated,
Standards based
Clinical Data
Repository

Data Driven
Clinical Research

Figure 4.4   Karkinos oncology platform.

This platform provides knowledge-driven clinical decision support, automates care guideline creation, and helps visualize complex data. The platform natively supports major healthcare data exchange standards like openEHR, HL7 FHIR, DICOM, and terminology standards like SNOMED and LOINC, allowing a wide range of interoperability across partner hospitals supporting a variety of HIS, EMR, and internal systems.

Using the aforementioned 4D model powered by delivery model, Karkinos has evaluated the risk of cancer and noncommunicable diseases for over 1.1 million vulnerable citizens to date and has also assisted hundreds of patients in India through its distributed cancer care network utilizing the platform.

Karkinos: "Collaborate and Listen" Approach Highlights

Following are the key highlights of the innovative approach developed through "collaborate and listen":

■ *Enabling Precision Care:* With a relentless focus on data, analytics, and artificial intelligence (AI), Karkinos is dedicated to transforming cancer care and driving precision medicine forward. At the core of Karkinos' mission is the belief that data-driven insights have the power to revolutionize healthcare outcomes. Leveraging advanced analytics and AI algorithms, the company combines insights from vast amounts of medical data, ranging from patient records to genetic profiles, pathology data, imaging data, and treatment outcomes. Karkinos combines deep expertise in technology, analytics, cancer research, and medical science. Their team of experts collaborates with leading oncologists, researchers, and institutions to push the boundaries of cancer care. The company's platform enables precise analysis, interpretation, and utilization of data to enhance decisionmaking and treatment planning. By harnessing the power of AI, Karkinos empowers healthcare professionals with predictive models, personalized treatment recommendations, and clinical decision support tools that optimize patient care and outcomes.

■ *Multidimensional Approach*: During engagement with stakeholders, Karkinos discovered that early detection and prevention were critical areas in need of improvement. Recognizing that these challenges required a multidimensional approach, Karkinos sought collaboration opportunities with stakeholders, including government health agencies, NGOs, technology partners, and healthcare providers.

■ *Leveraging Technology*: Karkinos understood that technology would be the key enabler to address the identified challenges effectively. Leveraging the power of digital solutions, Karkinos embarked on the development of a user-friendly platform for cancer risk assessment and awareness. By collaborating with leading technology partners and engaging stakeholders throughout the design and development process, Karkinos ensured that the platform aligned with the needs of both patients and healthcare professionals.

■ *Enhancing Accessibility:* Equitable access to quality cancer care is a pressing concern in India. To address this, Karkinos collaborated with health-care providers, offering the platform as a tool to enhance early detection and prevention efforts. By integrating digital solution into existing health-care systems and training healthcare professionals on its usage, we successfully bridged the gap between urban and rural areas, reaching underserved populations. Karkinos actively sought feedback from healthcare providers, adapting the platform to their needs, and ensuring seamless integration into their workflows.

■ *Empowering Patients and Caregivers:* A crucial aspect of digital cancer community risk assessment platform was its focus on empowering patients and caregivers. By providing personalized risk assessments, educational resources, and support networks, Karkinos aimed to ensure that individuals affected by cancer felt informed, supported, and connected. Karkinos actively sought input from patients and caregivers, incorporating their suggestions to enhance the platform's user experience and value.

■ *Measuring Outcomes and Continuous Improvements:* To assess the impact of digital solutions, robust measurement metrics were established by collaboratively working with stakeholders. Regular feedback loops allowed us to identify areas for improvement and iterate the platform accordingly, ensuring that it remained responsive to the evolving needs of the community.

■ *Addressing Health Disparities:* India is a vast and diverse country with significant health disparities between urban and rural areas. Recognizing this, Karkinos actively collaborated with community leaders, NGOs, and government health agencies to ensure that Karkinos digital cancer community risk assessment platform reached underserved populations. By conducting targeted outreach programs, organizing health camps, and partnering with local healthcare providers, Karkinos aimed to bridge the gap and address the unique challenges faced by rural communities. Through active listening and continuous engagement, Karkinos gathered insights from these communities, adapting Karkinos platform to suit their specific needs and cultural nuances.

■ *Privacy and Data Security:* Implementing a digital solution in the healthcare sector necessitates utmost attention to privacy and data security. To address these concerns, Karkinos collaborated closely with data privacy experts, legal advisors, and technology partners. By adhering to stringent data protection protocols, including encryption, anonymization, and secure storage, Karkinos ensured the confidentiality of patient information. Transparent communication with stakeholders about Karkinos privacy practices built trust and confidence in the platform, encouraging widespread adoption.

■ *Training and Capacity Building:* Introducing innovative technology in healthcare requires adequate training and capacity building among health-care professionals. Karkinos collaborated with medical associations, academic institutions, and professional bodies to design comprehensive training programs. By actively listening to the needs and challenges faced by healthcare professionals, Karkinos tailored the training modules to address their specific requirements. The focus was not only on platform usage but also on enhancing their understanding of cancer risk assessment, prevention strategies, and patient-centered care. Through collaboration and knowledge sharing, we aimed to create a skilled and empowered healthcare workforce.

■ *Data-Driven Insights and Research:* One of the significant advantages of digital cancer community risk assessment platform was its potential to generate a wealth of anonymized data. Recognizing the value of this data in informing public health strategies and research, Karkinos collaborated with academic institutions and research organizations. By sharing deidentified datasets and partnering on research initiatives, Karkinos aimed to contribute to evidence-based practices and scientific advancements in the field of cancer care. Collaborative research projects allowed Karkinos to explore emerging trends, identify high-risk populations, and develop targeted interventions.

■ *Scaling and Expansion:* As the digital cancer community risk assessment platform gained traction and demonstrated its impact, Karkinos explored opportunities for scaling and expansion. Collaboration with investors, philanthropic organizations, and strategic partners became crucial in securing the necessary resources for growth. By actively listening to their perspectives and aligning with their goals, Karkinos formed partnerships that fueled Karkinos' expansion plans. Through their support, Karkinos aims to extend the reach of the platform to other regions in India and potentially explore international collaborations to tackle the global burden of cancer.

- *Sustainability and Long-Term Impact:* Creating sustainable solutions in healthcare requires careful planning and collaboration. Karkinos engaged with policymakers and government health agencies to ensure the long-term viability and integration of Karkinos digital platform into the broader healthcare ecosystem. By actively participating in policy discussions and sharing Karkinos insights, Karkinos contributed to the development of a supportive regulatory framework. Collaboration with insurance providers and healthcare payers also enabled to explore reimbursement models, making the platform accessible and financially viable for all segments of the population.
- *Empowerment of Community Workers:* Community health workers (CHWs) play a vital role in delivering health-care services, especially in rural and underserved areas. Recognizing their importance, Karkinos collaborated closely with CHWs and trained them to utilize Karkinos digital cancer community risk assessment platform effectively. By actively listening to their feedback and understanding their on-ground experiences, Karkinos improved the platform's usability for CHWs, making it an invaluable tool in their daily work. The collaboration empowered CHWs to provide accurate risk assessments, educate communities about cancer prevention, and facilitate early detection efforts, ultimately strengthening the overall impact of the platform.
- *Virtualization of Care:* Telemedicine has emerged as a critical component of healthcare delivery, particularly during the COVID-19 pandemic. Understanding the potential of telemedicine to enhance cancer care accessibility, Karkinos collaborated with telemedicine providers to integrate the digital platform seamlessly. By enabling remote consultations, Karkinos platform facilitated risk assessment discussions between patients and healthcare professionals, ensuring continuity of care while reducing the need for in-person visits. This collaboration not only expanded the reach of the platform but also optimized the utilization of healthcare resources.
- *Public-Private Partnerships:* Karkinos recognized the importance of public-private partnerships (PPPs). Collaborating with government health agencies, Karkinos explored opportunities to align Karkinos goals with national health policies and initiatives. By actively listening to the priorities of the government and engaging in dialogue, Karkinos established partnerships that allowed the company to leverage existing infrastructure, funding mechanisms, and public health campaigns.

The collaboration helped Karkinos reach a wider audience, maximize resources, and create sustainable models for scaling platform's impact. To amplify the impact of Karkinos digital cancer community risk assessment platform, Karkinos took an API-driven approach to be able to connect with various stakeholders in public and private seamlessly. This approach has enabled Karkinos to become the initial adaptors of Ayushman Bharat Digital Mission (India's Digital Healthcare Initiative).

■ *Addressing Language and Cultural Barriers:* India's linguistic and cultural diversity presents unique challenges in healthcare delivery. To address language barriers, the company collaborated with language experts and developed multilingual versions of the platform. By actively listening to the needs of diverse communities, Karkinos ensured that the platform was accessible and culturally sensitive. Collaborating with community leaders, Karkinos incorporated culturally appropriate content and tailored educational resources to resonate with different regions and populations. The collaboration helped the company overcome linguistic and cultural barriers, fostering trust and engagement among diverse communities.

■ *Collaboration of Policy Advocacy:* Transforming healthcare systems often requires policy changes and advocacy efforts. Karkinos actively collaborated with patient advocacy groups, NGOs, and professional associations to raise awareness about the importance of cancer risk assessment and early detection. By listening to the experiences and challenges shared by these groups, Karkinos amplified their voices and supported their advocacy initiatives. Through collaborative efforts, Karkinos aimed to influence policies that prioritize cancer prevention, improve access to care, and allocate resources for comprehensive cancer-control programs.

■ *Addressing Technology Barriers:* While technology has immense potential, it is crucial to address technological barriers to ensure equitable access. Karkinos actively collaborated with technology companies and internet service providers to tackle issues such as connectivity, device accessibility, and digital literacy. By listening to the challenges faced by underserved communities, Karkinos advocated for improved infrastructure, subsidized internet access, and digital skills training programs. Collaborative efforts with technology partners helped bridge the digital divide, ensuring that Karkinos platform reached even the most marginalized populations.

Conclusion

With the various challenges posed in oncology care, Karkinos leveraged the "collaborate and listen" approach, which helped in developing an innovative delivery model, namely 4D powered by a robust technology platform driven by insights and analytics. The delivery model along with the platform has demonstrated enormous potential in transforming cancer care by leveraging the care network, reimagined process flow, people, and technology with much-needed "care and compassion."

References

Relevant published papers and articles from Karkinos

1. *Developing institutions for cancer care in low-income and middle-income countries: from cancer units to comprehensive cancer centers* by Sirohi, B., Chalkidou, K., Pramesh, C. S., Anderson, B. O., Loeher, P., El Dewachi, O., et al. (2018). Developing Institutions for Cancer Care in Low-Income and Middle-Income Countries: From Cancer Units to Comprehensive Cancer Centers. *The Lancet Oncology,* 19(8), E395–E406. https://www.thelancet.com/journals/lanonc/ article/PIIS1470-2045(18)30342-5/fulltext
2. Ramachandran, V., Pradhan, A., Kumar, A., Sarvepalli, B. K., Rao, S., Oswal, K., Kommu, R. S., Sharma, M., Pathak, S., Kunnambath, R., Kuriakose, M. A., Rengaswamy, S., Alajlani, M., & Arvanitis, T. N. (2022). A Distributed Cancer Care Model with a Technology-Driven Hub-and-Spoke and Further Spoke Hierarchy: Findings from a Pilot Implementation Programme in Kerala, India. *Asian Pacific Journal of Cancer Prevention,* 23(9), 3133–3139. doi: 10.31557/APJCP.2022.23.9.3133. PMID: 36172676, PMCID: PMC9810301. https://www.ncbi.nlm.nih.gov/pmc/articles/PMC9810301/
3. *Digital Inequalities in Cancer Care Delivery in India: An Overview of the Current Landscape and Recommendations for Large-Scale Adoption* by Venkataramanan, R., Pradhan, A., Kumar, A., Purushotham, A., Alajlani, M., & Arvanitis, T. N. (2022). Digital Inequalities in Cancer Care Delivery in India: An Overview of the Current Landscape and Recommendations for Large-Scale Adoption. *Frontiers in Digital Health,* 4, 916342. doi: 10.3389/fdgth.2022.916342. https:// www.frontiersin.org/articles/10.3389/fdgth.2022.916342/full

Chapter 5

Communicate and Eliminate Barriers

Cross communication is essential to promote innovation. By stripping virtual or physical barriers to communication, ideas have a better chance of being realized.

Transparency is key to effective relationships, which are required for innovation to thrive. The depth and width you share will determine the size of your success. Look for every opportunity and platform to share while actively eliminating barriers to communication. Effective communication will make or break innovation. If active or passive resistance rises, so must your communication. While technology provides great tools to reach many, do not neglect the power of in-person eyeball-to-eyeball dialogue.

A NEW MODEL FOR MEMBER ENGAGEMENT | BY FRED W. KOPPLOW

Digital health has revolutionized the healthcare landscape, promising improved outcomes, increased accessibility, and enhanced patient-provider communication. However, the rapid proliferation of technologies and complex health stacks has disconnected patients and healthcare providers. Patient engagement is a critical component of the digital health ecosystem to bridge this gap. Examining the significance of patient engagement today from a payer's perspective, my intention is to highlight the challenges patients and providers face in navigating digital health technologies with the

DOI: 10.4324/9781003381983-5

ever-growing need for innovative solutions to improve patient engagement. This will foster meaningful patient interactions and ensure better health outcomes for stakeholders.

Patient engagement refers to the active involvement of patients in their healthcare journey, encouraging patients to take ownership of their health and collaborate with healthcare providers for better outcomes. However, despite the potential benefits, challenges hinder the effective implementation of patient engagement strategies. Let's start grounding where we began getting our hands dirty, defining an overall approach to tackling patient engagement to define the right technology and moving from a once-a-week batch world to a near-time patient engagement model within the new payer enterprise. The premise and challenge for payers and digital healthcare stakeholders were some of the reasons I got into healthcare with the hope of leveraging technology to see when patients were diagnosed and needed further care. Yet many times, payers needed to learn how to navigate the many health systems.

Let us begin with technology fragmentation. The rapid proliferation of digital health technologies has resulted in a fragmented ecosystem where patients, providers, and health plans use various applications, portals, and platforms to manage health information. This need for interoperability makes it taxing for patients to access comprehensive health records and for healthcare providers to obtain a holistic view of patient's medical history. Today's health literacy and the digital divide show that not all patients possess the same health literacy or digital proficiency level. Patients need help understanding complex medical information or navigating digital health tools effectively. Additionally, disparities in access to technology create a digital divide, limiting patient engagement among vulnerable populations. Data privacy and security concerns have also risen, even though most payers have aligned disparate patient databases in the last five years. The increasing use of electronic health records (EHRs) and digital health apps continues to climb based on rapid chronic disease growth within the payers market. Patients are hesitant to share sensitive health information due to fears of potential breaches or unauthorized access. Building trust with patients and ensuring robust data protection measures are critical to encouraging patient engagement. The other side of patient engagement leads us to provider buy-in and workflow integration For patient engagement initiatives to be successful, healthcare providers must be willing to embrace and integrate digital health tools into their workflows. Resistance to change and concerns about added administrative burdens hinder the adoption of patient engagement strategies. Another area for attention is communication issues within the health tech stacks. Patients have difficulty accessing care but have yet to be advised or informed what care is available. Effective and adaptive patient engagement relies on clear and open communication between patients and healthcare providers.

Today's gap between our former written and coded cloud-based journeys for the patient and provider has left both sides stuck. The easier-forgotten side includes time constraints during appointments, language barriers, and varying communication preferences, which impede meaningful interactions, leaving care at a standstill for patients. Encouraging patients to engage actively in their healthcare requires appropriate incentives and motivation and is one opportunity for payers.

Payers need to head back and redesign programs that provide tangible results to patients for their participation, such as improved access to care, reduced out-ofpocket expenses, or rewards for healthy behaviors. Such programs dovetail us into care coordination and continuity in a complex healthcare system; patients often receive care from multiple providers across various settings. Ensuring seamless care becomes challenging, making it easier for patients to feel engaged in their healthcare. Today's state of digital health technology, such as electronic health records (EHRs), EMRs, telemedicine, wearables, and RPM and home health monitoring apps, has rapidly integrated into the healthcare system. While these innovations have offered numerous benefits, barriers exist to their implementation. It is necessary to examine the adoption of various technologies that have led to the fragmentation of healthcare data, making it difficult for patients and providers to access comprehensive and integrated health information.

Technology is surely moving healthcare forward. We now have the digitalization of payers with EHRs, EMRs, platforms, portals, and dashboards. Aligning the associated patient data has been a plus for patients and providers in real time, yet overcoming digital health fatigue is a big hurdle. With an overwhelming number of health apps and wearables without a clear-cut path to accessing medical information or records on either side (patients/ payers or providers), patients experience disengagement. To prevent patient disengagement, payers must streamline point solution offerings and support adopting user-friendly, integrated digital health solutions. A distinguished professor at Babson College, Thomas Davenport, highlights in his former report that patient engagement and adherence have long been seen as the "last mile" problem of healthcare—the final barrier between ineffective and good health outcomes. "The more patients proactively participate in their own well-being and care, the better the outcomes—utilization, financial outcomes, and member experience." Big data and AI are increasingly addressing these factors. In a survey of more than 300 clinical leaders and healthcare executives, more than 70% of the respondents reported having less than 50% of their patients highly engaged, and 42% of respondents said less than 25% of their patients were highly engaged.

Another growing focus in healthcare is on effectively designing the "choice architecture" to nudge patient behavior more anticipatively based on real-world evidence. Through information provided by provider EHR systems, biosensors, watches, smartphones, conversational interfaces, and other instrumentation, the software can tailor recommendations by comparing patient data to other effective treatment pathways for similar cohorts. The recommendations can be provided to providers, patients, nurses, callcenter agents, or care delivery "coordinators."

Payers are becoming vital in facilitating patient engagement on the reimbursement and financial front today, but reimbursement models must align with these strategies. Providing financial incentives to healthcare providers to engage patients can assist in driving the integration of patient engagement practices when bundling in payment program options. New companies integrating Fin-tech (Healthbridge, Kareo, and Paymedix) into healthcare are coming into the space to relieve the financial impact on patients with the growing costs of care and emergency out-of-pocket care that still needs an answer. Measuring and determining patient engagement initiatives' effectiveness and return on investment (ROI) are arduous for payers. Establishing meaningful metrics and gathering relevant data to assess the impact of these strategies is essential to demonstrate their value. Recognizing the transformational potential of patient engagement in an evolving digital health landscape is essential. Pat Geraghty, CEO of GuideWell/Florida Blue Cross Blue Shield, a thought leader whom I've admired as a leader for years, states, in healthcare, "This work isn't easy. It requires imagination, courage, and collaboration. We're creating a better healthcare system for us all."

The proliferation of health technologies and complex health stacks has left patients and healthcare providers disoriented and disconnected, leading to obstacles that hinder the delivery of efficient and effective healthcare services. Addressing these issues and fostering a patient-centric digital health ecosystem aims to underscore the importance of patient engagement. Devising a digital patient engagement plan today needs a real focus on human-centered design and user experience (UX).

Chief Innovation Officer of Modus, Jay Erickson, rewrote his white paper titled "To Achieve Patient Centered Health, Get to Know the Three 'e's' of Engagement." Describing patient engagement now as three components of engagement from a user experience perspective, he writes: As UX professionals, our focus was on the "Little e"—engagement with the experience itself. The behavioral scientists were tasked with narrowing in on the "Big E"—the desired effects of the experience—enacting a behavior change (exercising more, doing a group meditation, and so on). We always used this distinction: **Little e = experience, Big E = effect.** The term "little" was not intended to demean our work but rather keep the focus and primacy on what we were trying to accomplish with these prototypes: the Big E of positive, healthier behavior change. We also collectively acknowledged that good "little e" is a prerequisite for impactful "Big E." After all, you can't get to the behavior change with poor UX standing in the way. The newest addition of adding the easy E in "Empathy" is "easy" because most of us can do it. Like any muscle, for some, it may be in better shape than others—and for some, perhaps overworked—but our ability to connect is part of what makes us human. It is widely acknowledged that a health professional's ability to empathize with a patient leads to better therapeutic results. Patients are more likely to follow their treatment plan and practice self-care when they feel heard and understood. However, while empathy is a natural human instinct, incorporating empathy into patient experience design takes much work.

With crucial health data scattered across various platforms, lost patient and provider dilemmas and its use of disparate digital health technologies have resulted in a fractured patient experience. Patients need help managing their health information, making informed decisions, and actively participating in their care.

Similarly, healthcare providers need help with interoperability issues that lead to communication gaps and inefficiencies in care delivery. Lack of capabilities to do so leads to consequences of a lost patient and provider dilemma, impacting healthcare quality and cost. True patient engagement encompasses strategies and technologies encouraging patients to participate in their healthcare journey actively. It is crucial to explore the concept of patient engagement and its various dimensions, such as health literacy, shared decision-making, and self-management. Highlighting ways to increase patient engagement will lead to better health outcomes, improved patient satisfaction, and reduced healthcare costs.

Patient engagement is not just a buzzword but a vital aspect of digital health transformation. From my payers' perspective, the discussion emphasizes the importance of patient engagement from the potential cost savings associated with improved patient adherence, reduced hospital readmissions, and better disease management. Several healthcare organizations and payers have recognized the significance of integrating UX and behavioral science into their patient engagement plans, implementing various initiatives to promote it. Now another large component to be considered is behavioral science as it's not new, but it's being included now as a key component to better solve for patients getting into the care they need.

Amy Bucher, Chief Behavior Officer at Lirio Company, states that

> Behavioral Science seeks to understand human behavior in context, accounting for individual factors such as knowledge, prior experience, and values, as well as situational factors such as work or family obligations, social norms and cues, and environmental factors. Focusing specifically on behavior as an outcome, behavior science can increase the chances that someone takes a recommended action and develop an understanding of that person that makes it easier to guide them in future actions. Behavior Science leverages theories and frameworks from the social sciences that allow us to understand the factors influencing behavior and identify the right approaches to help people act based on their particular barriers. Ideally, behavior science is part of a personalized approach to patient engagement, given that people are different from each other and may respond to different approaches depending on the context.

It is necessary to examine successful patient engagement programs and technologies, including patient portals, personalized health applications, and virtual care platforms. Equally important is analyzing the impact of these initiatives on patient outcomes and provider efficiency. Addressing barriers that impede the tremendous promise of widespread patient engagement adoption is also needed. Common challenges patients and healthcare providers face include limited digital health literacy, concerns about data privacy, and resistance to change. It outlines potential strategies to overcome these barriers, including patient education, data security measures, and provider training.

Communicate and Eliminate Barriers. Future trends in patient engagement rely on integrating and optimizing the initial patient and provider journeys with newer advanced technologies such as artificial intelligence (AI), machine lea rning, UX and behavior science, and big data analytics. Payers will continue to play a pivotal role in fostering patient engagement as stakeholders with a vested interest in the health and well-being of their members. Patient engagement is no longer an option but is required in the digital health era. To bridge the gap between lost patients and providers, payers must prioritize patient engagement initiatives that empower patients, streamline care delivery, and enhance healthcare outcomes. By embracing innovative technologies and overcoming barriers, payers will lead toward a patient-centric, technology-driven future in healthcare. In closing, patient engagement has become and will remain a critical component of the digital health revolution, but it comes with varied challenges that must be examined for successful implementation. As a thought leader in digital health for payers, understanding these demands can help design effective strategies that promote patient engagement, improve healthcare outcomes, and enhance patient satisfaction. By addressing these obstacles proactively, payers can create a patient-centric healthcare ecosystem that benefits all stakeholders.

IMPLEMENTING AN ENTERPRISE-LEVEL PATIENT ENGAGEMENT STRATEGY LEADS TO BETTER OUTCOMES | BY CARRIE KOZLOWSKY

In today's ever-evolving healthcare landscape, patient engagement has shifted from a mere buzzword to a critical strategic imperative. The days of hoping to achieve meaningful engagement by sending impersonal text messages and relying on portals are over. Trailblazers like Amazon leverage data to curate consumer experiences that convert to additional purchases by deploying advanced personalization techniques. In fact, Upfront and Ipsos conducted a study that found that 41% of people under 45 years old felt Amazon knew them better than their doctor.[1] The breadth and depth of historical health data and personal information that providers and health plans collect about each patient far surpass even Amazon, yet we aren't putting that data to work. Payers must transform patient engagement into a top organizational priority and invest in technologies that can better leverage their robust dataset to orchestrate personalized experiences that convert into every patient getting the care they need.

Personalized care can significantly improve patient experiences and health outcomes, as research from McKinsey[2] has shown. Personalizing communications with patients can help them feel known and compel them to engage with their health, while strengthening their ties with the health plans and networks that serve them.

To truly engage and activate patients, payers need to adopt a holistic approach that intelligently leverages patient data and seamlessly integrates digital communication into the patient journey, augmenting in person clinic visits with proactive, *personalized* nudges in between. It's all about building trust, fostering loyalty, and optimizing access—and it's a process that demands buy-in from stakeholders across the spectrum, from IT and operations to marketing and care delivery.

Addressing the Systemic Problem of Disengaged Patients

Today, people expect more responsive, open, and transparent healthcare experiences. They want to be seen and heard as unique individuals with specific needs and preferences. But payers and providers across the network are often missing the mark by not reaching patients with personalized, engaging, and connected communications at each phase of their health journey. Despite spending an estimated $19.4 billion for healthcare customer relationship management (CRM) software solutions in 2022 alone,[3] healthcare providers still face an uphill battle to reach and motivate patients to take ownership of their own health. In fact, only 8% of patients get the recommended preventive care, and only half take their prescribed medication.[4] Furthering this disconnect, payers are failing to adequately inform consumers about preventive services they are entitled to receive at no additional cost,[5] according to a new report from the consumer representatives to the National Association of Insurance Commissioners (NAIC).

Recent studies indicate that patients are looking for more personalized connections. In fact, 61% of patients in one recent industry survey found that they wanted better patient engagement[6] to help them with preventative screenings and wellness checks. These types of touchpoints historically come from primary care physicians (PCPs). Patients with a strong PCP relationship experience tend to report better health outcomes, yet only 43% of patients have a relationship with their primary care provider.[7] That's unlikely to change since many patients do not trust doctors and/or favor convenience over a long-term relationship. We cannot leave those patients without care simply because of their barriers and preferences. Personalized engagement can ensure everyone gets the care they need, even in the absence of an established PCP relationship.

Too often, healthcare takes a one-sizefits-all approach to patient engagement that assumes everyone with the same health condition thinks and acts alike. But patients are people, with distinct personalities, priorities, and motivations. Stakeholders need to demonstrate that they recognize their patients' unique preferences and needs, and engage them at relevant points to help them get or stay well.

Engaged Patients = Better Outcomes = Healthier Networks

In the intricate, intimate relationship between the patient and their provider, health plan, and health system, alignment across the enterprise reaps rewards for all involved. An enterprise-level engagement strategy doesn't just enhance patient experiences and outcomes; it bolsters the entire system's efficiency and effectiveness.

For the patient: Imagine a healthcare experience that doesn't just happen to you but is thoughtfully orchestrated to guide you through it seamlessly. A comprehensive, personalized approach to patient engagement would ensure that your care needs are intelligently prioritized and sequenced, creating a journey tailored to your unique requirements. For example, if you needed an annual wellness visit, a colonoscopy, and a referral to endocrinology, patient engagement solutions could prioritize scheduling the referral, demonstrating an intelligent sequence of care. Bundling appointments, such as combining a wellwoman exam with a mammogram on the same day, can both enhance convenience and promote proactive care. This type of orchestrated experience is underpinned by the ability to provide outreach in myriad ways to suit each patient's preferences, with a focus on digital channels. This is critical; we know it's not just young people who prefer digital experiences. In fact, Upfront sees a 25% higher engagement rate among people 61–90 years old than those 18–60.

For the healthcare team: Deploying a comprehensive patient engagement strategy doesn't solely benefit patients; it's a boon for healthcare teams as well. By offloading tasks like scheduling, rescheduling, enrollment, benefits adoption, or the arduous and manual collection of post-visit symptom assessments or post-surgical outcomes surveys, an enterprise-level patient engagement platform can free up valuable human resources to focus on the needs of truly complex patients. A comprehensive patient engagement solution also opens the door to learning more about patients, aiding in addressing barriers to care and tracking long-term quality-of-life improvements.

For the health plan: Payers are under more pressure to maintain and own their network. Their current business model is under attack as providers continue to form new partnerships, causing health plans to lose leverage.[8] Payers must maintain a highquality provider network to win new business because engaging patients to complete preventative care will meaningfully grow provider loyalty by driving visits, revenue, and value-based incentives.

In addition, payers are on a journey to redefine their perception in the market and to move beyond their traditional role of claims and risk management. This is an opportunity for health plans to transform into "health solutions companies," a transition intended to capture legacy health insurance functionality while offering the attractive new patient solutions they hope to bring to market.[9] More strategic, modernized patient engagement will be crucial to health plans realizing this vision and remaining competitive. New enrollees want to go beyond chronic condition management and care coordination. They desire a seamless experience, with a focus on wellness programs and supplemental benefits. Payers with an enterprise-level engagement strategy will have the distinct advantage of presenting benefits in a differentiated way—personalized to the patient to promote benefit and program adoption.

The Building Blocks of a Patient Engagement Strategy

Barbara Bartosch, Upfront's former vice president of services, passed away from ovarian cancer on May 31, 2020. Her care journey during the COVID-19 pandemic highlighted the importance of building patient trust. Barbara had 30 years of healthcare industry experience, working in every arena, every facet, and every workgroup available, and took pride in herself for knowing the full cycle of care delivery. She previously worked with frontline caregivers all the way to the board of directors in almost 65 plus health systems across the country as well as health plans, medical groups, and healthcare technology companies. She believed those years of experience provided her with a deep understanding of the country's healthcare delivery systems, but during her treatment journey, she experienced a lack of system communication and care compromises that crucially impacted her journey, as well as that of other patients.

Sadly, Barbara's care journey is not unique, and patients fall through the cracks every day and lose trust. With a sharp focus on patient engagement strategy, we work with partners to implement a unified enterprise-level patient engagement and access solution that can enhance existing technology investments and personalize the care experience For instance, sending a singular email blast to 50,000 women in October for Breast Cancer Awareness Month to remind them to get a mammogram does not communicate that providers "know" their patients. Instead, a targeted platform could deliver highly personalized messages based on when patients need it, using messaging and engagement tactics backed by behavior and consumer science. Rather than campaigns, this approach embraces continuous and personalized care navigation.

A personalization framework serves as a strategic starting point for this enterprisewide mission. Developing and implementing an enterprise-level personalization framework that combines advanced technology, behavioral science, and humanpowered outreach can help close gaps in care, improve patient engagement, reach hard-to-engage and chronic care populations, and streamline operations.

There Are Three Critical Considerations to Keep in Mind When Developing Such a Framework

Timing it right—It's not just about sending a message; it's about sending the right message at the right time. For instance, sending a mammogram reminder in October, when it's breast cancer awareness month, might seem like a routine campaign. However, sending the reminder precisely 11 months after the patient's last appointment and guiding her to the same in-network location shows a deeper level of understanding of that person and her specific needs. Datadriven insights can allow healthcare providers to intervene at the most opportune moments, demonstrating a familiarity that fosters patient trust. That trust builds loyalty, and loyalty drives revenue.

Making it relevant—Patients are individuals with diverse motivations and preferences. The idea that "doctor knows best" doesn't hold true for all patients, with Americans' confidence in their doctors on the wane,[10] yet many networks still market to and communicate with patients as if it were. It's important to utilize language and content that align with each patient's unique motivations. For example, for those patients who value their providers' guidance, a video message from their provider might be the key to engagement. For others, understanding the evidence behind their care might be more compelling. Achieving this level of personalization in patient outreach is key to making the patient feel truly known. When information is relevant, it drives better patient understanding and can drive better outcomes.

Minimizing action barriers and making care access seamless—Barriers to care, information overload, and technical obstacles can deter patients from engaging with their healthcare. Patient data can be leveraged to simplify the patient's journey, make the interactions frictionless, and eliminate barriers to care. For example, if a patient faces transportation challenges, you can intelligently surface a link to add transportation services when they're scheduling their appointments, just like we add on products or services when we schedule a massage or purchase clothes.

Making the patient experience as frictionless as possible is important. Provide only the most essential information needed to motivate action and integrate scheduling into the call to action so the patient can simply do what's needed and have it automatically entered into the system. Empower patients to do as much as possible without having to call and sit on hold and without requiring them to repeatedly input their username and password.

Leveraging Technology and Behavioral Science to Achieve Personalization at Scale

Upfront Healthcare was founded on the belief that understanding each patient's unique needs and delivering hyperpersonalized healthcare experiences is crucial for better outcomes. To that end, Upfront provides patient engagement solutions that leverage rigorous science combined with data to provide patients with customized, culturally competent information when it matters most, based on their motivations and unique characteristics. Unlike traditional approaches to patient activation, Upfront's platform engages patients through omnichannel personalization, leveraging actionable data, and insights to guide them. This innovative approach enhances patient loyalty, reduces healthcare staff resource burdens, increases utilization, and boosts profits and operational efficiency.

The Upfront platform is powered by insights identified by the company's Bartosch Patient Activation Institute, which helps Upfront achieve best-in-class patient activation outcomes through data science, content, and design, incorporating best practices from the fields of health communication and behavioral science. Psychographics provide a key source of insights pertaining to people's attitudes, personalities, and lifestyles and are core to their motivations and communication preferences.

Upfront leverages this science and its proprietary technology to enable a content, messaging, and channel mix (personalized microsite, email, text/SMS, interactive voice response, print, interpersonal) designed to enhance the likelihood of patient activation. While psychographic segmentation has hitorically been challenging to operationalize and scale at the individual consumer level, Upfront achieves this to help its clients succeed with their clinical and business goals.

Upfront and Prisma Health: Closing Care Gaps

Upfront has demonstrated time and again that implementing an enterprise-level patient engagement strategy that leverages advanced and personalized insights can transform patient activation and generate unmatched clinical, operational, and financial performance results. We achieved it with our partner Prisma Health, a large network in South Carolina, which over a two-year period of engagement, resulted in recalling over half a million patients (onethird of their population) across all plans and payer types to complete preventive screenings and close care gaps without staff effort—generating $2 million in operating savings, the equivalent of 133,000 FTE hours of phone calling. Prisma also realized better outcomes: 50% of Medicare Advantage patients previously off track with medication adherence were activated to refill their prescriptions or flag a barrier to care for their care team to address. And over 40% of patients engaged in the next steps to complete preventive care, including scheduling care and reporting care completed outside the system, so gaps could be closed.

Upfront and OSF Healthcare: Advancing Health Equity

OSF HealthCare, an IL-based integrated health system owned and operated by the Sisters of the Third Order of St. Francis, is another example of patient engagement in action. OSF, with a focus on health equity, collaborated with Upfront to eliminate disparities in mammogram screenings among Medicaid patients, leveraging the company's expertise and technology to develop a scalable intervention to close breast cancer screening care gaps and get patients in for mammograms before they were overdue— preventing deaths and advanced-stage disease.

Using a multipronged intervention approach, Upfront combined its evidence-based research and technology to identify access barriers and deliver hyperpersonalized digital communication to proactively engage target patients and inform them of their breast cancer screening status. These communications included personalized text reminders, digital voice calls from community healthcare workers, and an invitation to a health fair offering onsite mammograms. Upfront additionally used microsites to educate patients about the value of completing preventative screenings with embedded scheduling links to help patients easily set up mammogram appointments.

Through these personalized digital communications and targeted interventions, Upfront was able to help OSF double its mammogram screenings and achieve a screening rate of 3.7% higher compared to patients deemed to have fewer barriers to care. Building on that success, OSF extended its partnership with Upfront to proactively communicate with all patients, engaging nearly 45,000 women before they were overdue for their mammograms. This personalized approach resulted in 52% of patients scheduling their mammograms within two weeks of Upfront's outreach, $450,00 in operating savings generated, and a 7× ROI resulting from revenue generated from completed mammograms.

The Future of Healthcare Must Be Personalized

The days of generic patient communications and experiences are over. Today's patients demand and deserve personalized, comprehensive engagement that guides them through their health journeys seamlessly. By embracing a technology-enabled, enterprise-level patient engagement approach, networks can align patient needs, system efficiency, and team empowerment, leading to improved patient outcomes, substantial cost savings, and a network truly optimized for the 21st century.

In Barbara's final call to action in her last blog entry, she implored, "We should be able to do better." She was right. With personalized patient engagement solutions, we can help every patient get the care they need.

References

1. Upfront Healthcare and Ipsos. (2020). *Annual Market Research Study of National Consumer Attitudes, Behaviors and Needs Regarding Healthcare in the United States. Data on File Available by Request.* https://upfronthealthcare.com/

2. McKinsey & Company. (2021, August 5). *The Role of Personalization in the Care Journey: An Example of Patient Engagement to Reduce Readmissions.* McKinsey. https://www.mckinsey.com/industries/healthcare/our-insights/the-role-of-personalization-in-the-carejourney-an-example-of-patient-engagement-to-reduce-readmissions

3. BioSpace. (2022). *Healthcare CRM Market Size to Worth Around US$ 27.8 bn by 2030.* BioSpace. https://www.biospace.com/article/healthcare-crm-market-size-to-wortharound-us-27–8-bn-by-2030/

4. Borsky, A., Zhan, C., Miller, T., Ngo-Metzger, Q., Bierman, A. S., & Meyers, D. J. (2018). Few Americans Receive All High-Priority, Appropriate Clinical Preventive Services. *Health Affairs,* 37(6), 925–928. https://doi.org/10.1377/hlthaff.2017.1248

5. Georgians for a Healthy Future. (2023, August 7). *Preventive Services Coverage and Cost-Sharing Protections are Inconsistently and Inequitably Implemented—Georgians for a Healthy Future.* https://healthyfuturega.org/ghf_resource/preventive-services-coverage-and-cost-sharing-protections-are-inconsistently-and-inequitably-implemented/

6. Actium Health. (2023, May 16). *Tracking American Sentiment: Managing Healthcare is Hard.* Actium Health. https://actiumhealth.com/reports/tracking-american-sentimentmanaging-healthcare-is-hard/

7. Meltzer, E. (2023). *45+ Patient Retention and Churn Rate Statistics—ETACTICs.* Etactics | Revenue Cycle Software. https://etactics.com/blog/patient-retention-statistics

8. KFF. (2022, July 21). *Price Regulation, Global Budgets, and Spending Targets: A Road Map to Reduce Health Care Spending, and Improve Affordability.* KFF. https://www.kff.org/health-costs/report/price-regulationglobal-budgets-and-spending-targets-a-road-map-to-o-reduce-health-care-spending-andimprove-affordability/

9. The Advisory Board. (2023, April). *Best Bets for Payer Growth.* The Advisory Board. https://www.advisory.com/content/dam/advisory/en/public/success-pages/best-bets-for-healthplan-growth.pdf.coredownload.pdf

10. Jones, B. J. M. (2022, November 29). *Republicans Less Trusting of Doctor's Advice than in the Past.* Gallup.com. https://news.gallup.com/ poll/357821/republicans-less-trusting-doctoradvice-past.aspx

KAISER PERMANENTE'S INTEGRATED PAYER-PROVIDER MODEL | ANONYMOUS

Kaiser Permanente's integrated payer-provider model is an excellent exemplifier of the "communicate and eliminate barriers" innovation pathway. This strategy combines payer and provider groups together, which can assist in enhancing communication and care coordination. This can result in better patient outcomes and lower expenses. Kaiser Permanente is leveraging technology and innovative organizational structures to improve care quality and patient outcomes and address health disparities.[1] As a payer-provider organization, Kaiser Permanente's integrated payer-provider model positions it for success. Members pay the organization, which is in charge of their care. This encourages preventative care and health maintenance, which leads to improved health outcomes.

The Challenge and Motivation

Kaiser Permanente describes prevailing issues that prompted the adoption of the integrated, coordinated high-quality care approach. The challenges prompting the innovative approach emanated from the limitations of the current healthcare system in the United States as highlighted in the following.

Disconnected Clinical Practices

According to Kaiser Permanente,[1] the US healthcare system is primarily reliant on disconnected clinical practices, which result in fragmented patient care. Health professionals frequently function independently of one another, resulting in a lack of information exchange and cooperation. Kern et al.[2] observe that American healthcare is often described as "fragmented," with patients routinely receiving care from multiple ambulatory providers.

Fee-for-Service Model

The main fee-for-service payment structure produces inefficiencies and uncertainty for patients. Billing for distinct services, tracking spending, and waiting for insurance payments all contribute to a convoluted process. Furthermore, this payment method might lead to conflicts regarding needed services and encourage quantity over quality.

Quantity at the Expense of Quality

The fee-for-service paradigm encourages a focus on the number of services delivered, perhaps at the expense of care quality. Healthcare providers may prioritize providing more services for financial motives, even if they are neither essential nor helpful, thus resulting in waste and injury.

Healthcare Professionals' Challenges

Clinicians have difficulties as a result of their limited interactions with other healthcare professionals.[2] This restricts their access to complete patient information, and they must manage different payers and varying standards, complicating their practices even further.

Population Health Issues

The emphasis on acute expenses under the fee-for-service system stymies investments in long-term population and community health. This inhibits efficient monitoring of patient care and the use of aggregate data for improvement.

To address the aforementioned challenges, Kaiser Permanente opted for an integrated and coordinated care strategy to eliminate most of the barriers to communication and coordination, guarantee high-quality treatment, streamline service access, and concentrate on enhancing member and population health outcomes. The integrated care model addresses the previously mentioned hurdles by offering remedies to the deficiencies of the traditional healthcare system.

Communicate and Eliminate Barriers Innovation Pathway

By stressing cooperation, openness, complete data sharing, and coordinated treatment, the Kaiser Permanente integrated care approach strongly matches with the "communicate and eliminate barriers" innovation route. The interconnection of many organizations within Kaiser Permanente's system shows an intentional attempt to break down communication barriers, boosting innovation and better patient outcomes.[1] The succeeding segments examine how the Kaiser Permanente model relates to the principles of "communicate and eliminate barriers."

Cross-communication and Barrier Elimination

To deliver appropriately coordinated care, Kaiser Permanente stresses integration and coordination across its many organizations (health plans, medical groups, hospitals).[1] This structural integration eliminates conventional boundaries between healthcare groups, allowing for seamless communication and collaboration. Dismantling the communication barriers that frequently separate healthcare professionals is accomplished by grouping hospitals, physician groups, and health plans under a single umbrella organization. Better communication and care coordination made possible by this integration may result in better patient outcomes.

The linkage of physicians, specialists, lab technicians, pharmacists, and other healthcare workers enables efficient communication, which is critical for encouraging innovation. The emphasis on coordinated care teams and data sharing allows for a full perspective of patients' medical histories and treatments, as well as the elimination of communication gaps and hurdles. Even when patients require the services of several different physicians, this team approach helps to guarantee that they receive coordinated care.

Kaiser Permanente's providers have access to the same electronic health record system. This makes it simpler for providers to interact and work together because they can access patient data from anywhere in the system.

Transparency and Sharing

The Kaiser Permanente approach values extensive data collection and sharing. The linked data system collects a large amount of data, which is subsequently shared with physicians, care teams, and members. This transparency allows for educated decisionmaking and prompt care delivery. The availability of personal health data via the member portal allows people to participate in their healthcare decisions, which align with the principle of sharing information to remove obstacles. On its website, Kaiser Permanente shares statistics on its quality and performance. This enables patients and other stakeholders to assess the organization's performance.

Cooperation for Better Outcomes

The Kaiser Permanente model encourages care team cooperation by encouraging cross-functional teamwork among doctors, specialists, and other healthcare providers. The model's approach to aligned incentives also encourages healthcare providers to prioritize prevention, health promotion, and effective management of both acute and chronic diseases, which necessitate excellent communication and teamwork.

The approach makes better use of technology to enhance cooperation and communication. For instance, the electronic health record system used by Kaiser Permanente enables doctors to access patient information from anywhere in the system. This makes it simple for them to collaborate and exchange information to deliver the best treatment possible.

As a result of effectively implementing its scalable integrated care model across several markets, Kaiser Permanente has grown to become one of the biggest and most prosperous healthcare organizations in the country.

Effective Communication in Resistance

You mentioned in your presentation that whether there is active or passive resistance, communication must be enhanced. Transparent communication can overcome any difficulties to integrated care or opposition to changes in the healthcare system in the context of Kaiser Permanente. The model's emphasis on data sharing, clinical recommendations, and quality improvement discoveries aids in overcoming opposition and fostering a cohesive approach.

Furthermore, Kaiser Permanente holds its providers responsible for their work. Numerous methods, including financial incentives and initiatives for quality improvement, are used to achieve this. Kaiser Permanente makes statistics on its performance and quality available so that patients and other stakeholders may assess how well the company is performing. This openness fosters the collaboration and trust necessary for creativity.

Case Study of Resultant Outcomes

To address the difficulty of discovering deleterious genetic abnormalities associated with breast and ovarian malignancies, Kaiser Permanente established a hereditary cancer program.[3] Care teams comprised professionals from many domains, including genetics, breast care, gynecologic cancer, plastic surgery, and supporting services, are involved in the initiative. This interdisciplinary approach removes the disparate therapeutic practices that frequently impede integrated treatment. Kaiser Permanente care teams provide coordinated assistance for high-risk patients. This integrated approach guarantees that patients receive complete treatment that is tailored to their requirements, removing the hurdles associated with fragmented care. The Hereditary Cancer Program has helped to improve cancer outcomes for women who have deleterious gene abnormalities. For example, the program has contributed to a 70% reduction in the risk of breast cancer and a 90% reduction in the risk of ovarian cancer.[3] Also, the program has helped to save expenses by preventing cancer and providing early care. For example, the initiative is anticipated to save $1 million each year in cancer care expenditures avoided.

By achieving significant success in lowering hip fracture rates, Kaiser Permanente's integrated care model demonstrates the efficacy of the "communicate and eliminate barriers" innovation approach. From 2002 to 2018, they reduced hip fracture rates by roughly 50% using data analysis, care coordination, and proactive outreach.[4] This result demonstrates their dedication to excellent communication and collaboration across clinicians and care teams. The program's fiscal flexibility, researchdriven quality improvement, and emphasis on individual and population health all played a part. The strategy demonstrates how removing obstacles, sharing data, and coordinating treatment may result in demonstrable gains in patient outcomes and cost savings.

With their advance alert monitor (AAM), Kaiser Permanente's integrated care strategy emphasizes the "communicate and eliminate barriers" pathway.[5] This approach provides care teams with 12 critical hours to respond to deteriorating conditions by quickly exchanging patient data, resulting in personalized therapies. All 21 Kaiser Permanente hospitals in Northern California have embraced the AAM program. This demonstrates the significance of efficient communication and the removal of barriers to adoption. The AAM program has resulted in earlier patient rescue, shorter ICU stays, lower all-cause mortality, and lower expenses. This demonstrates the program's favorable influence on patient outcomes. A team of academics created the AAM software by analyzing data from over 1.5 million individuals to determine ratings that indicate the severity of a patient's condition. This demonstrates the significance of using data to drive decisionmaking. The AAM program is managed by a team of highly qualified nurses who analyze the data to determine when they need to notify the nurse who is working directly with the patient. This demonstrates the need of having a coordinated care team that can respond rapidly to changes in a patient's health.

HCSC's AI-Aided Processing of Prior Authorization Requests

The purpose of the stress simplicity approach to innovation is reflected in the Health Care Service Corporation's (HCSC) drive to design solutions that operate better for everyone involved, including providers and members. The use of AI to speed up the process and give auto-approvals when appropriate seeks to enhance the experience for all stakeholders. Prior authorization denotes the requirement for a health professional to obtain clearance from a patient's health plan before proceeding with treatment, procedure, or medicine. When prior authorization is necessary, various health plans have different regulations.

HCSC has used AI and augmented intelligence to process prior permission requests 1,400 times faster than before. The AI-powered prior authorization tool was first created in 2021 and piloted the following year, with a focus on specialty pharmacy and behavioral health. In a considerable number of situations, quick approvals were given. Based on the program's effectiveness, HCSC expanded it to accommodate prior permission requests from a variety of healthcare services, including skilled nursing facilities, hospice care, home health, and outpatient services. The technology enables the automatic approval of requests that fulfill criteria, allowing clinical staff to focus on more complex cases. All requests are either automatically granted or sent to an HCSC clinician for a hands-on review. No requests are denied simply based on the judgment of the AI tool. The HSBC model fits into the innovation pathway's concept of stress simplicity as highlighted in the discussions later.

The Need and Motivation and Outcomes of Communicating and Eliminating Barriers

Lenert et al.[6] (previous studies by McKinsey & Company and other researchers) give excellent insights into why automating the prior authorization process is crucial and how incorporating artificial and augmented intelligence might positively improve it. The debate emphasizes that PA is viewed as a crucial component of the healthcare system to reduce costs and prevent needless care. However, it is known that PA can result in physician fatigue, treatment delays, and patient and provider dissatisfaction. This gives the background for why the PA process needs improvement.

Lenert et al.[6] observe that automated approaches for PA review have gained popularity, with initiatives like the HL7 DaVinci Project offering rule-based ways for automation. The limits of these techniques, however, are acknowledged. Because of the complexities of medical choices, as well as differing stakeholder viewpoints and interests, strictly rule-based systems are insufficient for dealing with the nuanced decision-making necessary in many medical circumstances. Lenert et al.[6] suggest an alternate strategy that uses AI algorithms to calculate permission choices while taking into account expert panels' assessments, including patient representatives. This method is said to be more human-centric since it attempts to imitate the decision-making process of expert panels.

BREAKING DOWN BARRIERS: PAYER HEALTHCARE INNOVATION THROUGH EFFECTIVE COMMUNICATION | ANONYMOUS

Introduction

The healthcare industry is undergoing a profound transformation, with innovation playing a pivotal role in improving access, quality, and efficiency of care. Payer models, including insurance companies and government programs, are at the heart of this transformation. The theme of "communicate and eliminate barriers" underscores the importance of fostering effective communication among all stakeholders in the healthcare ecosystem. This chapter explores the significance of communication in payer healthcare innovation and how it can be used to break down barriers that hinder progress.

The Crucial Role of Payer Models in Healthcare

Before delving into the "communicate and eliminate barriers" theme, it is important to understand the vital role of payer models in the healthcare system.

Payers as Healthcare Enablers

Payers act as intermediaries between patients and healthcare providers, overseeing financial aspects such as claims processing, reimbursements, and coverage verification. Their role extends beyond financial management to shape healthcare delivery, policies, and innovations.

Payers Driving Innovation

Innovative payer models have emerged as dynamic players in healthcare innovation. They are redefining the payer's role by promoting patient-centered care and valuebased models and leveraging technology to improve overall healthcare experiences.

The "Communicate and Eliminate Barriers" Approach

The "communicate and eliminate barriers" theme underscores the importance of effective communication and collaboration among all stakeholders in the healthcare ecosystem. By fostering open and transparent communication, payer models can identify and dismantle barriers that hinder progress and innovation.

Effective Communication Strategies

Member-Centered Communication: Payers must communicate with patients in ways that are clear, empathetic, and considerate of their diverse needs and preferences. Patient education, accessible communication channels, and language support services are essential components.

Provider Collaboration: Effective communication with healthcare providers is vital to streamline care coordination. Payers should establish channels for rapid, secure information exchange and cultivate strong relationships with providers to ensure smooth healthcare delivery.

Inter-organizational Collaboration: Payer models should promote collaboration among various healthcare organizations, including hospitals, clinics, and pharmaceutical companies. Transparent communication between these entities can lead to more efficient care pathways and innovative solutions.

Breaking Down Communication Barriers

Interoperability: Ensuring that healthcare systems can seamlessly exchange information is critical. Payers should advocate for and invest in interoperable healthcare IT solutions that enable data sharing across the continuum of care.

Health Information Exchange: Payers should actively participate in and promote health information exchanges (HIEs) to facilitate secure data sharing among healthcare providers, improving care coordination and patient outcomes.

Cultural Sensitivity: Recognizing and addressing cultural differences in communication is essential. Payers should provide training and resources to ensure culturally competent interactions with diverse patient populations.

The Benefits of Effective Communication in Payer Healthcare Innovation

Embracing the "communicate and eliminate barriers" approach offers several notable benefits within payer healthcare innovation.

Improved Member Engagement

Effective communication fosters patient engagement, empowering individuals to take an active role in their healthcare decisions. Patients who feel heard and understood are more likely to adhere to treatment plans and participate in preventive care.

Enhanced Care Coordination

Seamless communication between payers and healthcare providers results in more efficient care coordination. This leads to a reduction in duplication of services, fewer medical errors, and ultimately better patient outcomes.

Innovative Solutions

Transparent and open communication encourages the exchange of ideas and expertise. Payers, providers, and other stakeholders can collaboratively develop innovative solutions to address complex healthcare challenges.

Data-Driven Insights

Data analytics can provide valuable insights into patient needs and preferences. Payerscan leverage these insights to inform decisionmaking, personalize care plans, and enhance the overall healthcare experience.

Challenges and Considerations

Despite the clear benefits of effective communication, several challenges must be considered when implementing the "communicate and eliminate barriers" approach.

Data Privacy and Security

With increased data sharing comes the responsibility to protect sensitive health information. Payers must adhere to strict data privacy and security regulations, such as HIPAA, to ensure that patient information remains confidential and secure.

Technological Integration

Effective communication often relies on the integration of advanced healthcare technologies. Payers should invest in IT infrastructure and ensure the interoperability of systems to facilitate seamless data exchange.

Resistance to Change

Resistance to change is common in healthcare. Stakeholders may be hesitant to adopt new communication strategies or technologies. Payers must implement robust change management strategies to overcome resistance and promote a culture of communication.

Health Disparities

Payers must be mindful of health disparities that may exist among patient populations. Effective communication must take into account the unique needs and challenges faced by diverse communities.

The Future of Payer Healthcare Innovation

The "communicate and eliminate barriers" approach is poised to shape the future of payer healthcare innovation in significant ways.

Telehealth and Remote Monitoring

Effective communication will continue to drive the expansion of telehealth and remote monitoring services. These technologies facilitate real-time communication between patients and healthcare providers, improving access to care.

Value-Based Care Models

The transition to value-based care models relies heavily on transparent communication and collaboration. Payers, providers, and members must work together to measure and incentivize outcomes over volume of services.

Patient-Centered Innovation

Patient-centered care will remain at the forefront of payer healthcare innovation. Payers will continue to invest in strategies that prioritize patient engagement, communication, and shared decision-making.

Health Equity

Transparent communication and active listening are essential components of addressing health disparities and achieving equitable healthcare access for all individuals.

One real-world business case where payer organizations communicated and eliminated barriers in healthcare, leading to disruptive innovation, is the collaboration between Blue Cross Blue Shield of Massachusetts (BCBSMA) and Iora Health to create a unique primary care model known as "Landmark Primary Care."

Case Example: Blue Cross Blue Shield of Massachusetts And Iora Health—Landmark Primary Care

Background: BCBSMA, like many health insurers, recognized the challenges associated with rising healthcare costs, fragmented care, and the need for more patient-centric, valuebased care models. In response, BCBSMA sought to collaborate with healthcare providers to develop an innovative primary care model that would address these challenges.

Collaboration and Innovation

Partnership with Iora Health: BCBSMA partnered with Iora Health, a health-care company focused on transforming primary care. Iora Health had a unique approach to primary care centered around team-based care, care coordination, and technology.

Shared Vision: Both organizations shared a vision of delivering patient-centered, value-based care that prioritized the needs and preferences of patients. They aligned on the goals of improving patient outcomes and reducing healthcare costs.

Eliminating Barriers: Together, BCBSMA and Iora Health worked to eliminate barriers to care, such as high deductibles and copayments, which often deter patients from seeking primary care services. They designed a payment model that incentivized high-quality, comprehensive care.

Technology and Data Sharing: The partnership leveraged technology to support care coordination and communication between patients and their care teams. Patients had access to digital tools to schedule appointments, communicate with providers, and access health information.

Innovation and Impact

Patient-Centric Care: Landmark Primary Care focused on providing patient-centric care by offering extended office hours, sameday appointments, and longer visits. The care team included not only PCPs but also health coaches and behavioral health specialists.

Improved Health Outcomes: By prioritizing preventive care, chronic disease management, and care coordination, the model aimed to improve patient health outcomes and reduce hospitalizations.

Reduced Healthcare Costs: The valuebased payment model and emphasis on primary care aimed to reduce overall healthcare costs by addressing health issues early, avoiding unnecessary emergency department visits, and promoting costeffective care.

Enhanced Member Engagement: Patients had increased access to their care teams and were encouraged to actively participate in their healthcare decisions. This approach disrupted the traditional, often passive, patient-provider relationship.

Population Health Management: The collaboration enabled proactive population health management by identifying at-risk patients and providing tailored interventions.

Scalability and Expansion: The success of the Landmark Primary Care model led to its expansion to serve more BCBSMA members, demonstrating the scalability and potential for disruptive innovation in healthcare delivery.

The collaboration between BCBSMA and Iora Health to create Landmark Primary Care exemplifies how payer organizations, through effective communication and the removal of barriers to care, can drive disruptive innovation in healthcare. The innovative primary care model focused on patient needs, emphasized value-based care, and demonstrated the potential to improve patient outcomes while reducing healthcare costs, ultimately reshaping the delivery of primary care services.

Another example is the partnership between UnitedHealthcare and Optum to create "OptumCare."

Case Example: Unitedhealthcare and Optum—Optumcare

Background: UnitedHealthcare, one of the largest health insurance companies in the United States, recognized the need to address inefficiencies and fragmentation in the healthcare system. The company sought to collaborate with Optum, its subsidiary focused on health services and technology, to develop an innovative and integrated care delivery model.

Collaboration and Innovation

Unified Vision: UnitedHealthcare and Optum shared a unified vision of transforming healthcare by creating a patientcentric, value-based care model. They aimed to break down the traditional silos between payers and providers.

Integration of Services: The partnership involved the integration of health insurance (payer services) with healthcare services provided by Optum. This integration aimed to streamline the healthcare experience for patients, eliminating administrative barriers and improving care coordination.

Data and Analytics: The collaboration leveraged data and analytics capabilities to gain insights into patient health, treatment outcomes, and cost patterns. This datadriven approach helped identify areas for improvement and cost savings.

Eliminating Barriers: The integrated model aimed to eliminate many of the barriers that often hinder patient access to care, such as complex billing and referral processes. It focused on simplifying the patient experience.

Value-Based Care: OptumCare prioritized value-based care delivery, emphasizing preventive care, care coordination, and population health management. Providers were incentivized based on patient out-comes and cost savings.

Innovation and Impact

Coordinated Care: OptumCare's integrated approach ensured that patients received coordinated care across a spectrum of services, from primary care to specialty care. This reduced fragmentation and improved care continuity.

Cost Efficiency: The value-based care model aimed to reduce overall healthcare costs by focusing on preventive care, reducing hospital readmissions, and avoiding unnecessary tests and procedures.

Member-Centered Care: The model emphasized patient needs and preferences, providing a more patient-centric experience. Patients had access to care navigators who helped guide them through the healthcare system.

Improved Health Outcomes: Through proactive care management, population health initiatives, and data-driven interventions, OptumCare aimed to improve patient health outcomes, particularly for individuals with chronic conditions.

Scalability: The success of OptumCare led to its expansion to serve a broader population, demonstrating scalability and the potential for disruptive innovation in healthcare delivery.

Alignment of Incentives: The partnership successfully aligned the incentives of payers and providers, encouraging them to work together to achieve better patient outcomes.

The collaboration between UnitedHealthcare and Optum to create OptumCare illustrates how payer organizations, through effective communication and the elimination of barriers to care, can drive disruptive innovation in healthcare. The integrated care delivery model focused on value-based care, improved patient experiences, and demonstrated potential cost savings, ultimately reshaping how healthcare services are delivered and accessed.

Conclusion

In conclusion, the "communicate and eliminate barriers" theme is a powerful driver of innovation within payer healthcare models. By fostering open and transparent communication among all stakeholders, payer models can break down barriers that hinder progress and innovation in the healthcare ecosystem. In an ever-evolving healthcare landscape, embracing this approach is essential for achieving meaningful and sustainable innovation that benefits members, patients, providers, and communities alike.

References

1. Kaiser Permanente. (2023). *Integrated Care Stories: An Overview of Our Integrated Care Model.* Kaiser Permanente Institute for Health Policy. https://www.kpihp.org/integrated-care-stories/overview/ (Accessed: 21 August 2023).
2. Kern, L. M., Safford, M. M., Slavin, M. J., Makovkina, E., Fudl, A., Carrillo, J. E., & Abramson, E. L. (2019). Patients' and Providers' Views on Causes and Consequences of Healthcare Fragmentation in the Ambulatory Setting: A Qualitative Study. *Journal of General Internal Medicine,* 34(6), 899–907. https://doi. org/10.1007/s11606-019-04859-1
3. Kaiser Permanente. (2023). *Integrated Care Stories: Cutting Cancer Risk through Targeted Expansion of Genetic Testing.* Kaiser Permanente Institute for Health Policy. https://www. kpihp.org/integrated-care-stories/womens-hereditary-cancer-program/
4. Kaiser Permanente. (2023). *Integrated Care Stories: Early Warning System for Hospitalized Patients.* Kaiser Permanente Institute for Health Policy. https://www.kpihp.org/integrated-care-stories/early-warning-system-forhospitalized-patients/
5. KaiserPermanente.(2023).*Integrated Care Stories: Reducing Hip Fracture Rates in At-Risk Patients.* Kaiser Permanente Institute for Health Policy. https://www.kpihp.org/integrated-care-stories/ healthy-bones-program/
6. Lenert, L. A., Lane, S., & Wehbe, R. (2023). Could an Artificial Intelligence Approach to Prior Authorization Be More Human? *Journal of the American Medical Informatics Association: JAMIA,* 30(5), 989–994. https://doi. org/10.1093/ jamia/ocad016

Chapter 6

Stress Simplicity

Do not overcomplicate a solution to a problem; keep the following principle in mind: "When you have two competing theories that make exactly the same predictions, the simpler one" is better to implement.

It seems counterintuitive, but the majority of innovations are rather simple. The temptation to take a problem and create a complex solution exists in most of us. We tend to overthink an opportunity and therefore overengineer a fix. Innovation is often as basic as developing an elegant yet simple solution to a complex issue or opportunity, not the opposite way around. If the innovation can't be easily explained, start again.

THE PURSUIT OF PARSIMONY | BY VISHAKHA SANT

The healthcare payer industry is a labyrinth of financial transactions, regulatory roundabouts, and a nuanced state of affairs called patient care coordination. In this intricate landscape, the guiding principle of "parsimony" (/ˈpärsəˌmōnē/) emerges as a beacon for efficiency and effectiveness. Derived from Occam's Razor, the concept of parsimony advocates for simplicity—choosing the most straightforward solution with the fewest assumptions. In the realm of healthcare payers, where precision and clarity are paramount, the application of this principle has established more merit. This chapter explores the multifaceted application of parsimony based on consumer-centric access, claims processing and adjudication, and the transformative potential of time-driven activity-based costing (TDABC).

DOI: 10.4324/9781003381983-6

What do you consider to be the biggest barriers to access to healthcare in the U.S. health care system?

share of respondents (2,519 people surveyed; survey-takers could select multiple options)

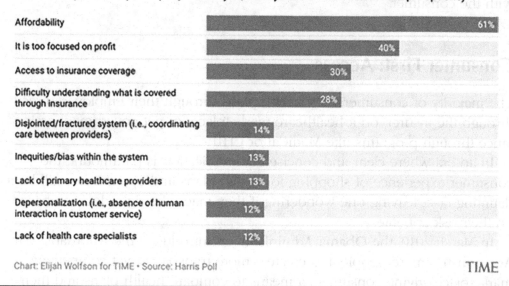

Affordability	61%
It is too focused on profit	40%
Access to insurance coverage	30%
Difficulty understanding what is covered through insurance	28%
Disjointed/fractured system (i.e., coordinating care between providers)	14%
Inequities/bias within the system	13%
Lack of primary healthcare providers	13%
Depersonalization (i.e., absence of human interaction in customer service)	12%
Lack of health care specialists	12%

Chart: Elijah Wolfson for TIME • Source: Harris Poll   TIME

Figure 6.1   Biggest barriers to access

Understanding Healthcare Payer Parsimony

The foundation of healthcare payer parsimony is not just simplicity for the sake of it but a strategic and intentional pursuit of straightforward solutions that balance operational efficiency, thereby, delighting the customer. Unfortunately, consumers are not delighted. TIME magazine published findings from a survey measuring *"What are the biggest barriers to access healthcare in the U.S. health care system."*

The first two, *"affordability"* and the *"sentiment that healthcare is focused on profit,"* are systemic issues requiring an ecosystem of actors to behave better along the healthcare delivery value chain—actors and organizations with deep pockets, lobbying for the best interests of their "consumers" to Congress.

The level of complexity required to solve the first two barriers goes deeply against the grain of simplicity, so we move to the next set of challenges. Here, we have *"access to insurance coverage"* and *"difficulty understanding what is covered."* These barriers are the basic tenets of any other consumer purchase we make—wanting to know what you are paying for and whether you are overpaying for the value you received?

This leads us to our first pillar of the healthcare payer parsimony, starting with the consumer.

Consumer First: Access

The majority of consumers buy health plans through their employer, directly through the insurer, on a healthcare marketplace, or get government assistance through programs like MediCal or CHIP.

In an era where clear and concise communication is paramount, the consumer experience of shopping for health plans and options can still be a daunting task, leaving one wondering if they made the right decision based on their risk appetite.

In March 2010, the Obama Administration introduced the Affordable Care Act to insure more people and create a more transparent yet competitive marketplace, giving consumers a means to compare health plans and their associated value. Both worked, uninsured rates dropped from 33.2 M in 2019 to 27.6 M in 2022. Furthermore, the share of individual market enrollment in ACA-compliant plans has increased to 93% in mid-2022, compared to 71% in mid-2015. However, a study published by the National Library of Medicine in 2019 revealed that while more people have coverage and are largely satisfied with their coverage, providers, and health plan selections, only 50% of enrollees found it easy to find the right coverage and only 41% believed it was easy to find an affordable plan.

What Does This Suggest?

First, it's an acknowledgment to the US government to follow through on a strong belief that *access to healthcare is a right, not a privilege*. As important, if not more, acknowledge the millions of *people trying to do the right thing by seeking coverage* despite their lifestyle choices. It also suggests the wobbly Healthcare.gov, which launched on October 1, 2013, with CBC news headlines that read "On first day, health marketplaces' glitchy at best, offline at worst'," has improved over the years. It also suggests a healthy *breeding ground for co-opetition*, the positive offspring of collaboration and competition. Payers and providers are looking for partners that stand out from their competition and bring substantive differentiation. In the long term, payers and providers alike may prioritize a smaller number of strategically aligned partners in a given market.

But more simplistically, there is a large opportunity for the *user experience to get at least half better.*

Call to Action: Simplify the Interaction

There are more than 900 health insurance companies operating throughout the United States, but not all offer health plan products on the commercial marketplace. For simplicity, let's assume each payer offers a tiered or subscription at each metal level: bronze, silver, and gold. We have exponentially made it confusing to access and understand insurance coverage compared to the others to enable marketplace simplicity.

Inherently, pricing can never be simple with so many products and parameters to consider. But a parsimonious solution would be thoughtful about how plan and product information is represented within the user experience.

How about evolving to an online health plan shopping experience like Amazon or Netflix?

Why not have a health plan marketplace where *all health plans* are offered including government, private, offmarket, commercial, and so on. Imagine a standard and simplified way to shop for health plans with dropdowns, categories, and ability to get served-up recommended plans, wellness programs, or family packages based on conditions. Make it easier by prioritizing information that matters to how money and/or time is spent. Uberize the need for a health plan based on life changes, consumption metrics, and utilization. Enable a marketplace that brings wellness to consumers, not woes of annual open enrollment. If GenAI is applied, why not go a step further and use historical claims, payment, and financial information to offer up government programs and fill out the right forms if I consent?

But that just solves the access portion of the problem. Here, the transition is from being shoppers in the marketplace to patients in the healthcare ecosystem. This is where we find the next area of focus—the messy middle, where the alphabet soup of DRGs, ICDs, CPTs, and APQs prevail— where claims go to be processed or sometimes possessed and where physician practices spend upward of $30 billion each year on claims and billing costs.

Messy Middle: Claims Processing and Adjudication

Healthcare payer operations, claims processing, and adjudication represent a critical juncture where the principle of parsimony can wield significant influence.

A recent landmark study on the complexity of billing and paying for physician care found that 30% of healthcare resources are tied up in administrative costs, one-seventh of total annual spending in the United States. Why is that?

Claims, just like carbs, can be simplified into two kinds: simple and complex. Around 80% of claims are simple while the remaining 20% of claims are complex and expensive. One in seven claims is denied, and of those, 65% are never resubmitted. Denied claims are passed on to a medical claims examiner for a detailed manual review. The administrative costs associated with claims appeals have reached a staggering $8.6 billion.

Streamlining this process involves adopting simple yet effective algorithms that prioritize accuracy, minimize the risk of errors, and enable fraud detection. Let's use Medicare Advantage, the segment of private plans that now cover about half of the government's health program for older Americans as a backdrop for applying the principles of parsimony to claims processing and adjudication.

Medicare Advantage aka the Gluttonous Cash Cow

In 2022, there were 3,834 Medicare Advantage plans available nationwide for individual enrollment, an 8% increase from 2021 and the largest number of plans available in more than a decade. In October 2022, the *New York Times* reported, "How Insurers Exploited Medicare Advantage for Billions."

It went on to claim that four of the largest five insurers either have settled or are currently facing lawsuits claiming fraudulent coding. Similar lawsuits have also been brought against an array of smaller health plans not found in the marketplace.

Since then, the Biden Administration responded with proposals that the US government would significantly lower payments—by billions of dollars a year—to Medicare Advantage. The proposed changes have unleashed lobbyists and insurance executives flooding to Capitol Hill to engage in their fiercest fight in years.

The Principles of Parsimony Applied to Claims Processing

1. **Look to confirm claims are not duplicated or paid already. If yes, a denial is sent.**
   - *Categorize into Simple versus Complex Claims (Occam's Razor):* Develop automated rules for straightforward claims to reduce complexity.
   - *Technology Application:* Simplify real-time adjudication through flexible benefit selection, iterative authorization matching, and automated filing limit detection. This is enough to be decided either entirely by the automatic review or with only a quick scan by a human medical reviewer.

2. **Basic review to ensure all details of the claim are present** (i.e., alphabet soup of procedure codes, diagnosis codes, ID, matching patients to records, and so on)
   - *Complex claims are complex due to the large dependency on system integration:* Occam's Razor suggests favoring the simplest, most interoperable path forward.
   - *Application:* Prioritize modern, interoperable health information systems to streamline real-time claims adjudication. Maximize existing investments to take a platform and workflow automation approach to tackle claims adjudication.

3. **Confirm and conform to provider network participation and agreements.**
   - *Data Accuracy and Completeness (Data Quality Standards):* Occam's Razor advises simplifying data processing by enforcing stringent data quality standards.
   - *Application:* Implement straightforward data validation checks and promote standardized code sets to ensure accurate and complete information.

4. **Apply patient contract benefits and spending rules.**
   - *Categorize into Simple versus Complex Claims (Occam's Razor):* Develop automated rules for straightforward claims to reduce complexity.
   - *Technology Application:* Simplify real-time adjudication through flexible benefit selection, iterative authorization matching, and automated filing limit detection.

5. **Final determination—payment.**
   - *Standardization of Codes and Terminology:* Occam's Razor suggests choosing standardized code sets to simplify claims processing.

- *Application:* Emphasize the use of standardized codes and medical terminology to reduce complexity and ensure consistency in claims submissions.

By aligning these solutions with each step, we create a comprehensive approach that not only simplifies the claims-processing steps but also leverages technology and system integration to enhance efficiency and accuracy. However, we haven't solved the issue at its core and within its simplest form. **Cost.** This is the final segment with the largest promise of change, not only in systems but in mindset.

Costs: The Healthcare Hot Potato

Amidst the intricate web of financial complexities and regulatory challenges, the healthcare industry grapples with a daunting cost crisis. Addressing this crisis necessitates a fundamental reevaluation of how we measure and assign costs. Any true healthcare reform will require moving away from fee-for-service and into covering bundled payments for the full life cycle of care. For comparisons, the average cost for a hip replacement in Germany and Sweden is approximately $8,500 versus the comparable figure in the United States of $30,000. Key reasons are attributed to a highly fragmented care delivery system with a number of distinct entities involved trying to pass along the costs to the next actor like a doomed game of hot potato. However, it can be better, right from the core. It will take us away from the traditional structure of charge-based accounting where cost allocations are problematic because they misrepresent drivers of cost and enable utilization. The recommended measure is time-driven activity-based costing (TDABC). As elaborated by Robert S. Kaplan and Steven R. Anderson in their seminal work, *TimeDriven Activity-Based Costing,*[1] TDABC brings clarity to the healthcare cost landscape by accurately assigning costs to each process step, including personnel, drugs, supplies, devices, space, equipment, and so on, for each step. This ultimately gives you two parameters: resource-attributable expenses divided by the available capacity of the resource.

MD Anderson intentionally used TDABC in their opening of a new cancer center in 2011. They launched a pilot project with the head and neck center to assess the feasibility of applying TDABC. They assembled a team of clinicians and financial staff and began developing a care delivery value chain that mapped out the full treatment of the patient. Each segment represented of therapy, outpoint, diagnostic, imaging, and operating room; all had process maps and costs of people, process, and technology for each step. They applied measured capacity costs and time taken to perform tasks. They estimated a per-patient cost per step of the process and ultimately came to transparent pricing of services. The modified process resulted in an 11-minute reduction in process time, 67% reduction in costs for professional stuff, and total costs per patient drop from $250 to $160. Capturing costs at a point in time can only be achieved with a platform-based approach focused on the adoption of process mining to unlock operational efficiencies.

Unlocking Operational Efficiencies: The Power of TDABC and Process Mining Traditional cost measurement systems in healthcare often lead to fragmented and highly customized structures, perpetuating cost shifting and hindering a comprehensive understanding of resource utilization. The cornerstone of resolving the cost crisis lies in embracing TDABC, which precisely measures the cost of each resource used in a process and the time each patient spends with that resource. This not only ensures accurate cost allocation but also provides a holistic view of the entire care pathway. By reorganizing healthcare units based on conditions, providers can standardize protocols and treatment processes, fostering a more efficient and streamlined approach to healthcare delivery.

Process Mining as a Catalyst for Change: Going beyond TDABC, process mining emerges as a catalyst for transformative change in healthcare operations. Delving into the intricacies of each step in the healthcare process, process mining uncovers associated costs and inefficiencies. The call to action is clear—providers must leverage process mining to reorganize into units focused on conditions. This not only optimizes resource utilization but also lays the foundation for standardized protocols. The outcomes are profound, ranging from a total revamp of reimbursement structures to enhanced compliance with regulatory processes. As healthcare embraces the power of TDABC and process mining, the industry can pave the way for a more costeffective, transparent, and patient-centric future.

Call To Action

To fully support time-driven activity-based costing (TDABC), payers would need to implement several key changes in their operational and strategic approaches. Here are some crucial adjustments:

1. **Process Reorganization:** Payers traditionally organize their structures around departments and services, leading to fragmented cost measurement.

- **Change Needed:** Adopt a processoriented approach by reorganizing units based on conditions or medical processes. This involves grouping activities and resources according to the specific conditions they address, allowing for more accurate cost assignment.

2. **Standardized Protocols and Treatment Processes:** Varied protocols and treatment processes across different departments or units contribute to cost ambiguity. Start with owned care provider entities or partnerships.
   - **Change Needed:** Encourage standardization of protocols and treatment processes to create consistency in healthcare delivery. Standardization enhances the accuracy of time and resource allocation, facilitating more precise cost calculations.

3. **Implementation of TDABC Methodology:** Many payers may still rely on traditional cost measurement methods that lack the granularity of TDABC.
   - **Change Needed:** Invest in the adoption of TDABC methodology, including the accurate measurement of the cost of each resource used in the process and the quantity of time each patient spends with the resource. This shift ensures a more detailed and accurate understanding of costs associated with each process step.

4. **Technology Integration for Process Mining:** Limited utilization of advanced technologies for analyzing and optimizing processes.
   - **Change Needed:** Embrace process mining tools and platforms to delve into the intricacies of each step in the healthcare process. Process mining allows for the identification of inefficiencies, bottlenecks, and opportunities for improvement, contributing to operational efficiency.

5. **Data Quality Standards and Interoperability:** Inconsistent data quality and lack of interoperability can hinder the effectiveness of TDABC.
   - **Change Needed:** Enforce stringent data quality standards and promote interoperability among different systems and data sources. Consistent and standardized data ensures accurate calculations and meaningful insights from TDABC.

   The success story at MD Anderson illuminates the potential—marked reductions in process time and costs, transparent pricing, and a shift toward operational efficiencies. To fully embrace TDABC, payers must embark on a journey of reorganization, standardization, technological integration, and data quality enhancement.

This comprehensive approach doesn't just address the symptoms; it reshapes the core, paving the way for a healthcare future that is costeffective, transparent, and, above all, consumer centric.

Conclusion

In the grand theater of healthcare, where costs often resemble a precarious game of hot potato and complexities seem insurmountable, the principles of parsimony beckon us to simplify, to clarify, and to prioritize the needs of the very individuals the system was designed for to serve—patients who are consumers of their health.

As the curtain falls on this exploration, we stand at a crossroads. The healthcare and payer industries, laden with challenges, hold the promise of a transformative future. By embracing the tenets of simplicity and parsimony, we can pave a new path—one marked by transparency, efficiency, and, above all, unwavering focus on the wellbeing of the individuals journeying through the healthcare ecosystem.

The pursuit of parsimony is not just a strategic choice; it's a revolution—a call to arms for a healthcare system that champions clarity over complexity, simplicity over convolution, and, ultimately, the well-being of its users over bureaucratic entanglements. In this pursuit, we find not just a solution to the challenges at hand but a vision for a future where healthcare is not just a system but a compassionate ally in the well-being of us all. Be kind and be well.

CUTTING THROUGH THE COMPLEXITY OF PAYER SYSTEMS | BY MANISH MEHTA

Introduction

In my two decades immersed in healthcare IT with a significant portion of that time dedicated to the healthcare payer sector, I've gained an above-average understanding of the dynamics driving this industry. My experience has afforded me insights into the persistent challenges and evolving needs that shape the healthcare value chain, especially the payer value chain. Carrying a good amount of battle scars reflecting many successes and failures, I've come to appreciate the intricate complexities that exist in the realm of healthcare payers and often find myself longing for a simpler and streamlined approach to harmonize the people, processes, and technology in this sphere.

Description of Opportunity

Healthcare payer IT systems, particularly the legacy ones, are intricate. At the heart of these networks is the claims administration system, which integrates with numerous modules like care management, contract oversight, and user portals. Persistent business requirements strain these systems, frequently accumulating technical debt. There's an essential need to revisit these demands, aiming for more streamlined IT solutions that address operational needs without adding further complexities.

Background and Challenges in IT

Every year, payer organizations see changes across their people, processes, and technologies. These shifts cater to a range of needs, from regulatory compliance and enhanced security to efficiency improvements and cost-cutting. Payers primarily lean on commercial off-the-shelf systems (COTS) for crucial tasks, like managing claims and contracts. These COTS systems form the bedrock for all records and transactions. But as needs change, these systems often require updates or integrations. This presents a challenge for both business and IT teams as they strive to quickly deliver solutions without escalating costs. Sometimes, the response is to add complexities when a simpler process or configuration tweak would suffice. From my experience, the introduction of a ROI framework for enhancements and change requests often acts as a guiding light in such situations.

Building Block of the ROI Framework

The foundation of the ROI framework can be understood through three primary pillars:

1. Assessment: This phase dives deep into the following:
   a. Differentiating between core products and custom features.
      Determine if the change or enhancement should be a COTS product feature or a customization is important. Incorrectly categorizing these

can lead to increased complexity, escalated costs, and diminished performance metrics

b. Evaluating the COTS product roadmap and understanding potential future enhancements that might support newer healthcare regulations or payment models.

c. Analyzing the criticality and complexity of the request like the importance and intricacy of integrating a new telehealth billing feature.

2. Classification: At this juncture, the focus is on the following:

a. Reviewing past implementations for insights. For example, understanding the challenges and successes of a prior adoption of a value-based payment model can offer significant insights. Evaluating the possibilities of reusing the past changes or tweaking the past change versus building from scratch needs to be factored in.

b. Consider adjusting workflows to match product capabilities. This could mean choosing configuration over coding when trying to adjust for newer billing codes. Often, the solution lies in slight configuration adjustments without waiting for a full system overhaul.

c. Weighing the benefits of waiting for a future product upgrade, especially if the next release promises better features like better integration with electronic health record systems as an example.

d. Scouring for alternative solutions that might be more efficient, such as adopting third-party APIs that provide real-time eligibility checks.

3. Projection: This stage involves the following:

a. Making forecasts based on each solution category, factoring in variables like potential cost savings, efficiency gains, or improved member experiences.

b. Evaluating how snugly each solution aligns with the set requirements, quantifying it in terms of a percentage fit. This could mean assessing how a proposed IT solution might cater to 80% of the needs of a new care coordination initiative.

GTM Strategy/Adoption

Adoption of a framework like this may sound simple but requires a fair bit of work. What works best is to co-evolve the framework with the key stakeholders involved and should include elements like

a. Framework Branding—Assign a unique name and/or logo to the ROI framework to make it more personalized to your organization.

b. Template and Calculator Tool—Create a standardized template for the ROI framework. Additionally, introduce a user-friendly ROI calculator tool that integrates with the template for instant ROI projections like an estimate of time it takes to build versus configure.

c. Entry Points Integration—Encourage the use of the ROI framework in all change management or PMO meetings.

d. Approval Mechanism—Make it as part of budget approvals for better transparency and tracking.

e. Feedback Loop—Set up a simple channel for feedback on the framework's use and make periodic refinements based on inputs.

Summary/Benefits

For a healthcare payer, simplicity often paves the path to efficiency, cost-effectiveness, and clarity. When we advocate for streamlined processes, we're not just promoting an abstract ideal; we're highlighting the tangible benefits like the ones described in the following:

a. Optimal Utilization of Standard Solutions: By focusing on out-of-the-box implementations, healthcare payers can harness the full potential of solutions that have been predesigned for their needs, thereby avoiding the pitfalls of excessive customization.

b. Mitigation of Risks: A simpler approach reduces the complexities of integrations and operations, leading to fewer errors and more predictable outcomes, which is crucial for ensuring member satisfaction and regulatory compliance.

c. Reduced Need for Customizations: By leaning toward standard functionalities, the need for custom tweaks diminishes. This means lesser technical debt, leading to easier upgrades and maintenance down the line.

d. Enhanced Return on COTS Investment: Leveraging COTS solutions to their fullest allows for significant cost savings in the long run, ensuring that healthcare payers get the best value for their investment.

e. Informative Feedback for COTS Roadmaps: Utilizing COTS solutions in their intended manner provides valuable insights that can be channeled back to product developers, ensuring that future versions of the product are even more aligned with healthcare payer needs.

Stressing Simplicity Outcomes

Embracing simplicity not only streamlines processes but also brings about a culture of clarity and efficiency, enabling healthcare payers to navigate the ever-evolving landscape with agility and foresight.

ADOPT SECURE DIGITAL COMMUNICATION TO SIMPLIFY ENGAGEMENT AND OPERATIONS | BY KRISHNA KURAPATI AND BOBBI WEBER

Don't make the process harder than it is.

—Jack Welch

Most healthcare organizations are in the early pilot stage focusing on streamlining operations and improving patient experience. While large hospitals were purchasing ultra-expensive enterprise-class systems and consultants, less financially robust hospitals had to make do with what they could afford. Interestingly, patient experience[2] and financial and clinical outcomes[3] were not markedly different. Our advisor Edward W. Marx has dubbed this lowercost, do-it-yourself, agile approach "scrappy innovation"—a lesson he learned from contributors to the original *Voices of Innovation* book.

Fueled by a commitment to digital transformation, more and more providers, aka scrappy innovators, are focused on rapidly delivering value. They seek affordable, simple, and workable patient-friendly online interactions that

- streamline operations
- improve the patient and staff experience
- improve profitability
- can be deployed with less effort and time.

These organizations adopt an agile mindset and drive a culture of iterative innovation and continuous improvement. Health IT innovators work collaboratively in a test-and-learn team approach divided into sprints, or phases, following the 80/20 rule of process improvement (20% of the effort, or input, leads to 80% of the results or output)

The goal is to drive alignment, prioritizing a series of digital care projects targeted to organizational pain points and grounded in reality. Ideas are developed and executed collaboratively, setting up an environment of super-charged creativity. The "perfect design and plan" is not the goal. Gone are the days of meticulously addressing every possible IT situation, with development handed *to* the front line. These organizations work hand in hand *with* the front line, IT, and other key players to develop, test, and iterate to success using digital communication tools.

With scrappy innovation, providers are not handcuffed to a specific vendor. They are willing and able to make low-cost, fast, and easy-to-implement digital investments to automate clinical and operational processes that yield measurable results. Everything is in the pursuit of simplification, removing manual steps from what was a cumbersome and fragmented process. By simplifying and connecting their workflows with digital communications, technologies, hospitals, and medical practices are achieving new levels of performance, staff and patient satisfaction— quickly and at an affordable cost.

Scrappiness Excels Through Trial and Error

Virtual Health

The digital transformation journey of Virtua Health, a nonprofit regional health system that serves southern New Jersey and the Philadelphia area, is a testament to the success of scrappy innovation. As a matter of necessity when facing the COVID-19 pandemic, Virtua became lean and agile, keeping their workforce involved with a new digital transformation office.

Virtua's cross-functional project groups applied agile methodology practices to digital solutions using conversational chatbots and virtual visits, aimed at responding proactively to the increasing demands of patients and clinicians. Tarun Kapoor, MD, MBA, senior vice president and chief digital transformation officer at Virtua Health, said:

> By addressing the needs of patients and multidisciplinary clinicians
> situated in different departments and care settings, agile helps
> Virtua Health achieve substantial change by helping our patients
> and employees embrace these iterative changes and engage with
> the new digital solutions quickly.

Virtua Heatlth's virtual care tools are built upon a purely browser-based platform that enables them to communicate with patients outside of their four walls. This web-based platform has been transformational in expanding the health system's patient engagement capabilities, which focus on delivering hospital-at-home monitoring services to prevent repeat ED visits and readmissions and streamlining urgent care patient check-in.

"The web-based platform's benefits are continually validated by patients through positive, real-time feedback, such as a short internal 2021 survey of patient users," said Angela Skrzynski, DO, board-certified in Family Medicine and Sleep Medicine and Clinical Lead for digital programs at Virtua Health. "We learned that meeting patients when, where, and how they want to receive care is the foundation of quality virtual care, especially the use of chatbots."

Virtua launched projects that are 100% clinically relevant and sound while the technology and related processes may only be 80–90% completed. For example, the user interface may need a bit more work, or some patient features aren't fully developed yet. By launching earlier, staff can gather feedback about what's working while optimizing functionality issues and incorporating feedback into future iterations.

Not every program will prove successful, but that's OK. The goal is to keep thinking about how digital technologies and workflows can transform interactions with patients. This includes trying new things, expanding those that resonate with patients and deliver value to the organization, adjusting those that don't meet expectations, and eliminating programs that aren't working.

While digital transformation doesn't happen overnight, it also doesn't require six to nine months to implement. An agile, iterative approach succeeds best when each initiative is limited to what can be implemented within two to three months.

Explained Danielle Wilson, Assistant Vice President of Digital Transformation, Virtua Health,

> Many organizations strive to do things that get to 99%. So many people have been ingrained with this "MBA Six Sigma" type mentality. The reality is that for healthcare, the solution has to be good enough and it has to be safe and medically sound. But if you get 80% of automation or 80% of patients taking on the self-service themselves, you're essentially allowing your workforce to take care

of the complex patient or the information that is highly complicated to schedule or engage with the patient.

Virtua Health reports the following positive outcomes resulting from virtual care:

- Increased volume of patients in urgent care telehealth
- 32% relative reduction in readmissions
- Reduced recurring ED visits
- 43% reduction in 14-day ED return visits
- An NPS score of 80 demonstrating high patient satisfaction using digital tools.

First Choice Neurology

Growing consumer expectations for patient engagement solutions coupled with managing the COVID-19 pandemic spurred medical groups into rethinking safety strategies. How, for instance, should they manage dramatic increases in patient volume while reducing risks posed by the respiratory viral illness?

First Choice Neurology (FCN), the nation's largest neurology group based in Medley, Florida, rose to the challenge at a time when digital adoption was limited. While physicians regularly use sophisticated tools to perform innovative procedures, their operational practices often are stuck in decades-old workflows that stifle productivity and frustrate patients.

FCN selected a HIPAA-compliant, consumer-friendly digital care solution initially to provide relief to overwhelmed healthcare workers and reduce in-person patient volume in an at-risk infectious environment. They engaged parents and caregivers responsible for their diverse 1,600-patient mix: children with congenital and cognitive conditions and adults aged 50-plus with memory issues.

Adapting new technology requires culture and behavior change, and trying to make that happen can be a daunting prospect. FCN initially started with one care center and incrementally added workflow changes. They started with secure texting and virtual visits to improve the efficiency of the care team. Next, they expanded to offloading repetitive, manual patient registration and intake tasks away from the care team to conversational chatbots. They involved the front line and IT automating manual, routine processes. They monitored and refined their approach until it was deemed ready and added EHR implementation to further remove work from the staff.

Experimentation, reassessing, and adjustment with each digital roll-out were the catalysts to digital transformation as FCN leaders and staff focused on user needs to arrive at the simplest way to be successful. Another lesson learned was that digital solutions should never be imposed on employees and patients. To be successful, practices must learn from the people who will be using the technologies—patients and staff to make sure the experience is positive and simple. The results speak for themselves. Fully 95% of FCN patients opt-in to their digital intake process, eliminating clipboards and hassle for patients and staff.

FCN also tracked and shared performance metrics. The combination of increased patient throughput, reduction in staff overtime, and patient satisfaction and engagement contributed to a 22% increase in clinic profitability, creating demand from other clinics eager to receive these benefits.

Within three years, FCN successfully digitized patient intake, orders follow through, and payment notification tasks to support all 90 adult and pediatric neurologists and other physician specialists working at 50-plus care centers across five counties.

Through digital self-services, FCN has empowered their patients to perform routine intake activities online, such as preparing for appointments, completing insurance forms for preapproval, accessing test results at their convenience, and receiving patient education. These efforts improve efficiency and increased clinical revenue by 24% by

- reducing staff overtime by 22%
- saving 19 minutes per patient seen
- scoring 4.8/5 in a patient satisfaction survey
- streamlining physician workflow, which saved 8 to 10+ minutes per visit and enabled two to three more patient visits per day.

"The biggest challenge in shifting to virtual care was facing our own fears," said Jose Rocha, First Choice Neurology's Director of Central Business Office.

> The future is here, and we knew we had to adapt to serve our patients better online, which meant giving up our comfort with pens, paper and clipboards. Initially, we were concerned that chatbots would be impersonal and difficult to use, but the results have been amazing.

ACOs are Ripe for Scrappy Innovation

The Biden administration's priorities include a continued focus on value-based care, especially access to specialty care, with accountable care organizations (ACOs) playing an integral role. Most significantly, in November 2022, the Centers for Medicare and Medicaid Services (CMS) Innovation Center set a goal to enroll the majority of Medicare (original and Medicare Advantage) members in valuebased programs by 2030.[4] Medicare and Medicaid cover nearly one out of every three Americans.

CMS' beneficiary timeline is expected to accelerate accountable care and value-based models and fundamentally transform how healthcare is paid for and delivered over this decade. ACO participants, including physicians, hospitals, practices, payers, and others, are challenged with a combination of delayed incentive payments and startup costs to build out population health and care coordination abilities that can stress practice finances. They need scrappy innovation.

"The goal of value-based care is a great one, but the revenue is in the back end, so you have to succeed for quite a while, sometimes a year or two, in order to reap the benefits," explained Chad Anguilm, Vice President of Growth at Medical Advantage, part of the Doctors Company Group.[5]

Managing Costs with an ACO

Five cost-reduction methods help ACOs succeed by reducing patient expenses and maximizing incentive revenue. They are as follows:

1. Implement care coordination and management
2. Launch disease management and preventive care programs
3. Monitor patients to avoid unnecessary emergency department (ED) visits and hospitalizations
4. Optimize medication management processes
5. Encourage end-of-life planning

These value-based strategies provide a long-term impact on patient health and outcomes. They also incur new operational costs as hospitals and medical practices hire additional personnel to build extended care teams and capabilities to coordinate care.

By laser-focusing on operational efficiency and reducing operational costs, healthcare organizations can remain profitable during the period of lower reimbursement. This approach requires practices to critically look for ways to manage operations differently.

A nationwide 2022 survey of healthcare workers found staff retention and administrative busywork stand out as top pain points[6]:

- Retention remains a challenge: Half (48%) are worried about their health system's ability to retain and hire staff if they do not prioritize automation.
- Staff spend too much time on documentation and not on patients: On average, respondents said staff at their organization spend 57.5% of · their time on repetitive tasks such as data entry and documentation.

An acute need exists for ACOs to implement innovative solutions aimed at retaining staff and skilled healthcare professionals including nurses.

A Promising Future for ACOs

ACOs embrace digital communication to help alleviate these problems. The digital world is revolutionizing every aspect of consumers' lives—and is fundamentally altering the advancement of provider-patient engagement. In addition to reducing costs by streamlining patient intake, digital health transformation is driving higher incentive payments improving gaps in care performance.

ACO risk-sharing contracts are designed to emphasize wellness and prevention through incentive payments and financial risk arrangements. Most ACO participants can identify which patients are due for preventive screening. However, few possess the outreach tools to foster patient engagement and provide relevant patient education at a population level. Since hiring extra staff is rarely an option, the opportunity to invest in a digital communication platform rapidly becomes a must-have commodity.

AllianceChicago

AllianceChicago, a national network of more than 70 community health centers across 19 states, successfully launched a patient outreach campaign supported by an innovative chatbot strategy. The network's medical researchers took note that well-child visits and immunizations among children in the United States declined at the pandemic's onset, leaving vulnerable populations disproportionately affected.

AllianceChicago identified patients due for exams using analytics and then employed campaigns to send conversational chatbots to their parents doing three simple things:

■ Outreach to tell parents their children were due for a visit and why it was important
■ Provide basic information on age-specific normal development
■ Make it easy to schedule an appointment.

Conversational chatbots facilitated a relative increase in well-child visits and immunizations by 27% in the intervention group of in-network parents and guardians who engaged with the chatbot.

Today, AllianceChicago is realizing comparable results expanding the use of chatbots to adult wellness and screening services, which include identifying and addressing social determinants of health (SDOH) barriers that influence health outcomes.

In addition to improving the health of their patient population, they are

■ generating more revenue by bringing in patients previously lost to follow-up,
■ reducing staff costs and effort from previously manual follow-up, and
■ increasing incentive payments for preventative services and SDoH screening.

"By engaging patients and caregivers, chatbots present the potential to proactively engage patients in care, optimize vaccination uptake and realize one of societies' greatest public health achievements—decreasing the spread of communicable diseases," said Nivedita Mohanty, MD, Chief Research Officer, AllianceChicago.

As federal initiatives are setting ambitious goals for value-based care approaches, the shift to new ways of interacting with patients doesn't have to be hard. Maturing digital solutions can be a key factor in your success and is a win-win proposition for everyone. They are simple solutions that are simple to deploy and simple for patients to understand.

Simple digital outreach strategies can yield positive health and incentive payment results starting in the first month of use and are critical to cost-effectively managing effectively at a population level.

Adopting Secure Digital Communication to Simplify Engagement and Operations Outcomes. As the real-world examples demonstrate, secure digital communications are a key enabler for success. Payers and payviders of all kinds can benefit from these approaches. Not only are they simple to develop and execute, but they do not require enormous investments, providing value from day one.

References

1. https://www.hbs.edu/ris/Publication%20 Files/04045_d62528d4–79314ea1-a205-d9683c639d6e.pdf
2. https://www.qliqsoft.com/blog/want-toimprove-patient-engagement-ditch-the-app-other-barriers
3. https://www.qliqsoft.com/customer-success/ first-choice-neurology
4. https://www.cms.gov/blog/cms-innovation-centers-strategy-support-person-centered-value-based-specialty-care
5. https://www.medicaleconomics.com/view/ solutions-to-common-physician-practice-challenges
6. https:// www. busines swire. com/news/home/20220426005250/en/Majority-of-Healthcare-Workers-Worry-About-Burnout-from-Increasing-Burden-of-Administrative-Work

HCSC'S AI-AIDED PROCESSING OF PRIOR AUTHORIZATION REQUESTS | ANONYMOUS

The purpose of the stress simplicity approach to innovation is reflected in Health Care Service Corporation's (HCSC) drive to design solutions that operate better for everyone involved, including providers and members. The use of artificial intelligence (AI) to speed up the process and give auto-approvals when appropriate seeks to enhance the experience for all stakeholders. Prior authorization denotes the requirement for a health professional to obtain clearance from a patient's health plan before proceeding with treatment, procedure, or medicine.[1] When prior authorization is necessary, various health plans have different regulations.

HCSC has used AI and augmentedintelligence to process prior permission requests 1,400 times faster than before.[2] The AI-powered prior authorization tool was first created in 2021 and piloted the following year, with a focus on specialty pharmacy and behavioral health. In a considerable number of situations, quick approvals were given. Based on the program's effectiveness, HCSC expanded it to accommodate prior permission requests from a variety of healthcare services, including skilled nursing facilities, hospice care, home health, and outpatient services. The technology enables the automatic approval of requests that fulfill particular criteria, allowing clinical staff to focus on more complex cases. All requests are either automatically granted or sent to an HCSC clinician for a hands-on review. No requests are denied simply based on the judgment of the AI tool. The HSBC model fits into the innovation pathway's concept of stress simplicity as highlighted in the discussions later.

The Need and Motivation

Choudhury and Perumalla,[3] Lenert et al.,[1] and McKinsey & Company[4] give excellent insights into why automating the prior authorization process is crucial and how incorporating artificial and augmented intelligence might positively improve it. The debate emphasizes that PA is viewed as a crucial component of the healthcare system to reduce costs and prevent needless care. However, it is known that PA can result in physician fatigue, treatment delays, and patient and provider dissatisfaction. This gives the background for why the PA process needs improvement.

Choudhury and Perumalla,[3] Lenert et al.,[1] and McKinsey & Company[4] observe that automated approaches for PA review have gained popularity, with initiatives like the HL7 DaVinci Project offering rulebased ways for automation. The limits of these techniques, however, are acknowledged. Because of the complexities of medical choices, as well as differing stakeholder viewpoints and interests, strictly rule-based systems are insufficient for dealing with the nuanced decision-making necessary in many medical circumstances. Lenert et al.[1] suggest an alternate strategy that uses AI algorithms to calculate permission choices while taking into account expert panels' assessments, including patient representatives. This method is said to be more human-centric since it attempts to imitate the decision-making process of expert panels.

How The HSBC Model Stresses Simplicity

It Simplifies and Simplifies the Process as Much as Feasible

The AI-powered prior permission tool is intended to be simple and easy to use for both providers and members.[2] The tool simply asks providers the questions essential to analyze and expedite claims, and it takes an average of six minutes to submit a request. This coincides with the innovation pathway's emphasis on simplicity, where the objective is to make procedures easy to comprehend and utilize. HCSC intends to use AI technology to expedite approvals and decrease administrative burdens for both healthcare providers and members. In HCSC's approach, the notion of "when you have two competing theories that make exactly the same predictions, the simpler one is better to implement" is reflected. HCSC simplifies the decision-making process by employing AI to process requests, concentrating on speedy approvals for requests that fulfill particular criteria.[5] This approach is consistent with the notion that most inventions are basic yet effective. The AI tool references the essential information to allow treatment in seconds by fast reviewing past authorizations and claims data. This rapid decision-making simplifies and expedites the process for providers, allowing them to respond to permission requests more quickly.

According to Choudhury and Perumalla,[3] Lenert et al.,[1] and McKinsey & Company,[4] electronic ePA speeds up the sharing of information between payers and providers by digitizing procedures and resulting in shorter response times. The AI-enabled workflow architecture automates previously manual operations such as finding, aggregating, and cross-checking information.

It Gets Rid of Superfluous Stages and Bureaucracy

Many of the procedures in the prior authorization process are automated by the AI technology, which avoids unnecessary paperwork and delays. This allows health-care professionals to concentrate on more challenging patients. The stress simplicity approach model explains how to resist the desire to devise complicated solutions to issues. Rather than complicating the process, the firm uses AI technology to handle previous authorization requests simply and effectively. This is consistent with the innovation pathway's focus on preferring simpler solutions over more complex ones.

Since 2018, HCSC has pledged to eliminate prior authorization requirements for roughly 1,000 procedure codes, which is a big step toward simplifying the process.[5] This decrease in the number of operations that require PA clearance reflects a proactive attitude to removing excessive bureaucracy, making the system more efficient and less burdensome for both providers and members. HCSC's "Gold Card" program displays a deliberate approach to removing superfluous stages. The initiative expedites the process for hospitals adhering to evidence-based standards of care by asking chosen Illinois healthcare facilities to join and auto-approving prior authorization requests fulfilling specified criteria. This program avoids bureaucratic delays and guarantees that eligible operations are approved on time. By establishing criteria for adhering to evidence-based standards, HCSC speeds the process even further by automatically accepting requests that match the criteria. This tailored strategy eliminates needless delays and speeds up permits for suitable facilities.

Choudhury and Perumalla,[3] Lenert et al.,[1] and McKinsey & Company[4] note that AI-enabled workflow architecture can automate low-value, time-consuming jobs. It enables computer-based systems to undertake duties such as acquiring medical evidence and cross-validating data against patient records. The automation engine, driven by AI and NLP, accelerates decision-making and predicts success for various outcomes, decreasing the need for manual involvement in many circumstances.

It Is Accountable and Transparent

All requests are either granted automatically or routed to an HCSC physician for a hands-on examination.[5] No requests are refused solely based on the AI tool's assessment. This guarantees that all choices are made consistently and equitably. By automating the approval process for requests that match specific criteria, HCSC's technology frees up clinical professionals to focus on more complicated situations while alternately helping with accountability. This smart approach solves the difficulty of managing numerous forms of previous authorization requests and directs human resources to the areas where they are most required. The HCSC's method comprises AI algorithms that take into account past data and claims, but no request is refused without human evaluation. This two-pronged strategy assures a balanced decision-making process, with AI providing speed and efficiency and humans providing supervision and responsibility.

The HCSC's reliance on proprietary algorithms that reference past authorization and claims data demonstrates a data-driven decision-making strategy. This strategy improves openness by guiding permission choices with historical data, resulting in consistent and accountable outcomes. The dedication of HCSC to assessing procedures that require prior authorization regularly and reducing extraneous restrictions indicates a data-driven approach to continuous improvement. This dedication to system improvement promotes openness by demonstrating an ongoing effort to align the process with medical best practices and minimize redundancies. The future objective of the HCSC to develop AI technology to incorporate a larger variety of process codes demonstrates an inclusive attitude. By embracing a broader set of codes, HCSC guarantees that a broader range of healthcare services benefit from expedited approvals, improving openness in decision-making across a wide range of medical circumstances.

Choudhury and Perumalla,[3] Lenertet al.,[1] and McKinsey & Company[4] explain how the triage engine uses data from a variety of sources, including member eligibility and benefits information, clinical claims, past authorization requests, and aspects of electronic health records (EHRs). Triage choices are made utilizing classification algorithms that are dynamically produced, demonstrating a methodical and transparent methodology. The AI-powered process makes recommendations, evaluates information for consistency, and optimizes communication routes, assuring accountability and tracking decision progress.

Conclusion

Industry experts advanced the need for an AI-driven strategy as a possible "disruptive innovation" for PA. It is characterized as a strategy that seeks win-win-win results for payers, providers, and patients. It tries to increase decision-making efficiency, save costs, and eliminate delays by simplifying the process with standardized data and AI. Furthermore, it seeks to promote justice by taking into account socioeconomic determinants of health and assuring just results. HCSC hopes to simplify approvals and reduce administrative constraints on providers by automating the PA process, which is consistent with the efficiency goals outlined. Furthermore, the emphasis on incorporating expert judgment and maintaining justice is consistent with the authors' approach.

References

1. Lenert, L. A., Lane, S., & Wehbe, R. (2023). Could an artificial intelligence approach to prior authorization be more human? *Journal of the American Medical Informatics Association: JAMIA, 30*(5), 989–994. https://doi.org/10.1093/jamia/ocad016
2. Diamond, F. (2023, July 17). *How HCSC Is Using AI to Speed Up Prior Authorization.* Fierce Healthcare. https://www.fiercehealthcare.com/ payers/ hcsc-using-augmented-and-artificialintelligence-quicken-speed-prior-authorization

3. Choudhury, A., & Perumalla, S. (2021). Using machine learning to minimize delays caused by prior authorization: A brief report. *Cogent Engineering, 8*(1), 1944961. https://doi.org/10.1 080/23311916.2021.1944961

4. McKinsey & Company. (2022, April 19). *AI Ushers in Next-Gen Prior Authorization in Healthcare.* https://www.mckinsey.com/indus-tries/ healthcare/our-insights/ai-ushers-in-next-gen-prior-authorization-in-healthcare

5. Health Care Service Corporation. (2023, July 13). *HCSC Transforms Prior Authorization Process.* Health Care Service Corporation (HCSC). https:// www.hcsc.com/newsroom/ news-releases/2023/artificial-intelligence-prior-authorization-process-helps-members-providers#:~: text=HCSC,%20 which%20 received%20over%201.5,up%20to%201,400%20times%20faster

6. Dowd, B. E., & Laugesen, M. J. (2020). Fee-for-service payment is not the (main) problem. *Health Services Research, 55*(4), 491–495. https://doi. org/10.1111/1475-6773.13316

Chapter 7

Recognize and Reward

Recognize or reward the efforts of stakeholders to innovate even at the smallest levels.

To maximize innovation potential, we must not forget the power of motivation in human behavior. People will largely do what they are primarily rewarded and recognized for. For innovation to thrive, consider launching multiple reward and recognition programs to reinforce culture, enhance engagement, and encourage collaboration. Programs should reward not only those who generate ideas but also all the support teams enabling the success. That which is rewarded and recognized is repeated. Innovation will multiply commensurate with affirmation given.

CELEBRATING AN END TO A GREAT PAYVIDER | BY EDWARD W. MARX

We tend to think about recognition and rewards when there is a growth marker to celebrate or a time milestone surpassed. I never gave much thought to celebrating the end of an innovative era until I became the CIO at University Hospitals in Cleveland Ohio. In fact, it was my first major task following my CIO promotion. Assist in the winddown of our innovative payer division.

DOI: 10.4324/9781003381983-7

Background

University Hospitals long had an insurance product called QualChoice. When I was Deputy CIO, I spent a fair amount of time with the QualChoice VP of technology who reported to me. It was my first significant exposure to the payer side of healthcare. What an awakening it was. It makes sense in retrospect, but the payer arm of our healthcare system knew much more about our members than did the provider know about our patients. The QualChoice systems were more sophisticated than our provider side, especially when it came to data and sophisticated analytics. I presumed this was a fundamental reason perhaps why payers always seemed to have the upper hand in contract negotiations and why much of the success of our payer arm came at the mercy of financial losses on the provider side. Their innovation capabilities were ahead of our provider side for sure.

Winding Down

It is not the point of this example to go into the why behind the winding down of an innovative payer plan, but the reasons were very strategic. There were a combination of factors including politics, focus, provider relations, and so forth. All I know is the mandate was given, and we began the process of smartly dismantling an otherwise strong organization. Working with senior management, I argued how important it was to celebrate QualChoice even in such a contrite situation. They agreed.

Philosophy

You see, we often only think of recognition and reward when it comes to growth. But what about failure or death or just the strategic need to shut something down? I postulate that recognition and reward are more important in these circumstances than any other! Recognition and reward events are highly visible and set the foundation for culture. If you don't celebrate failure, you will foster a culture of fear, which may set forth a series of behaviors that hurt your organization. These include lack of risktaking, increased likelihood of deception, and failure to report. You're sending an implicit message you think is silent but is actually very loud—that failure or missing a KPI is shunned and shamed. I encourage the opposite approach where if you celebrate such negatively perceived events, you will actually free your leaders, teams, and organization to improve overall performance. You will create a safer work environment.

The Celebration

I grabbed a few people of all levels, and we planned an amazing celebration. While we would recognize a few individual contributors, we came up with a plan to celebrate each team and the organization. We would allow for a period of mourning, recognizing the negative impact this would have for those losing their jobs but not let that damper the joy of all the great things QualChoice did for its members.

The Event

While we did some individual events for those that preferred to be recognized and rewarded privately, we had one amazing, combined evening.

- Everyone was allowed to bring guests, and families were encouraged to join in.
- Again we acknowledged the sad part of what was taking place and reminded the audience of all the services being made available to help in transition.
- We had a professional video and slideshow developed, which elicited laughter and tears.
- We recognized a few individuals from every level of the organization. Not just VPs but at every level to include analysts.
- We spent most of the evening acknowledging the role of every team. Someone from those teams was chosen to share 2–3 highlights.
- We ended with a talk from our key organizational leaders demonstrating support and acknowledging the great services to the community and members served.

Unexpected Benefits

Many years have passed, and I still have strong relationships with many of my former co-workers. I attribute this in part to our culture of recognition and reward. The winddown could have been handled very differently and in a negative way. We chose the opposite approach, and as a result, many relationships grew from the experience.

Always Celebrate

I was young back then, but that winddown celebration reinforced the need for recognition and reward throughout the rest of my career. I realized how important it is to celebrate even those events that are not typically positive. They make a difference.

STRIVE FOR CREATIVE THINKING AND INNOVATION SHALL FOLLOW | BY SAKSHIKA DHINGRA

From several organizations I have worked for in my career, I have only seen a couple that are able to retain their talent and keep them motivated to do good valuable work.

Long-term employees accumulate valuable knowledge about the company's culture, processes, and operations. Retaining them ensures that this institutional knowledge remains within the organization, benefiting overall efficiency and continuity, and this is crucial to maintain in a highly competitive industry like healthcare. Experienced employees tend to be more productive and perform better. They are familiar with their roles, possess specialized skills, and require less supervision, leading to higher performance levels. When employees feel valued and appreciated, they are more engaged and motivated. Retaining talent involves creating a positive work environment, fostering loyalty, and boosting morale, which in turn enhances productivity. Continuity in talent ensures a consistent pool of skilled individuals capable of driving innovation and adapting to changing market trends. They bring fresh perspectives and contribute to the company's growth and competitiveness.

In my experience, one key element that significantly influences associate engagement and retaining top talent is the concept of "recognize and reward." Thus, this plays a pivotal role in driving innovation. This involves acknowledging and incentivizing individuals or teams for applying a creative approach and experimenting with their way out of problem-solving.

Recognizing and rewarding innovation not only motivates existing employees but also serves as a powerful recruitment tool. Talented professionals are more likely to join organizations that appreciate and reward their innovative contributions.

Recognition and rewards create a positive and motivating work environment. When individuals or teams know that their innovative efforts will be acknowledged and rewarded, it fosters a culture that values creativity and continuous improvement. One way to ensure innovative ideas keep flowing is to have a dedicated set of individuals or a team that looks at areas of stagnation that need overhauling and modernization and formalizes ways to foster innovation around and within.

I am going to share my experience where the organization I worked for prioritized this concept by doing exactly this. They created a team, whose sole focus was "innovation," and their instrument of change was "recognition and reward." The innovation team in the organization initiated an innovation challenge around member experience. They invited employees from various departments to submit innovative ideas and solutions to streamline and improve the member experience. The best part, there was a tangible reward associated with winning the challenge. Healthy competition will always get people excited and spirited to strive for higher results. I am sharing the benefits and outcomes of this initiative, as witnessed by me and my colleagues firsthand, with you later for all to leverage as best practices.

Driver of Employee Engagement

Right from the time this team was introduced, they started pulling the right level of leaders together to drive engagement at the highest levels and equipped these leaders with the right tools for that engagement to trickle down further into their respective teams. Engaged employees are more likely to contribute ideas and actively participate in innovation initiatives. Recognizing and rewarding their efforts reinforces their sense of purpose and connection to the organization, leading to higher levels of engagement.

Accelerating the Innovation Cycle

Anyone who works for healthcare knows that it's a rapidly evolving space, and the beauty of this framework is that it helps you stay ahead, which is key. The work that team was doing accelerated the entire innovation cycle. As we all know, the best strategic ideas come from people who are the closest to it. And this challenge encouraged individuals and teams to experiment, learn from failures, and iterate quickly, ultimately leading to more rapid and effective innovations.

Encouraging Collaborative Innovation

This is the one pleasant side effect that I didn't see coming. We know innovation unequivocally requires collaboration across disciplines and departments, but putting everyone up to a challenge will break down silos, encouraging interdisciplinary collaboration, and knowledge sharing was something that I didn't expect. Leaders and their teams took it upon themselves to reach out to the cross-functional teams, which their solutions were dependent upon and asked for participation, thought partnership, and collaboration, which seemed effortless and not forced—the kind of joining of hands and coming together that is vital for holistic and impactful innovations.

Enhancing Organizational Reputation

The world is a small place, and/or industry is even smaller. Words get around, and it's not hard to imagine the way an organization is being run and the kind of culture its leaders are trying to foster quickly builds its reputation within the industry. Once it's established that your org has a keen focus on innovation and is perpetuating it by rewarding it, you start attracting the right partnerships, investments, and collaborations, which in turn creates a virtuous cycle of innovation and success.

Now that we know how beneficial this framework can be, let's review some simple steps in which you can adopt and replicate the same framework within your own organization:

Transparent Evaluation Criteria

We established a transparent criterion for evaluating the submissions. They emphasized factors such as efficiency improvements, error reduction, and positive impact on provider and member experiences.

Recognition Events

Throughout the innovation challenge, organized recognition events were conducted to showcase the efforts of participants for continued interest, momentum, and engagement. Shortlisted teams presented their ideas to leadership, creating a platform for visibility and acknowledgment. And the final selection of initiatives that got rewarded and the necessary funding to be executed went on to be showcased in the All Employee Townhall. The progress of delivery was then shared on an ongoing basis through successful completion, and even afterward, we knew what kind of impact was being made and whether that was close to what was expected. Success stories were brought back to all associates so this cycle of innovation could continue.

Monetary Rewards and Incentives

We know that incentives and performance are closely related and are a well-studied aspect of organizational behavior and management. Incentives, whether monetary or nonmonetary, can have a significant impact on individual and collective performance within a workplace. The leaders who ran the challenge knew this very well, and recognizing the financial aspect, monetary rewards were introduced for the winning teams. These rewards were linked to the actual implementation and success of the proposed innovations, creating a direct correlation between effort and reward.

Skill Development Opportunities

This one was my personal favorite. Just as growth can mean different things to different people, so do rewards. While the monetary incentives do add a certain competitive spirit to spice up the challenge, the real motivation for some select associates can come from an opportunity to learn and develop their skills further. The innovation team launched a program in parallel to this challenge that included access to training programs, workshops, and mentorship, enhancing the professional growth of individuals involved in the innovation challenge.

Outcomes: As expected, both the concept of the innovation team and their first challenge were a huge success. The winning ideas were implemented, leading to significant improvements. The innovation team continued working on multiple initiatives, all focused on driving innovation and bringing work forward, which was potentially going to give our organization the disruptive advantage that is much needed in the industry today.

Conclusion

This is just one technique to orchestrate a reward for associates to engage their creative faculties and do out-of-the-box thinking. Recognizing such individuals and teams and rewarding them to encourage more of the same must be embedded at every step of the implementation and delivery cycle. That is the only way the work we do will result in tangible improvements, increased employee engagement, and positive impact on customer satisfaction. In conclusion, the "recognize and reward" framework is instrumental in driving healthcare innovation, and as the industry continues to evolve, it will remain a cornerstone for success and progress in the industry. And if we continue to reward creativity, innovation will follow.

INCENTIVIZING PAYER HEALTHCARE INNOVATION | ANONYMOUS

Introduction

In the dynamic landscape of healthcare, innovation is essential for enhancing member and patient care, accessibility, and cost-effectiveness. Payer models, including insurance companies and government programs, play a central role in healthcare innovation. The theme of "recognize and reward" underscores the importance of acknowledging and incentivizing innovation within payer models. This chapter explores how recognizing and rewarding innovation can drive positive change in payer healthcare systems, ultimately benefiting patients and the healthcare industry as a whole.

The Evolving Role of Payer Models

To understand the significance of recognizing and rewarding innovation in payer healthcare, we must first appreciate the evolving role of payer models.

Payers as Crucial Players

Traditionally, payers have focused on administrative tasks, risk assessment, and claims processing. However, the healthcare landscape has evolved significantly, necessitating a more proactive and innovative approach from payers.

Payer-Driven Innovation

Innovative payer models are stepping up to meet the evolving needs of the healthcare system. These payers are not merely financial intermediaries; they are proactive drivers of innovation, seeking to improve patient outcomes, lower costs, and enhance the quality of care.

The "Recognize and Reward" Approach

The "recognize and reward" theme underscores the importance of acknowledging and incentivizing innovation within payer models. By establishing mechanisms that recognize and reward innovative efforts, payers can create a culture that fosters and sustains innovation.

Acknowledging Innovation

Highlighting Success Stories: Payers can share stories and case studies of successful innovations within their organizations. This showcases the value of innovation and inspires others to contribute their ideas.

Awards and Recognition: Establishing awards and recognition programs within payer models can be an effective way to celebrate innovative achievements. These programs can range from acknowledging individual contributions to team efforts and even recognizing external partnerships that drive innovation.

Internal Communication: Regularly communicating innovative initiatives and their impact to employees can help create a culture that values and encourages innovation. Employees who feel their efforts are recognized and valued are more likely to contribute innovative ideas.

Incentivizing Innovation

Financial Rewards: Payers can provide financial incentives to employees or teams that develop and implement successful innovations. This can include bonuses, profit-sharing, or equity participation in the innovation's success.

Professional Development: Offering opportunities for professional growth and development can incentivize innovation. Payers can support employees in pursuing advanced degrees, certifications, or training that enhances their ability to drive innovation.

Resource Allocation: Allocating resources, such as time, personnel, and funding, to support innovation projects signals a commitment to fostering innovation. Payers should establish dedicated budgets for innovation and allocate resources strategically.

Benefits of Recognizing and Rewarding Innovation

Embracing the "recognize and reward" approach offers several notable benefits within payer healthcare innovation.

Encouragement of Creativity

Recognizing and rewarding innovation encourages employees to think creatively and seek innovative solutions to healthcare challenges. This ultimately leads to the development of more effective and efficient healthcare processes and services.

Increased Employee Engagement

Employees who feel their innovative efforts are acknowledged and rewarded are more likely to be engaged and motivated. This can lead to higher levels of job satisfaction and a more productive workforce.

Enhanced Competitive Advantage

Payers that actively recognize and reward innovation are better positioned to compete in the healthcare market. They can differentiate themselves by offering innovative solutions and services that attract both patients and healthcare providers.

Improved Member Care

Innovation in payer models can lead to improved patient care, better health-care outcomes, and increased patient satisfaction. Patients benefit from more accessible and effective healthcare services.

Challenges and Considerations

While recognizing and rewarding innovation has numerous benefits, there are challenges and considerations that payer models must address.

Measuring Innovation Impact

Determining the impact of innovation can be challenging. Payers must estab-lish clear metrics and evaluation criteria to assess the success and effective-ness of innovative initiatives.

Balancing Risk and Reward

Innovation inherently involves some level of risk. Payers must strike a bal-ance between encouraging innovation and managing potential risks, such as financial investments that may not yield immediate returns.

Fostering a Culture of Innovation

Creating a culture that values innovation requires a concerted effort. Payers must ensure that all employees feel empowered to contribute their ideas and that leaders actively champion innovation.

Avoiding Innovation for Its Own Sake

Innovation should be driven by a genuine desire to improve patient care and healthcare processes, rather than simply pursuing novelty. Payers must ensure that innovation efforts are aligned with their mission and goals.

The Future of Payer Healthcare Innovation

The "recognize and reward" approach is poised to shape the future of payer healthcare innovation in significant ways.

Technological Advancements

Recognizing and rewarding innovation will drive the adoption of cutting-edge technologies in payer models. This includes advancements in data analytics, telehealth, and artificial intelligence, which can revolutionize healthcare delivery.

Member-Centered Care

Innovation efforts will increasingly focus on enhancing patient-centered care. Payers will develop and implement initiatives that improve patient experiences, engagement, and satisfaction.

Value-Based Care Models

Payers will continue to transition toward value-based care models, which emphasize quality over quantity. Recognizing and rewarding innovations that support these models will become a central focus.

Collaboration and Partnerships

Payers will actively seek partnerships and collaborations with healthcare providers, tech companies, and other stakeholders to drive innovation. These partnerships will lead to the development of novel solutions and services.

One real-world business case where payer organizations achieved transformation in healthcare by recognizing and rewarding innovation is the collaboration between Independence Blue Cross (IBC), a prominent health insurer, and Comcast NBCUniversal to launch the "Independence@Home" program.

Case Example: Independence Blue Cross and Comcast NBCUniversal—Independence@Home Program

Background: Independence Blue Cross (IBC) recognized the need to transform the way healthcare services are delivered to its members, particularly seniors with complex healthcare needs. Comcast NBCUniversal, known for its expertise in technology and content delivery, saw an opportunity to leverage its capabilities to improve the healthcare experience for seniors.

Recognizing and Rewarding Innovation

Shared Vision: IBC and Comcast NBC Universal shared a vision of using technology to enable seniors to age in place while receiving high-quality healthcare services. They recognized that this vision required innovative solutions and a patient-centered approach.

Strategic Collaboration: The partnership involved the creation of the Independence@ Home program, which aimed to leverage technology, telehealth, and home-based care to support seniors' health and wellbeing. The program outlined a roadmap for achieving these goals.

Provider Engagement: IBC and Comcast NBCUniversal actively engaged with healthcare providers, including primary care physicians, specialists, and home health agencies, to build a network that could deliver comprehensive care to seniors at home.

Data and Analytics: The program leveraged data and analytics to monitor seniors' health, track outcomes, and identify potential issues. This data-driven approach informed decision-making and personalized care plans.

Innovation and Impact

Value-Based Care at Home: Independence@ Home introduced a value-based care model that encouraged seniors to receive healthcare services at home rather than in institutional settings. This disruptive approach aimed to reduce healthcare costs while improving patient outcomes.

Remote Monitoring and Telehealth: The program provided seniors with remote monitoring devices and access to telehealth services, enabling healthcare providers to monitor their health remotely and conduct virtual visits.

Rewards for Healthy Behavior: Independence@Home included reward programs that incentivized seniors to engage in healthy behaviors, adhere to their care plans, and actively participate in their healthcare decisions. This recognition and reward system encouraged positive health choices.

Improved Member Outcomes: By focusing on preventive care, early intervention, and ongoing monitoring, the program aimed to improve health outcomes, reduce hospital admissions, and enhance the quality of life for seniors.

Enhanced Member Experience: Seniors received more personalized, patientcentered care in the comfort of their homes. The program aimed to reduce the burden of traveling to healthcare facilities for appointments.

Scalability: The success of Independence@ Home demonstrated the potential for scaling home-based care models and disruptive innovation in senior healthcare.

Alignment of Incentives: The program aligned the incentives of payers, providers, and patients by promoting healthier behaviors, reducing healthcare costs, and improving patient outcomes.

The collaboration between Independence Blue Cross and Comcast NBCUniversal through the Independence@Home program exemplifies how payer organizations can recognize and reward innovation in healthcare. By embracing technology, telehealth, and value-based care, they disrupted traditional healthcare delivery models, improving the quality of care for seniors and transforming the way healthcare is delivered to this demographic. This innovative approach has the potential to reshape senior healthcare and aging-in-place strategies.

Another great example is the collaboration between Humana and the University of Louisville to establish the "Humana Integrated Health System Sciences Institute."

Case Example: Humana and the University of Louisville—Humana Integrated Health System Sciences Institute

Background: Humana, a leading health insurance company, recognized the importance of advancing healthcare delivery and promoting innovative solutions to enhance the well-being of its members. The University of Louisville, a research-intensive institution, had expertise in healthcare research and innovation. Together, they sought to create an institute dedicated to driving innovation in healthcare.

Recognizing and Rewarding Innovation

Shared Vision: Humana and the University of Louisville shared a vision of promoting innovation in healthcare through research, education, and the implementation of cutting-edge solutions.

Strategic Collaboration: The partnership resulted in the establishment of the Humana Integrated Health System Sciences Institute. The institute was designed to be a collaborative hub that brought together researchers, health-care professionals, and innovators to work on transformative healthcare projects.

Funding and Resources: Humana provided significant financial support to the institute, recognizing the potential for innovation to improve healthcare outcomes, reduce costs, and enhance the patient experience. This funding served as a recognition of the value of healthcare innovation.

Research and Development: The institute focused on conducting research, developing new healthcare technologies, and implementing innovative care delivery models. It also offered educational programs to foster a culture of innovation in healthcare.

Innovation and Impact

Research and Development: The institute's research efforts led to the development of new technologies, care models, and strategies aimed at improving patient care. This included initiatives related to remote monitoring, tele-health, and data analytics.

Education and Collaboration: The institute provided a platform for collaboration between academia, healthcare providers, and industry partners. It promoted a culture of innovation by offering educational programs, workshops, and innovation challenges.

Improved Patient Outcomes: Through innovative research and solutions, the institute aimed to improve patient outcomes, enhance the quality of care, and increase the efficiency of healthcare delivery.

Cost Efficiency: Innovations developed by the institute had the potential to reduce healthcare costs through improved care coordination, early intervention, and more effective use of healthcare resources.

Recognition and Awards: Innovations and research outcomes from the institute received recognition and awards in the healthcare industry, further validating the importance of innovation in healthcare.

Fostering Innovation Ecosystem: The collaboration between Humana and the University of Louisville created an innovation ecosystem that attracted talent, entrepreneurs, and healthcare professionals interested in advancing healthcare through technology and research.

The Humana Integrated Health System Sciences Institute represents a real-world example of a payer organization recognizing and rewarding innovation in healthcare. By providing financial support, fostering research and development, and promoting collaboration, Humana and the University of Louisville contributed to the creation of innovative healthcare solutions that have the potential to transform patient care, reduce costs, and advance the field of healthcare delivery. This collaboration underscores the importance of recognizing and incentivizing innovation in the healthcare industry.

Conclusion

"Recognize and reward" is a powerful driver of innovation within payer healthcare models. By acknowledging and incentivizing innovation, payer models can foster a culture that values creativity, ultimately leading to improved member and patient care, increased employee engagement, and a competitive advantage in the healthcare industry. In an ever-evolving healthcare landscape, embracing this approach is essential for achieving meaningful and sustainable innovation that benefits patients, providers, and the healthcare industry as a whole.

Chapter 8

Co-create Solutions

Appreciate the complexity of attention that innovation requires, and expose the organization to demands from all stakeholders.

Innovation does not happen by innovators alone. We must be careful not to fall into a belief that innovation is reserved for one person or a special team whose primary function is to develop solutions to problems or invention to opportunities. Innovation is primarily cultural and thrives in team-based organizations. Avoid the trap that innovation is for a select few and all others are discounted. Innovation happens best when it becomes the culture of the entire organization and everyone has the opportunity to engage.

REVOLUTIONIZING THE MEMBER EXPERIENCE | BY TANVIR KHAN AND TINA HSINTING LIU

How are AI and generative AI-enabled digital human technologies improving health plan operation efficiency and health equity

Skyrocketing healthcare costs, as well as an alarming number of cases of healthcare inequity and lack of access in certain communities and demographics, have been one of the biggest issues in the United States over the last few years. National health expenditure was over $4.3 trillion in 2021, or $12,914 per person, and accounted for 18.3% of gross domestic product (GDP). National Health spending is projected to hit $7.2 trillion by 2031.

Is this sustainable, and are we, as a society, getting the right care to the right people with this colossal investment?

DOI: 10.4324/9781003381983-8

Triple Aim (2007)	Quadruple Aim (2014)	Quintuple Aim (2022)
• IHI (Institute of Healthcare Improvement) introduced the framework • Improving the patient experience of care (including quality and satisfaction) • Improving the health of populations • Reducing the per capita cost of health care • Donald M. Berwick, MD	• A term coined by Thomas Bodenheimer, MD in <u>Annals of Family Medicine</u> paper • The Quadruple Aim framework was designed to help health care organizations to achieve • Triple Aim + Improve provider satisfaction (professional well-being)	• Dr. Kedar Mate, CEO and president of IHI and a group of healthcare leaders proposed • Four essential steps to address health equity 1)identify disparities, 2)design and implement evidence-based interventions to reduce them, 3)invest in equity measurement 4)incentivize the achievement of equity

Figure 8.1   The quadruple aim.

According to WestHealth, an estimated 112 million (44%) American adults are struggling to pay for healthcare. Meanwhile, the Healthy People 2030 report states that about 1 in 10 people in the United States don't have health insurance. Healthy People 2030's emphasis on health equity is closely tied to its focus on health literacy and social determinants of health (Economic Stability, Education, Health Care Access & Quality, Neighborhood & Environment and Social & Community), which drive 70% of healthcare outcomes and are vital to healthcare transformation.

Efforts to address these issues have been made in the past. In 2007, the IHI (Institute of Healthcare Improvement) introduced the "Triple Aim," a concept of improved patient experience, better outcomes, and lower costs as key to healthcare transformation. There is no care without the clinician, so clinician well-being was added to turn it into the "Quadruple Aim."

However, the COVID-19 pandemic dramatically underscored how our healthcare ecosystem and the economy are inextricably linked. So IHI introduced "Quintuple Aim," which incorporates health equity as another key element to realize good health for everyone by improving access, reducing cost of care, and improving health outcomes.

These needs have placed increasing pressure on payers to implement innovative solutions. To help address these aims, US healthcare payers are prioritizing growth, experience, and technology modernization as top enterprise goals.

Can Generative AI and Digital Human Help?

The convergence of generative AI, digital human, and mobile technologies has created a unique opportunity to address challenges to access, cost, health outcomes, and clinician workloads. Generative AI, or GenAI, is a form of AI that enables computers to generate new, original, and human-like content using previously created content, such as text, audio, video, images, and code. Generative AI possesses the unique potential to transform work by creating new content, streamlining processes, enhancing efficiency through automation, and promoting creativity and innovation.

How is generative AI different from current technologies? Chatbots and self-service solutions are used like never before—they are fast, efficient, and flexible—but they lack emotions and a human touch. At the same time, there is a need for automating and utilizing the limited resources of employees in the best possible way.

The research and experience of the NTT DATA team have shown that the emerging discipline of "Human + Machine" solutions will help payers achieve their "Quintuple Aim." These findings have been further supported by Gartner's recent publication "Use-Case Prism: Generative AI for U.S. Healthcare Payers," which included 20+ GenAI use-case scorecards and stated that GenAI is an "enabler" of specific use cases.

NTT DATA's data and intelligence approach is based on two levers in which GenAI plays a very significant role.

Business Disruption through Data and Intelligence: Artificial Intelligence is a crucial technology that has the potential to revolutionize most industries and create cutting-edge solutions and business models. With the right technical and organizational capabilities in place, organizations can harness the full power of AI and data to bring innovative solutions to market quickly and at scale. The responsible use of AI and data, in accordance with regulatory compliance, ensures that organizations can maximize the benefits of this revolutionary technology. With the shift to Whole Person Health that combines Care and Wellness, Data & Intelligence driven understanding of members and their needs and the next best action that can be taken by the payers to drive Whole Person Health outcomes.

Data Democratization: Most payer organizations could greatly benefit from enhancing their data access and analytical capabilities. This can be achieved by removing barriers to accessing reliable data and providing equal access to all employees. Effective data governance is also crucial in ensuring that the data is trustworthy, secure, and of high quality. Additionally, it is essential to implement upskilling programs for users and data literacy initiatives to ensure the success of these efforts. Payers should implement programs to drive data literacy—that includes data governance, improving data reliability and quality. The next-gen technologies can enable guided actions for payers' employees to take actions and implement strategies that are member centric. To enable such capabilities, payers should pursue data and intelligence as an enterprise solution that directly impacts experience metrics (e.g., net promoter score [NPS]), outcome metrics (medical loss ratio [MLR]) optimization, health outcomes, and so on, and empower employees to unlock the power of data, analytics, and technologies through technology upskilling and data literacy.

HIPAA's privacy and security rules, healthcare ethics, and emerging data usage guidelines make the use of Generative AI in healthcare a compliance minefield and need a very strong governance policy before any meaningful generative AI-led transformation can be implemented.

It.human®: Combining the Best of Human and Digital Interactions

One of the biggest areas where generative AI's impact can clearly be seen is customer experience. By automating tasks, improving efficiency, and providing personalized service through a digital human, AI can help organizations provide a better customer experience, which leads to increased satisfaction and loyalty.

NTT DATA's digital human platform, It.human®, was built with the vision to add a "smiling face" to all self-service solutions worldwide. An It.human® platform works as an interaction between a user and persona on a screen. The main technology components are the following:

■ Digital Human: A high-fidelity, lifelike digital avatar looking like a human, with whom users can interact with, including movement and micro-expressions. In addition to the it.human® on the screen, it is also possible to display multimedia content including audio, video, and images. The user interface can also be augmented with touch elements.
■ Artificial Speech: Users can interact with the it.human® using natural spoken language. The it.human® is able to both hear and understand natural language, and responds using a natural-sounding voice.

- Computer Vision: The it.human® can detect when people are in front of it.
- Conversational Artificial Intelligence: The it.human® can understand what the user wants and gives an appropriate and informative answer. The answer can be enhanced by integrating with back-end systems and services.

In simple terms, the it.human® digital human has

- sight—can see and recognize people's faces and emotions
- memory—can remember facts, faces, and previous conversations
- voice—can speak in the natural tone and sound excited, empathetic, and neutral
- hearing—can hear people speak and understand natural language
- emotions—is always positive and empathetic
- appearance—can express emotions and is recognizable.

The platform has already been implemented in various use cases. At the world's oldest golf championship, the Open, NTT DATA helped take the spectator experience to the next level with its generative AI-powered, interactive digital human named "Lottie" to create a unique and engaging onsite experience.

it.human® platform is not just limited to installation via a kiosk. The it.human® technology can also be used on laptops, mobile phones, and

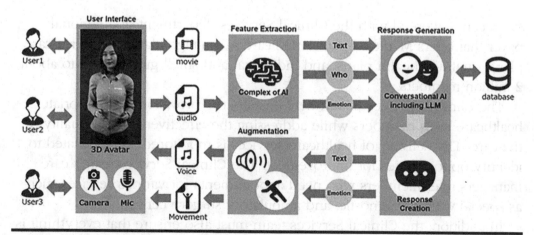

Figure 8.2   It.human® platform process.

QR codes. This flexibility has allowed the NTT DATA team to work with payers and other healthcare organizations to improve outcomes and solve "Quintuple Aim's" health equity and healthcare access challenges.

Staying Compliant When Using Digital Human Technology

Ethics and compliance are very important to digital human solution deployments. We need to make sure that data is protected by the most comprehensive enterprisewide security and compliance controls. For example, generated content must not infringe upon existing copyright or intellectual property rights. Addressing data privacy concerns is also a point of emphasis. With the it.human® platform, everything happens within your private cloud subscription.

One of the biggest issues when it comes to using digital human and other AI technology is ethical considerations and bias mitigation. When training on a large corpus of text data or image data, the model naturally replicates any representative biases in its source. Limiting the input dataset could, in turn, help limit the biases in training datasets and mitigate them. ChatGPT, for instance, has content moderation guardrails in place to prevent sexual, hateful, violent, or harmful content.

Payer Use Case: Improving the Member Experience with Digital Human Technology

We recently worked with the Clinical Services department of a regional payer that offers Medicaid plans, Medicare Advantage plans, long-term care plans, qualified health plans, and individual and small group plans to about 2 million members.

The Clinical Services department ensures the provision of appropriate healthcare to its members while addressing the effectiveness and quality of the care. The delivery of healthcare services is monitored and evaluated to identify opportunities for improvement. The Clinical Services team's care managers refer members who need appointments for various services such as specialty, PCP, diagnostic, and ambulatory surgery centers.

In addition, the Clinical Services team must also ensure that everything is up to HEDIS® (Healthcare Effectiveness Data and Information Set) standards. HEDIS includes 92 standardized performance measures under six categories. HEDIS reporting is required by NCQA and the Centers for Medicare and Medicaid Services (CMS) for use in payer accreditation, star ratings, and regulatory compliance.

The VP of Clinical Services told us that her biggest challenge was assessing and managing the medical appointment scheduling of members because many providers don't have electronic appointment scheduling and members are not tech-savvy.

To help the department address this, we started with a few collaborative workshops to learn more about priorities, workflow, KPIs, gaps, and business rules. From there, the NTT DATA team was able to identify how the it.human® digital human functions and benefits could help solve these challenges.

One of the biggest highlights was the ability to optimize the scheduling process, as well as the cancellation or modification of an appointment previously made. The digital human agent can also be configured to validate for various criteria such as language, age, area, and health conditions.

The digital human agent can handle individual queries at mass scale and provides 24/7 access to users using conversational self-service. At any time, the agent can walk the user through the process of selecting the closest location by zip code, finding a day and time, and securing an appointment for an appointment. This results in reduced hold times and alleviated pressure on the department's contact center. This capability, with a defined workflow-driven interface, allows users to locate as well as confirm, cancel, and change appointments in or near their location.

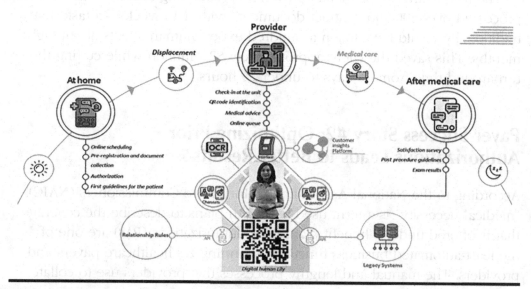

Figure 8.3   It.human® platform workflow.

Payer Success Story #1: Saving Million Dollars with Intelligent Document Processing

Our national payer client faced challenges related to the high volume of documentation, provider contracts, and regulation adherence associated with its speedy growth. To help the organization address these issues and improve its data processing capabilities, we co-created a "Human + Machine" solution that was scalable to the client's operational structure and needs.

Implementation of the solution was centered around NTT DATA's NUCLEUS™ Intelligent Document Processing (IDP)/Robotic Context Processor (USA patent pending application #62/636,074), rebooted traditional optical character recognition (OCR)-based document processing. This advanced cognitive automation engine identifies and extracts relevant information from unstructured documents and provides instructions based on the extracted information and intelligent algorithm to perform appropriate actions.

The solution uses a convolutional neural network (CNN) model and natural language processing (NLP) to dynamically identify the entities and values in a table and even analyzes sentiments. It works seamlessly with robotic process automation (RPA) platforms and includes an option to plug in third-party OCR/intelligent character recognition (ICR) engines via application programming interfaces (APIs) and dynamic link library (DLL) integrations to extend and enhance the engine's performance. Its self-learning capabilities continuously improve document processing accuracy while minimizing failures.

The results after implementation were a resounding success. The solution processed over 500,000 contract documents within 13 weeks—a task that traditionally would have taken a hundred expert human agents about eight months. This saved the client approximately $2.5 million while cutting the turnaround time from 45 days to under 24 hours.

Payer Success Story #2: Optimizing Prior Authorizations Leads to Better Results

According to the National Association of Insurance Commissioners (NAIC), "medical necessity" is a term used by health plans to describe the coverage that is offered under a benefit plan. Prior authorizations (PAs) are one of the least-automated business functions spanning US healthcare payers and providers. The manual and lengthy processes that providers use to collate patient data for submission and that payers use to evaluate requests are beyond cumbersome.

These inefficient, segmented, and siloed workflows result in claim process delays and member/provider dissatisfaction. According to the 2021 American Medical Association (AMA) Prior Authorization survey, 94% of respondents reported that prior authorization (PA) resulted in care delays. To make things worse, 86% of practicing physicians found the administrative burden associated with PAs as "high or extremely high." In an effort to fix this, the Centers for Medicare & Medicaid Services (CMS) issued a proposal in 2022 designed to address how burdensome prior authorization is on the healthcare system, calling for this process to join the digital world.

We co-created "Human+Machine" scalable solutions to help a mid-sized Blue plan client improve provider and member satisfaction and reduce cost by implementing Clinical Language Pro (CLP), which is an AI-integrated natural language processing (NLP) solution. It integrates with SNOMED CT, LOINC®, HCPCS, and IDC and can process over 16 million clinical terms and 4.4 million clinical concepts. The solution was built with an auto-prior authorization AI tool with manual prior-authorization review recommendations to expedite automatic decisions, improve process efficiency, and provide a continuous feedback loop with unstructured data supplements. The result was an estimated 3 million human hours saved annually across 1 million members with 45.6% auto-approval, 0.1% auto denial, 51.3% manual approval, 3% manual denial, and greater than 99% recall accuracy.

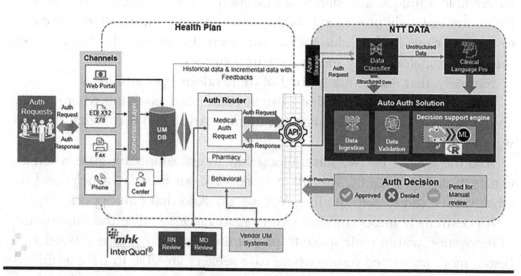

Figure 8.4   It.human® platform interface.

Co-create Solutions Can Yield Unprecedented Results

In conclusion, the integration of human and machine capabilities has immense potential to transform payer operations and care management to improve outcomes and experiences. We want to help payers send the right message to the right person at the right time with tailored communications that will motivate the member to act.

By embracing the collaborative approach of combining human expertise and empathy with the computational power and efficiency of machines, we are optimistic that our solutions can revolutionize payer operations and help them achieve the "Quintuple Aim" (lower costs with improved patient and provider experience, better outcomes, and health equity).

However, to fully harness these benefits, it is crucial to prioritize ethical considerations, data privacy, and equitable access to ensure that the human-machine partnership in healthcare remains patient-centered and inclusive. But when implemented correctly, the integration of human and machine capabilities has the immense potential to transform payer operations and care management by providing massive improvements in experiences and outcomes for everyone involved.

CREATING THE PERFECT ATMOSPHERE FOR INNOVATION | BY SAKSHIKA DHINGRA

Payers hold a unique and significant position in the healthcare ecosystem. Payers are uniquely positioned, as the aggregators of information and data to use it to drive health value for our members. Payers are also the next best action coordinators in the members' care journeys.

Naturally, that makes it a hotbed of tremendous opportunity.

Here's a quick litmus test that I use anytime I am assessing where we as an industry are on the innovation continuum. And I call this "What I would want for my family test."

And the answer is, "We have a long way to go" simply because when it comes to our own family, we call in favors, ask our friends for help, and do whatever we can to skip the line. Yes, we do. And that's an opportunity.

It is extremely important that payer organizations realize the importance of innovation within their space to propel the whole landscape toward a better, more integrated future where care seekers are able to have a unified experience.

In this chapter, I have attempted to shine a bright light on three basic guiding principles that payer organizations can follow to create an atmosphere that not only is conducive to innovation but fosters it from within.

As simple as this first principle may sound, I was amazed at how often this gets forgotten in day-to-day business discussions—keeping consumers at the front and center of every initiative. Being able to create ongoing value for our customers is what distinguishes the most successful organizations from others. I say "ongoing" because it's not a one-time thing and requires a mindset of excellence around the consumer. This would mean that the team puts the customer at the center of all their decisions, from their daily priorities to their processes to how they spend company dollars. Developing a mindset of how the customer will benefit from our actions will help connect decisions to serving the customer. It will also help connect actions to a greater purpose while strengthening team and culture. It's a great framework and helps embed continuous innovation by improvement into the very fabric of an organization.

One of the biggest barriers in creating a consumer-centric organization is that organizations are structured around the work they do within the four walls (virtual or otherwise). They start by organizing themselves by technology and then departments, and then there are some that are further along, and they organize themselves by consumer journey steps. But think about it from a consumer perspective. A consumer does NOT get value from these touchpoints; a consumer gets value from the whole stream. And frankly most organizations don't understand value. The key is to understand our consumers—whether they are providers or members—and what they value from our service. Once this is done, orgs can immediately see how structuring by specialization created a labyrinth of an org where no one fully understands how value is created.

Organizing around value streams is the first and the most foundational step a payer organization can take toward becoming a truly innovative org. Bringing everyone who touches a workstream closer together will enable them to co-create solutions that would maximize the value for our consumers.

Now that we have the form right, let's talk about function. "Form follows function" is a principle of design associated with late 19thand early 20th-century architecture and industrial design in general, which states that the shape of a building or object should primarily relate to its intended function or purpose. And it's extremely relevant to my next guiding principle, that is, to architect the right operating model.

An operating model describes how an organization delivers value. Healthcare is an industry that experiences constant change and disruption, and the digital acceleration during the pandemic has put us even more behind than other industries like retail as far as innovation is concerned. Naturally, market obsolescence is a growing threat for many organizations out there, especially with new, more tech-savvy market entrants that have the technology and the resources it takes to innovate. The result is a wave of transformative initiatives these organizations are going through. And many transformation efforts begin with reinventing the operating model.

The key to reinventing your operating model is to have a unified vision, a central strategy to which the model can be aligned to. Nothing brings an organization together to co-create solutions like a singular vision that can act as the North Star.

When asked in a survey what topics C-suite-level executives discuss most frequently as an organization, 57% of survey respondents put developing and creating new products in the top five. And many blame failure to innovate effectively on organizational inertia—focusing on protecting the current state while avoiding or delaying responses to marketplace disruptions. An organization that is not siloed and is structured to bring people together so they can collaborate, be inclusive, and co-create is in a better position to overcome the organization inertia referenced earlier.

The third guiding principle speaks to the age-old divide between business and technology—a technology-centric framework alone will never be an answer. Technology is a means to an end—not an end in itself. The starting point for any technological solution needs to be the customer or end user.

Sometimes, in a race to become a technology-driven organization and make use of new advances in technology to gain a competitive advantage, it's easy to forget the greater purpose, that is, to better serve customers while evolving with the marketplace. And this is where design thinking comes into play.

Design thinking is a human-centered approach to innovation that fundamentally rests on two essential principles: empathy and objectivity.

Empathy. In order to innovate, you must understand the people you're trying to serve, the environments and contexts in which they operate, and the interactions they have with the world. Innovation all begins with observation: through empathy, you can identify the problems people experience today as they try to get "jobs" done in their lives or work. It's important to document your observations carefully: notes, photos, videos, interviews, and customer quotes. These should be compiled in a diary that will help you understand what the customer "does," "thinks," and "feels." In turn, these observations will give you insights that can help you identify and prioritize opportunities to innovate.

Objectivity. In this phase, you also want to keep an open mind and avoid being prisoner of assumptions that might blur your thinking. The challenge for leaders is to act as anthropologists who immerse themselves in the user context to see the world from their perspective—and understand reality as it is, not as they wish it to be.

At the end of the day, design thinking is focused on having an end-user perspective for value creation and people orientation at the center of their approach, and it's pivotal to prevent us from ending up with technology-centric frameworks that are far from our customer needs. Instead, we need purpose-centric frameworks that are cutting edge and are focused on serving a customer need in the marketplace.

While we are on the subject of design thinking, I would like to touch on another competency that is fundamental in establishing a place where solutions get co-created: inclusive and transparent decision-making. Whether an org is transparent on how decisions get made and whether an org is transparent on the actual decisions are two very different concepts and realities. Even socializing the "how" of decision-making can be powerful and engaging. And what we hear often is that keeping everyone up on the actual decision-making in a growth atmosphere is almost impossible to do.

It's not impossible.

Being transparent about your decisionmaking process builds contractual trust. Contractual trust calls for honest and frequent communication. When people advocate for transparency, what they typically care about is not knowing every detail. We quickly realize that's impossible. But rather they care about understanding how and why the decisions are made and how and why they can participate in iterating on the actual solution.

Another key point to remember is that those impacted by decisions are often the best to determine whether those decisions were effective. Did we end up getting the desired effect? And within that maybe retrospectively thinking how the decisionmaking process could be improved. This is the "why" that people most crave. The why is scalable because it carries the original intent of the decision and not just the tactic. And then we enter into a partnership to continuously improve on those decisions.

It's the combination—trust and collaboration—that turns the typical hierarchical decision-making model into a partnership. And that lets information sharing scale.

To accelerate a culture where solutions are co-created keeping consumers in mind, payers will need to revisit what is the value they are creating for their consumers and how they deliver this value, all enabled by bringing people who create this value together and closer. Catalysts in this framework infusing collaboration are strategic alignment, consistent processes, and transparent decision-making. When you have all of these elements working in unison, innovation happens.

THE CATALYST FOR PAYER HEALTHCARE INNOVATION | ANONYMOUS

Introduction

In the contemporary healthcare landscape, innovation is not a luxury but a necessity. Payer models, encompassing insurance companies and government programs, hold a pivotal role in shaping healthcare systems. The theme of "co-create solutions" emphasizes the importance of fostering collaborative efforts among all stakeholders in payer healthcare models to drive innovation.

We took an academic approach to our chapter. Rather than stick to our experience exclusively, we spent time researching the topic in order to ensure a holistic understanding of our grand proposition, how to ensure innovation with payers??? You are reading our findings. This chapter explores the significance of co-creation as a strategy for payer healthcare innovation, shedding light on its potential benefits and challenges. As our outcomes continue to mature, we end with a few examples from our colleagues.

Payer Models: The Engines of Healthcare Transformation

Understanding the essential role of payer models in healthcare is foundational to comprehending the significance of co-creation in their innovation efforts.

Payers as Healthcare Orchestrators

Payers serve as intermediaries between patients and healthcare providers, managing financial aspects like claims processing, reimbursements, and coverage verification. However, their role extends beyond these administrative tasks to influence healthcare policies, delivery, and innovation.

Payers as Innovators

Modern payer models have evolved into catalysts of innovation, striving to enhance patient outcomes, reduce costs, and elevate the quality of care. They recognize that embracing technology and fostering collaboration are essential components of innovation in healthcare.

The "Co-create Solutions" Approach

The "co-create solutions" theme underscores the importance of collaborative cocreation efforts among payers, healthcare providers, patients, and other stakeholders. It emphasizes that innovation in payer models should not be a top-down process but a collaborative endeavor that includes the collective intelligence of all participants.

Collaboration Across Stakeholders

Member Involvement: Payers should actively involve patients in decision-making processes. Patients' first-hand experiences and insights can be invaluable in identifying gaps and co-creating solutions that meet their needs.

Healthcare Provider Collaboration: Effective communication and collaboration between payers and healthcare providers are vital. This can lead to more efficient care coordination, reduced administrative burdens, and improved patient care.

Community Engagement: Collaborating with community organizations, advocacy groups, and local leaders is crucial to understanding and addressing social determinants of health and healthcare disparities.

Breaking Down Silos

Interoperability: Payers should advocate for and invest in interoperable healthcare IT systems that allow seamless data sharing between different healthcare entities. Breaking down silos ensures that patient information is readily accessible and accurate.

Data-Sharing Initiatives: Payers can take a lead in developing data-sharing initiatives that encourage transparency and collaboration among various stakeholders. These initiatives can contribute to betterinformed decision-making and improved care coordination.

Cultural Competence: Recognizing and addressing cultural differences in healthcare practices and communication is essential for effective collaboration, especially in diverse communities.

The Benefits of Co-creating Solutions in Payer Healthcare Innovation

Embracing the "co-create solutions" approach offers several significant benefits within payer healthcare innovation.

Member-Centered Care

Collaborative efforts involving patients lead to patient-centric solutions. These solutions prioritize patient experiences, needs, and preferences, ultimately enhancing the quality of care and patient satisfaction.

Enhanced Care Coordination

Effective collaboration between payers and healthcare providers results in more streamlined care coordination. This leads to a reduction in duplicated services, fewer medical errors, and better patient outcomes.

Innovative Solutions

Co-creation fosters the exchange of diverse ideas and expertise. Payers, healthcare providers, patients, and other stakeholders can collaboratively develop innovative solutions that address complex healthcare challenges.

Health Equity

Collaboration with community organizations and leaders allows payers to better understand and address health disparities and social determinants of health. Co-created solutions promote equitable healthcare access.

Challenges and Considerations

While the benefits of co-creating solutions are evident, several challenges must be addressed.

Data Privacy and Security

Co-creation efforts often involve the sharing of sensitive health data. Payers must prioritize data privacy and security to ensure that patient information remains confidential and protected.

Resistance to Change

Resistance to change is common in healthcare. Stakeholders may be hesitant to adopt new collaborative strategies or technologies. Payers must implement robust change management strategies to overcome resistance.

Cultural Competence

Efforts to co-create solutions should be culturally sensitive. Payers must ensure that their communication and collaboration practices are respectful and inclusive of diverse patient populations.

Resource Allocation

Collaborative efforts may require additional resources, both financial and human. Payers must allocate resources strategically to support co-creation initiatives effectively.

The Future of Payer Healthcare Innovation

The "co-create solutions" approach is poised to shape the future of payer healthcare innovation in profound ways.

Advanced Digital Health Solutions

Collaboration among payers, technology companies, healthcare providers, and patients will drive the development of advanced digital health solutions.

These solutions will include telehealth, remote monitoring, and personalized healthcare experiences.

Value-Based Care Models

Co-creation will support the transition to value-based care models. Payers, healthcare providers, and patients will work collaboratively to measure and incentivize outcomes over the volume of services.

Personalized Healthcare

Patient involvement in co-creation efforts will lead to more personalized healthcare experiences. Solutions will be tailored to individual patient needs and preferences.

Holistic Population Health Management

Co-creation will lead to a more holistic approach to population health management. This includes addressing social determinants of health, preventive care, and early intervention.

One real-world business case of payer organizations co-creating solutions in healthcare that led to disruptive innovation is the partnership between UnitedHealth Group's subsidiary, Optum, and Mayo Clinic to form Optum Labs. Optum Labs is a research and innovation center that focuses on leveraging data and collaborative research to drive advancements in healthcare delivery and outcomes.

Case Example: Optum Labs—Unitedhealth Group and Mayo Clinic Collaboration

Background: UnitedHealth Group is one of the largest health insurance and healthcare services companies globally, while Mayo Clinic is a prestigious healthcare provider known for its excellence in patient care and medical research. Both organizations recognized the potential to disrupt traditional healthcare models by leveraging their respective strengths and expertise.

Co-creation and Innovation

Data Sharing and Analytics: Optum Labs was established as an open research collaborative, where payer data from UnitedHealth Group and clinical expertise from Mayo Clinic were combined. This allowed researchers to access a vast repository of patient data and clinical insights.

Research Partnerships: Optum Labs invited other healthcare stakeholders, including academic institutions, pharmaceutical companies, and technology firms, to join the collaborative effort. These partners contributed their expertise and resources to conduct research on pressing healthcare issues.

Healthcare Research and Insights: Optum Labs conducted research projects on a wide range of healthcare topics, including chronic disease management, treatment effectiveness, healthcare disparities, and cost containment. They used advanced analytics and big data techniques to extract valuable insights from the data.

Innovation and Impact

Evidence-Based Medicine: The collaborative research conducted at Optum Labs generated evidence that helped inform medical practice guidelines and treatment protocols. This data-driven approach has the potential to enhance the quality of care and improve patient outcomes.

Predictive Analytics: The partnership enabled the development of predictive models that identify patients at risk of specific health conditions. This proactive approach allows for early interventions and better management of chronic diseases.

Cost Containment: By studying healthcare utilization patterns and cost drivers, Optum Labs aimed to find ways to reduce healthcare costs while maintaining or improving the quality of care.

Data-Driven Decision-Making: Payers, providers, and policymakers have access to data-driven insights and research findings to inform healthcare policy and reimbursement decisions.

Innovation Ecosystem: Optum Labs has cultivated an innovation ecosystem, bringing together diverse stakeholders to collaborate on healthcare solutions. This ecosystem fosters a culture of innovation and collaboration.

Dissemination of Knowledge: Findings and insights from Optum Labs' research have been shared with the broader healthcare community, contributing to the dissemination of best practices and innovative approaches to healthcare delivery.

The collaboration between UnitedHealth Group's Optum and Mayo Clinic through Optum Labs exemplifies how payer organizations can drive disruptive innovation in healthcare. By co-creating solutions that leverage data, research, and diverse expertise, they have the potential to transform healthcare delivery, improve patient outcomes, and reduce costs. This innovative approach represents a shift toward a more data-driven, evidence-based, and collaborative model of healthcare.

Another great example is the partnership between Humana, a leading health insurance company, and the home healthcare company, Kindred at Home, to create the "Hospital at Home" program.

Case Example: Humana and Kindred at Home—Hospital at Home Program

Background: Humana recognized the need to address the challenges associated with traditional hospital-based care, such as high costs, overutilization, and inconvenience for patients. Kindred at Home, a home healthcare provider, had expertise in delivering healthcare services in patients' homes. Both organizations saw an opportunity to disrupt the healthcare industry by co-creating a solution that would enable certain medical treatments to be provided in the comfort of patients' homes.

Co-creation and Innovation

Hospital-Level Care at Home: Humana and Kindred at Home collaborated to develop the "Hospital at Home" program, which aimed to provide hospital-level care to patients in their homes. This included services such as acute care, monitoring, diagnostics, and treatment.

Technology Integration: The program leveraged technology to facilitate remote monitoring and communication between healthcare providers and patients. Patients were equipped with devices and tools to enable real-time data sharing and video consultations.

Care Team Collaboration: The partnership involved coordination between physicians, nurses, and other healthcare professionals to ensure that patients received comprehensive care at home. Care teams were designed to be interdisciplinary with a focus on patient-centered care.

Innovation and Impact

Reduced Healthcare Costs: By providing care in patients' homes, the Hospital at Home program aimed to significantly reduce the costs associated with hospitalization, including room and board expenses. This disruptive model had the potential to lower healthcare costs for both payers and patients.

Improved Patient Experience: Patients often prefer receiving care in the comfort of their homes rather than in a hospital setting. This approach could enhance the patient experience, leading to higher satisfaction and better adherence to treatment plans.

Enhanced Outcomes: Early results from the program suggested that patients receiving care at home experienced outcomes comparable to those in traditional hospital settings. Additionally, some patients reported faster recovery times and reduced risks of hospital-acquired infections.

Reduced Hospital Capacity Strain: By diverting certain patients to home-based care, the program had the potential to free up hospital beds and resources for patients with more critical needs.

Scalability: The partnership aimed to scale the Hospital at Home program to serve a broader population, potentially disrupting the traditional healthcare delivery model on a larger scale.

The collaboration between Humana and Kindred at Home to create the Hospital at Home program represents a disruptive innovation in healthcare. By co-creating a solution that challenges the status quo of hospital-based care and leverages homebased care, they aimed to provide more cost-effective, patient-centered, and scalable healthcare services. This innovative approach has the potential to transform how certain medical treatments are delivered and reshape the healthcare landscape.

Conclusion

In conclusion, the "co-create solutions" theme is a powerful driver of innovation within payer healthcare models. By fostering collaboration among stakeholders, payer models can harness the collective intelligence of members, healthcare providers, and the community to develop innovative solutions that enhance patient centered care, care coordination, and equity in healthcare access. In an ever-evolving healthcare landscape, embracing this approach is essential for achieving meaningful and sustainable innovation that benefits all members and communities.

We hope to share more details about our specific outcomes in the next edition of this book! We are trending in the right direction, and we hope some of our research we share is helpful to you in your journey. There is no better way to innovate than by embracing this "co-creation" concept. No more silos!

Summa Health Technology Governance Model for Payer and Provider Optimization | By Elbridge Locklear

Headquartered in Akron, Ohio, we are one of the largest integrated health-care delivery systems in the state. Our nonprofit system encompasses a network of hospitals; community-based health centers; a health insurance entity (SummaCare); a multispecialty group practice; an entrepreneurial entity; research and medical education; and a foundation. We have served millions of patients in comprehensive acute, critical, emergency, outpatient, and long-term/ home-care settings. We are known for high-quality care on the provider side and five-star member service on the payer side. Balancing the technical requirements for the diverse provider and payer divisions is both art and science.

Co-creation Is Art and Science

The art is enabled by Summa Health's strong culture, which focuses on organizational mission at its core. The mission of Summa Health System is to provide the highest quality, compassionate care to our patients and members and to contribute to a healthier community. We guide the organization by our values, which include "serve with passion," "personalize care," "value every person," "take ownership," "work collaboratively" and "partner with the community." With this strong foundation in place, we are able to set aside typical disagreements and friction and really focus on what is best for our patients and members. Co-creation is just a natural byproduct. That is the art.

The science is enabled by a strong technical governance structure that enables us to effectively co-create solutions to meet the needs of our patients and members. While the art may be specific to Summa Health, our governance model is extensible to most organizations, especially payviders like us. We call our model "X-Portfolio Alignment" (Figure 8.5).

We found the best way to manage the diverse requirements is to view our product and services in three specific verticals—clinical, health plan, and administration. Horizontally, we layer in the critical technical enterprise capabilities of architecture and cybersecurity. These are all managed by centralized tech leadership to ensure resource optimization and alignment. This is the science.

Co-creation Model

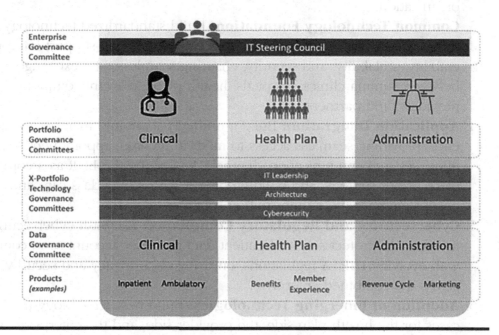

Figure 8.5   Summa technology governance X-portfolio alignment.

How It Works

Value co-creation and innovation for payer provider requires streamlined and scalable technology solutions that allow for sharing of ideas, applications, and data. Technology is a core driver of value in healthcare, and Summa Health technology leaders put processes in place to support the journey of unifying and driving the technology integration of the historically segregated sides of payer and provider.

Core Aspects

1. **Co-creation and Innovation Culture:** Cultivate a co-creation culture between Summa Health and SummaCare that empowers clinicians, IT staff, and administrative staff to collectively identify challenges, develop solutions, and implement improvements.
2. **Data-Driven Decision-Making:** Build a unified enterprise-wide data and analytics platform for insights into patient care patterns, health plan membership performance, operational trends, and financial performance (and more), enabling data-driven decision-making across the organization.
3. **Common Technology Foundation:** Build standardized technology infrastructure with smart use of cloud capabilities that support interoperability, scalability, and security, ensuring seamless data exchange between Summa clinics, hospitals, health plans, relevant community providers, and partners.
4. **Application Integration:** Build a unified patient and member experience, providing seamless access to medical records, appointment scheduling, secure communication channels, leveraging the EHR as a core piece of our strategy, and building onto it with world-class care and benefit/membership administration solutions.
5. **Cybersecurity and Regulatory Compliance:** Establish cybersecurity measures to protect sensitive patient data and user accounts and comply with evolving HIPAA regulations, ensuring data privacy and security across the combined enterprise.
6. **Adoption of Emerging Technologies:** Build new technology use cases for the health plan side, the provider side, and the enterprise as a whole to ensure that experimentation is a joint experience across payer and provider.

X-Portfolio Outcomes

Technology-focused co-creation and innovation in an integrated payer-provider organization like Summa demand a comprehensive approach targeting the platforms, processes, skills, and culture in IT. IT and business continue to work together more closely as all challenges, and opportunities need to be evaluated through operational and technology lenses for ultimate success.

Since we put the model in place, noise and redundancy have declined, and we have optimized many of our applications. The art has enabled the Summa Health leadership to come together and listen and collaborate, and we see this very actively inside and outside of our technology governance steering committee meetings. We eliminated the pointing of fingers and the "us versus them" mentality that plagues many organizations. Science is still being perfected, but the structure has moved us from the ice age to a renaissance of sorts. Art and science have moved us to the place where we are co-creating solutions that benefit both the patients and members simultaneously.

Index